CRIMINAL DEFENSE IN CHINA

The Politics of Lawyers at Work

Criminal Defense in China studies empirically the everyday work and political mobilization of defense lawyers in China. It builds upon 329 interviews across China, and other social science methods, to investigate and analyze the interweaving of politics and practice in five segments of the practicing criminal defense bar in China from 2005 to 2015. This book is the first to examine everyday criminal defense work in China as a political project. The authors engage extensive scholarship on lawyers and political liberalism across the world, from 17th-century Europe to late 20th-century Korea and Taiwan, drawing on theoretical propositions from this body of theory to examine the strategies and constraints of lawyer mobilization in China. The book brings a fresh perspective through its focus on everyday work and ordinary lawyering in an authoritarian context and raises searching questions about law and lawyers, and politics and society, in China's uncertain futures.

Sida Liu is Assistant Professor of Sociology at the University of Toronto, Faculty Fellow at the American Bar Foundation, and a Member of the Institute for Advanced Study in Princeton in 2016–2017. He received his LL.B. from Peking University Law School and his Ph.D. in sociology from the University of Chicago. He has written widely on Chinese law, sociolegal theory, and general social theory, including two books (in Chinese) on the legal profession in China.

Terence Halliday is Co-Director at the Center on Law and Globalization, Research Professor at the American Bar Foundation, Honorary Professor at Australian National University, and Adjunct Professor of Sociology, Northwestern University. He has written widely on global law-making, professions, and national law reforms across the world, including corporate bankruptcy and criminal procedure law reforms and on professional regulation in China.

CAMBRIDGE STUDIES IN LAW AND SOCIETY

Cambridge Studies in Law and Society aims to publish the best scholarly work on legal discourse and practice in its social and institutional contexts, combining theoretical insights and empirical research.

The fields that it covers are: studies of law in action; the sociology of law; the anthropology of law; cultural studies of law, including the role of legal discourses in social formations; law and economics; law and politics; and studies of governance. The books consider all forms of legal discourse across societies, rather than being limited to lawyers' discourses alone.

The series editors come from a range of disciplines: academic law; socio-legal studies; sociology; and anthropology. All have been actively involved in teaching and writing about law in context.

Series editors
Chris Arup, *Monash University, Victoria*
Sally Engle Merry, *New York University*
Susan Silbey, *Massachusetts Institute of Technology*

A list of books in the series can be found at the back of this book.

Criminal Defense in China

THE POLITICS OF LAWYERS
AT WORK

SIDA LIU
TERENCE C. HALLIDAY

CAMBRIDGE
UNIVERSITY PRESS

CAMBRIDGE
UNIVERSITY PRESS

University Printing House, Cambridge CB2 8BS, United Kingdom

Cambridge University Press is part of the University of Cambridge.

It furthers the University's mission by disseminating knowledge in the pursuit of education, learning and research at the highest international levels of excellence.

www.cambridge.org
Information on this title: www.cambridge.org/9781107162419

First published 2016

Printed in the United States of America by Sheridan Books, Inc.

A catalogue record for this publication is available from the British Library

Library of Congress Cataloging-in-Publication data
Liu, Sida, 1980– author. | Halliday, Terence C. (Terence Charles), author.
Criminal defense in China : the politics of lawyers at work / Sida Liu, Terence C. Halliday.
Cambridge [UK] : Cambridge University Press, 2016. | Series: Cambridge studies in law and society
LCCN 2016026625 | ISBN 9781107162419 (hardback)
LCSH: Criminal defense lawyers – China. | Defense (Criminal procedure) – China.
LCC KNQ4630.D43 L59 2016 | DDC 345.41/05044–dc23
LC record available at https://lccn.loc.gov/2016026625

ISBN 978-1-107-16241-9 Hardback
ISBN 978-1-316-61484-6 Paperback

Sida Liu would like to dedicate this book to his father

Liu Bao

Terence Halliday would like to dedicate this book to
Andrew, Charles, Gabriel, Olivia, and Reid

Contents

Tables and Figures

Tables

Figures

Prologue

In the autumn of 1731, the Parisian Order of Barristers went on strike. Provocations for such a dramatic protest against royal justice had been building for several years as the bar progressively articulated ideas that would require limits on royal power. The Absolute Monarchy initially counseled restraint, despite its exasperation at the Order, whose impertinence caused the Crown to describe it as "an independent little republic at the heart of state." However, this restraint disappeared when the Monarchy was confronted with a legal brief that proclaimed the subversive doctrine that "all laws are contracts between those who govern and those who are governed." The Council threatened disbarment of the brief's author and thirty-nine fellow barristers unless they retracted the document. After negotiations failed to defuse the confrontation, lawyers walked out of the courts, thereby denying the Crown a central function – the dispensing of justice. Confronted with an obdurate profession, the Crown held out for three months and then effectively conceded the battle to the lawyers. The work stoppage symbolized a moment where the very foundations of royal absolutism began to be eroded; it marked the beginnings of a movement, said Voltaire, where "simple citizens triumphed, having no arms but reason" (see Bell 1994; Karpik 1998 for details of this historical episode).

In December 2009, a Chinese criminal defense lawyer named Li Zhuang was arrested in Chongqing during Politburo member Bo Xilai's campaign against organized crime. Li was subsequently charged twice for the crime of lawyer's perjury. Labeled "China's trial of the century" by some observers, thousands of Chinese lawyers, legal scholars, and other legal professionals enthusiastically watched Li's dramatic trials and mobilized to defend him both in the courtroom and in cyberspace. While Li spent eighteen months in prison for his first charge in 2009, his second charge in 2011 was dropped by the

Chongqing authorities, thanks to the vigorous defense of his counsel as well as the online uproar generated by the legal profession. The Li Zhuang case marks not only a key turning point in the fallen political career of Bo Xilai from Communist Party leader to a life in prison, but also a watershed event in the history of the Chinese legal profession. It was the first time that lawyers across China mobilized collectively to defend a fellow professional whom most of them had never met or even heard of. After this *cause célèbre*, a loosely connected group of "die-hard lawyers," consisting of elite, activist, and grass-roots members of the Chinese criminal defense bar, emerged and took on controversial cases all over the country.

In July 2015, four years after the conclusion of the Li Zhuang trial, the Chinese authorities launched a large-scale crackdown against die-hard law-yers, with more than two hundred lawyers detained, disappeared, or brought in for questioning. Among the first detained lawyers was a woman named Wang Yu, who had been involved in cases of disability discrimination, religious freedom, land rights, and illegal restriction of personal freedom by govern-ment and law enforcement officials. Wang was taken from her home in the early morning on July 9 (and later accused of being part of a "criminal gang" and charged with subverting state power in January 2016). On the same day, 101 lawyers all over China signed a petition requesting to know her whereabouts and urging that "torture and abuse of power must not be tolerated." Since many of these 101 lawyers were also taken away by the police in the next a few days, more petitions were signed by bar associations and human rights orga-nizations in Hong Kong, Taiwan, England, Germany, Australia, and, finally, the United States. As this book goes to press, the fate of some detained lawyers remains unknown.

These three instances of lawyers' mobilization could not seem more differ-ent. Separated by continents, centuries, and circumstances, they seem at first glance to belong to different spheres of history, politics, and law. We will argue, however, that these episodes belong to a common theoretical problem regarding lawyers and politics, despite many variations on the theme (e.g., Karpik 1995: 92–116).

Illiberal political societies come with varieties of labels – absolute monar-chies, military dictatorships, authoritarian or totalitarian politics, Big Man regimes, or dual states. Yet they share key features in common – little or no restraint on arbitrary executive power, most especially as it is exercised through military, police, and security apparatuses; law that is distorted and circum-scribed and ultimately ineffectual in its protections of individuals and organi-zations offensive to the ruling power; little space for voices to speak freely about their rulers, their qualities of life, or their circumstances in times and places and organizations of their own choosing; severely constricted notions of rights-bearing citizens beyond those granted or withdrawn by the rulers themselves; and precariousness of property ownership, among others.

Yet the ubiquity of illiberal political societies, as they appear to invent themselves time and again at one historical moment or in another geographical location, cannot hide or suppress another powerful impulse deep within those societies. Over the last four hundred years and across the world, individual and collective action by lawyers, and often a wider range of legally trained occupations such as judges or legal academics, to transform illiberal politics into an open and liberal political society can repeatedly be observed. In this new political society, institutions and practices are both transformed and maintained such that the structures of society press insistently, even if unevenly and episodically, towards basic legal freedoms, vibrant civil societies, and moderate states.

There are many exceptions to this deep impulse; many reversals, many betrayals and retreats, many false starts and inept actions; but very often, in every type of illiberal political society that has been observed in decades of scholarly inquiries, lawyers have fought for basic legal freedoms. Their fight is often carried on in the name of the law but it is a fight, nonetheless, ultimately for political change. Among these activist professionals can be observed complex social structures of motivation and ideology, organization and collective action, historical trajectories and local dramas, sacrifice and vision, defeat and victory.

In these historical and comparative contexts of transformation, this book grapples with two broad questions, both far beyond its ability to answer definitively: Where are China's legal and political reforms going? And how do lawyers fight for basic legal freedoms in illiberal political societies?

WHERE ARE CHINA'S LEGAL AND POLITICAL REFORMS GOING?

Where goes China? This is arguably one of the great questions of the twenty-first century. There are "straight line" prognostications that China will get increasingly richer and more powerful, that it will become a superpower on the global stage. There are developmentalist predictions that are, in effect, new forms of the old modernization theory that as China grows progressively more prosperous it will also become ostensibly more democratic. There are warnings that China's fragilities may lead to domestic instability and international conflict. There are doomsday accounts that a desperate Chinese Communist Party (CCP) is losing its control of the population and that the

CCP itself is trapped in serious problems of corruption and organizational inertia. Optimists expect the rule *of* law to triumph in China, while pessimists believe that rule *by* law already overshadows economic reforms.

The correctness of any of these short- or longer-term projections lies beyond the determinations of any observers, scholarly or otherwise. China's future, especially in the legal-political turn since the ascendancy of Xi Jinping, remains acutely indeterminate and quite possibly becomes more so by the day. On the one hand, the CCP presented the most systematic proposal of legal reform in its history in the Fourth Plenum of its 18th Party Congress in October 2014. On the other hand, law's emancipatory potential seems eviscerated as openness in the political space is progressively closed and the nascent civil society is under constant harassment and attack from the state. At best, scholars like us can peer intently inside China with the historical and comparative awareness that many other illiberal and seemingly unassailable rulers have been confronted with a vanguard of lawyers, judges, and others, so much so that transitions sometimes have led to a very different sort of political society.

Our focus in this book, therefore, is on a particular *actor* and a particular *institution* that will be integral to China's future. The actor is manifest in many guises – barefoot lawyers on the margins of hardscrabble rural areas; headline-grabbing bar association leaders who are Party members while also champions of high-profile white-collar detainees; ordinary grassroots lawyers eking out a modest existence yet assured in themselves that their everyday practices are building, brick by brick, a rule-governed criminal justice system; law professors who believe and teach that historical precedents about legal proceduralism and arrangements of power have salience for China; human rights lawyers who defend desperate persons in every corner of China in the most politically sensitive cases; and constitutionalists who envision a society in which every citizen has a political voice and every person is guaranteed rights and duties inscribed in law.

These actors are not simply individual lawyers floating like professional flotsam on a sea of social and political turbulence. They connect with one another: some through local relational networks; some as law school classmates who never lose touch; some through temporary solidarity in a high-profile trial. Some self-identify as "human rights defenders" or "die-hard lawyers." Others seek informal and formal means of forging a professional community. And yet others reach fellow lawyers and publics through Internet forums, blogs, and, most recently, Weibo and WeChat.

Our focus spotlights a particular institution – criminal procedure law and the struggles around it in everyday criminal justice, most notably through lawyers' defense work. We shall show that for both theoretical and prudential reasons, the research site of criminal procedure law and practice puts a social scientist's fingers on a very sensitive pulse in China's social and political life. Criminal defense invokes laws and procedures that directly confront state power and potentially hold it at bay. It offers a case of law practice that has little glory and often less reward, yet it is also a grassroots place where great struggles for the future of a political society occur in microcosm. Although invisible to most ordinary persons, everyday criminal defense practice reveals both the limitations and distortions of formal law, such as China's 1979, 1996, or 2012 Criminal Procedure Law, and yet also law's underlying potential for individual freedom and collective action. The contradictions of Chinese law and politics become openly displayed in remote and notable places of criminal defense work.

In this particular institution, other legal occupations also come into conjunction or conflict with defense lawyers. Lawyers confront the police as they seek to meet with clients or collect evidence or point to instances of confession by torture. Lawyers face off against procurators who have supervisory powers over the judicial process and even the capacity to incarcerate lawyers under China's Criminal Law. Lawyers appear before increasingly professionalized judges, although they well know that out of sight there is an adjudication committee consisting of court leaders and, more troublingly, a Party Political-Legal Committee often chaired by the police chief that will determine the outcomes of important and difficult cases. Law professors play a significant role, too, sometimes as architects of criminal procedure reforms, and not infrequently as part-time lawyers or opinion-leaders in particularly controversial trials. Insofar as the police, the procuracy, and the court have historically constituted an "iron triangle" in China, their confrontations with lawyers and changing ethos and relations with each other also signal where China is headed. Towards a political society where law matters as a semi-autonomous force for freedom and restraint? Or towards a political society where law primarily is an instrument of power, a more respectable and less bloody means of repression?

The question of "Where are China's legal and political reforms going?" therefore may be answered by learning whether there are impulses among China's criminal defense lawyers that transform everyday work into a different kind of politics, and whether there are signs or prospects for collective action that might intimate a future China that has attributes in common with transformations in other times and places. This brings us to the second question.

HOW DO LAWYERS FIGHT FOR BASIC LEGAL FREEDOMS?

In an enormous diversity of times and places, lawyers and other legally trained occupations have fought against illiberal political regimes. What is particularly challenging and consequential are the scholarly findings that the fight is not inevitable, it does not involve all lawyers, it occurs despite deep conflicts within the legal profession, and very often lawyers are handmaidens of power to preserve an illiberal status quo (Karpik 2007). Efforts at mobilization are met with skepticism, counter-mobilization, or repression. Activist lawyers are abducted, imprisoned, tortured, and, on occasion, assassinated or executed. Within and beyond the legal profession, there are powerful forces that will inhibit the impetus towards the establishment of basic legal freedoms.

This book seeks to advance understandings of how and when lawyers mobilize by juxtaposing what we observe in China with other patterns of lawyer activism in other regions of the world. At the very least we seek to discover what forms and degrees of political mobilization are already occurring in China and whether these resonate with practices elsewhere or rather manifest distinctively Chinese characteristics.

Consider lawyer activism in other national contexts. In seventeenth-century Britain, the Crown complained bitterly that lawyers were like an "independent little republic" in their expectations of time-honored autonomy for the bar from control by the king. Likewise, in the France of the *Ancien Regime*, seventeenth- and eighteenth-century Paris advocates insisted that there should be limits on the king's power and that the strictures of censorship over political speech could not silence advocates in their oral presentations of *judiciaires mémoires* (court memorandums) (Bell 1994; Karpik 1995; Burrage 1997).

Consider also the marches of lawyers in Pakistan in support of a chief justice summarily dismissed by the president in 2007. Or the formation of an activist group of lawyers under military rule in South Korea who emerged as a vanguard of liberal politics. Or efforts by Kenya's lawyers in the 1980s to resist President Moi's one-party repressive rule, or the Zambia's Law Society's leadership of a national campaign to forestall a president intent on extending his rule beyond constitutional limits. Think too of the role of the Brazilian Bar Association which united with the Roman Catholic Church against torture, brutality, and killings under a military dictatorship in the 1970s (Falcao 1988; Ghias 2012; Gould 2012; Munir 2012).

From another angle, consider Sudan's bloody descent into despotism when its liberal lawyers were crushed. Or Lee Kuan Yew's campaign to silence the Law Society of Singapore when it dared critique the government's retreat from rule of law. Or the cutting off of overseas support for lawyers and other liberal groups by Egyptian President Mubarak, who was intent on preserving his illiberal one-party rule (Massoud 2012; Moustafa 2012; Rajah 2012).

In struggles for political futures, therefore, history reveals many occasions when the agents of transformation include lawyers, often beginning with very few voices and being subjected to harsh crackdowns, yet persisting until their impetus combines with facilitating circumstances and precipitating events to produce a transformed legal and political order. In other places, such as contemporary Singapore or Sri Lanka or Russia, that is a history unrealized.

This book therefore not only investigates the political struggles of Chinese lawyers, but also resonances of other times and places beyond contemporary China. Are lawyers, any lawyers, acting inside this highly authoritarian state in ways that point to liberal political futures? If so, how are they mobilizing? In ways seen elsewhere or uniquely? And what are they mobilizing *for*? In their work and in their political action, what instruments of authoritarianism do they confront? And how do they adapt or surmount a harsh criminal justice system and a repressive state apparatus? These questions will be pondered and answered with empirical data that point to far-reaching pragmatic and theoretical implications.

Acknowledgments

Even in the digital age, when human interactions are increasingly threatened by electronic devices and quantitative indicators, no good academic work could be completed without the help and support of friends, colleagues, and critics. The long journey for this book began from a brief meeting of the two authors at the American Bar Foundation (ABF) in 2004, having been kindly introduced by Andrew Abbott, our colleague and friend at the University of Chicago. Since then, we have become semi-permanent residents of the fifth-floor conference room of the ABF, with a gorgeous view of Lake Michigan, for more than a decade. The ABF provided us not only with excellent institutional and funding support, but also the best intellectual community that any socio-legal researcher could hope for. In the decade-long process of research and writing, we have benefitted enormously from our ABF colleagues for their enthusiastic, constructive, and insightful comments and critiques on our project as it evolved over time. For sustained support and encouragement we thank particularly ABF Directors Robert Nelson and Ajay Mehrotra and the ABF Board of Directors and Fellows. We are also very grateful to Amy Schlueter for her exemplary administrative support. It has been a privilege to be part of this outstanding scholarly community.

A major grant from the National Science Foundation (SES-0850432) covered much of our research and travel costs for this project. We gratefully acknowledge permissions to reprint parts of articles and chapters previously published by Hart Publishing (Terence C. Halliday and Sida Liu. 2007. "Birth of a Liberal Moment? Looking through a One-Way Mirror at Lawyers' Defense of Criminal Defendants in China." Pp. 65–108 in *The Legal Complex and Struggles for Political Liberalism*, edited by Terence C. Halliday, Lucien Karpik, and Malcolm M. Feeley), Wiley (Sida Liu and Terence C. Halliday. 2009. "Recursivity in Legal Change: Lawyers and

Reforms of China's Criminal Procedural Law." *Law & Social Inquiry* 34: 911–950; Sida Liu and Terence C. Halliday. 2011. "Political Liberalism and Political Embeddedness: Understanding Politics in the Work of Chinese Criminal Defense Lawyers." *Law & Society Review* 45:831–865), and Cambridge University Press (Sida Liu, Lily Liang, and Terence C. Halliday. 2014. "The Trial of Li Zhuang: Chinese Lawyers' Collective Action Against Populism." *Asian Journal of Law and Society* 1:79–97). Various pieces of the book were presented at universities and research institutions in both China and the United States, including China University of Political Science and Law, Council on Foreign Relations, Georgetown University, Harvard University, Northwestern University, Shanghai Jiao Tong University, Sichuan University, Stanford University, Yale University, University of California–Berkeley, University of California–Los Angeles, University of Chicago, University of Hong Kong, University of Michigan, University of Pennsylvania, University of Pittsburgh, University of Wisconsin-Madison, as well as the annual meetings of the Law & Society Association and American Sociological Association. We have benefitted from many discussions and coverage from the media, including the BBC, the *Guardian*, the *New York Times*, and the *Wall Street Journal*, partly owing to the Chinese government's harsh treatment of criminal defense lawyers in recent years. We are grateful for the comments and feedback from all of these academic and popular audiences of our work.

Many colleagues have been dedicated readers and friendly critics of our writings and speeches, especially Jerry Cohen, Cheng Jinhua, Laurie Edelman, Howie Erlanger, Malcolm Feeley, Fu Hualing, Mary Gallagher, John Givens, He Xin, He Yongjun, Kathie Hendley, Lucien Karpik, Heinz Klug, Lan Rongjie, Maggie Lewis, Li Xueyao, Lin Xifen, Stanley Lubman, Lynn Mather, Sally Engle Merry, Ethan Michelson, Carl Minzner, John Ohnesorge, Eva Pils, Gay Seidman, Rachel Stern, Alex Wang, Wang Qinghua, Erik Olin Wright, Wu Hongqi, Xu Shenjian, and Zuo Weimin, to all of whom we owe great debts. We were fortunate to work with a number of outstanding co-authors and research assistants since 2005, including Lily Liang, Cheng-Tong Lir Wang, Connor Steelberg, and twenty law students in China, as well as our Chinese translators, whose names must remain anonymous for their protection given the political sensitivity of our topic. We also thank Jerry Cohen, Frank Upham, Ira Belkin, and the US-Asia Law Institute at NYU School of Law for providing us many opportunities to learn from Chinese lawyers and legal academics at the final stage of completing this book. Reviewers of our book raised valuable issues for us to address. John Berger, Sarah Starkey, and Brianda Reyes at Cambridge University Press in particular provided some nuanced but critical touches to our manuscript and made it appealing to a broader audience.

Needless to say, we are most grateful to the hundreds of lawyers and other informants in China, without whose generous help this book would not have been possible. As the book goes to print, we are constantly mindful and pray for some of our bravest lawyer interviewees who remain in custody in China for the alleged crimes of perjury, subverting state power, or "picking quarrels and causing trouble," – a criminal charge beyond comprehension in the minds of the greatest experts on Chinese law. Their suffering and perseverance make all our challenges and difficulties of researching and writing this book pale into insignificance.

Abbreviations

ACLA	All China Lawyers Association
BBOJ	Beijing Bureau of Justice
BLA	Beijing Lawyers Association
CCP	Chinese Communist Party
CPL	Criminal Procedure Law
MOJ	Ministry of Justice
MPS	Ministry of Public Security
MSS	Ministry of State Security
NPC	National People's Congress
PLC	Political-Legal Committee of the Chinese Communist Party
PPC	Police, Procuracy, and Court
SPC	Supreme People's Court
SPP	Supreme People's Procuracy

1

The Politics of Criminal Defense Lawyers

Politics is everywhere in the legal profession, but nowhere is it as strong and complex as in the work of criminal defense lawyers. When handling criminal cases, lawyers often find themselves in an inescapable dilemma: on the one hand, they must pursue legal proceduralism and challenge the power of state authorities in order to mount a good defense for their clients; on the other hand, they often rely on their connections with judges and law enforcement officials to solve problems and reduce difficulties in practice. The tension between those two aspects of politics, which we call "political liberalism" (Karpik 1995; Halliday and Karpik 1997) and "political embeddedness" (Michelson 2007) in this book, is often amplified in authoritarian regimes where criminal defense is not only a matter of protecting individual rights in particular cases, but also a collective struggle for political change (Halliday, Karpik, and Feeley 2007; Ginsburg and Moustafa 2008).

At first glance, the story of lawyers and criminal justice in China is an unhappy story of difficulties and danger. Criminal defense lawyers encounter great difficulties in routine tasks such as meeting suspects, collecting evidence, and accessing case files (Yu 2002; Michelson 2007; Liu and Halliday 2011). Persuading judges to adopt their defense opinions in trial is rarely successful, thanks to the internal coordination among the "iron triangle" of Chinese criminal justice, namely, the police, the procuracy, and the courts (公检法, hereinafter "PPC") (Halliday and Liu 2007; Liang, He, and Lu 2014). Moreover, lawyers can be detained, prosecuted, or convicted under Article 306 of the 1997 PRC Criminal Law, which established the crime of lawyer's perjury (律师伪证罪). Labeled "Big Stick 306" (306 大棒) by Chinese lawyers, this article has been frequently abused in practice by the police or the procuracy to take revenge on those defense lawyers who dare to vigorously challenge the prosecution in court (Halliday and Liu 2007). As a result of all those difficulties and risks, many Chinese lawyers have stayed away from criminal defense for the sake of self-protection.

Nevertheless, thousands of lawyers all over China still persist in carrying out criminal defense work despite the harsh conditions for their everyday practice. This fact not only indicates a glimmer of hope for the reforms of China's criminal justice system, but also motivates several key research questions: What motivates them to do so? How do they survive in an extremely unfavorable criminal justice system? What are the various strategies that they adopt to mobilize for legal and political change? Based on more than three hundred interviews across the country and a variety of media and archival data that we collected during a decade of fieldwork in China from 2005 to 2015, this book explains these empirical questions at the key intersection between research on the legal profession, criminal justice, and political change.

Theoretically, this book draws China studies into comparative and historical socio-legal theory on lawyers in political change over the *longue durée*. Current struggles of Chinese lawyers are not unprecedented – they can be contextualized within a world history in which lawyers are episodically implicated in movements towards or away from liberal political societies, national sites where basic legal freedoms are a paramount terrain of struggle (Halliday and Karpik 1997; Halliday, Karpik, and Feeley 2007, 2012). These comparative-historical contexts offer theoretical propositions about forms of action by lawyers in China. While existing studies often point to a liberal orientation of lawyers in constituting the moderate state, civil society, and basic legal freedoms, our findings in this book suggest there is a nuanced balance in China between two distinct political orientations in lawyers' everyday practice. By closely examining the relationship between lawyers' liberal ideologies and their structural embeddedness, we seek to develop a potentially generalizable theoretical framework for understanding the individual choices and structural constraints of professional mobilization. Through this theoretical framework, our study also provides a unique lens for observing the Chinese criminal justice system from the perspective of defense lawyers.

A THEORY OF PROFESSIONAL MOBILIZATION

Political mobilization is a long standing research topic in social science, yet the vast majority of the social movement literature has focused on mass mobilization rather than the mobilization of professionals (e.g., Marwell and Oliver 1993; McAdam et al. 1996, 2001). Professions possess distinct forms of expertise and organizational structures that set them apart from political parties, labor unions, ethnic groups, and other major actors in social and political movements. Similarly, the vast scholarly literature on criminal justice has paid more attention to punishment and mass incarceration (e.g., Garland 1990; Western 2006; Wacquant [2004] 2009; Alexander 2012) than to the legal professionals working in the criminal justice system, such as judges, prosecutors, and defense lawyers (however, see Feeley 1979). One of our theoretical tasks in this book is therefore to present an analytical framework for understanding professional mobilization, particularly the mobilization of lawyers and other legal professionals in political change.

The starting point of our theory is that not all professionals are equally interested in politics or collective action. In comparison with other high-status professions, such as doctors, scientists, or engineers, lawyers have notable advantages in political mobilization because they are often uniquely able to exercise moral authority in the name of technical competence (Halliday 1985). But even within the legal profession, some lawyers are more likely to engage in politics and collective action than others. While the majority of lawyers are routine practitioners in ordinary cases, who are either politically conservative or apathetic, a critical mass of them may become vanguards of political change at key historical junctures.

From this basic insight, an extensive body of scholarship, often labeled "political lawyering" (Karpik 2007), has emerged since the late 1980s on the nexus of lawyers and legal-political change. Comparative and historical studies of more than thirty countries in all regions of the world indicate that frequently, though not always, lawyers are heavily implicated in the question of whether the legal and political institutions of a society will protect basic legal freedoms (Halliday and Karpik 1997; Halliday, Karpik, and Feeley 2007, 2012). While the "cause lawyering" literature, a parallel body of scholarship on lawyers and politics, extends the scope of analysis to a wide range of social and political causes such as labor rights or environmental rights (Sarat and Scheingold 1998, 2001, 2005; Marshall and Hale 2014), the political lawyering literature focuses more narrowly on the critical links between lawyers and a cluster of legal and political goals that scholars in this tradition term "political liberalism" (Halliday and Karpik 1997).

First of all, vanguards of lawyers, even entire legal professions, have fought for basic legal freedoms in various kinds of illiberal political societies. Basic legal freedoms include the core civil rights (e.g., *habeas corpus*, protections from arbitrary arrest or torture, and representation by counsel) and core political rights (e.g., freedoms of speech, association, movement, and religion) of individual citizens, but not their broader economic or social rights. Basic legal freedoms "rest upon the granting of legal personality to a citizen and the protection of all residents within a sovereign legal jurisdiction" (Halliday, Karpik, and Feeley 2007: 10). Many of these universal rights are enshrined in the covenants of the United Nations and signed by most of its members (including China), yet they have numerous forms of representation in different national contexts. Our first theoretical proposition is that, even in an authoritarian polity controlled by a single political party (e.g., China), there will be segments of the practicing bar that strive to institutionalize basic legal freedoms, although they may do so in ways that display different emphases and priorities than in other comparative and historical settings. One such setting, almost entirely neglected in earlier studies of lawyers and political liberalism, is the practice of criminal law. This book is intended to fill in this gap and provide a comprehensive account of how lawyers engage with the criminal justice system in their fight for basic legal freedoms.

Second, lawyers who strive for basic legal freedoms often insist that this is only possible if state power itself is fractured, most importantly through some independence or autonomy of the judiciary from control by the monarchy, the military, one-party leaders, or an executive branch of government, including the police – the domestic coercive arm of government itself. Professional mobilization for varieties of state moderation can be seen across East, Southeast and South Asia (Feeley and Miyazawa 2007; Ginsburg 2007; Jones 2007; Harding and Whiting 2012; Munir 2012; Rajah 2012). This leads to our second theoretical proposition: a fraction of China's lawyers, particularly criminal defense lawyers, will hold views and strive in practice for the restraint of state power through institutional re-arrangements of the judiciary and the political system. This book investigates the conceptions of state moderation in various segments of the criminal defense bar and how lawyers imagine future political and legal systems in China might be configured to protect basic legal freedoms.

Third, while lawyers play a role in constituting the justice system of a state, and hence might be thought of as officers of the court or servants of the state, historically they have also fought to position themselves as actors in civil society (Karpik 1988). They may do so through bar associations – in authoritarian societies these can take the form of insurgent and clandestine networks or associations; they may do so by defending other civil society groups or allying with civil society organizations, and hence constituting civil society itself (Karpik 1995; Tocqueville ([1835, 1840] 2000); and they may act as spokespersons for publics (Karpik 1988), thereby giving a voice to citizens and non-state actors and potentially opening up a deliberative public sphere (Habermas [1962] 1989). This leads to our third theoretical proposition: even in illiberal political regimes, some lawyers will mobilize either collectively in their capacities as lawyers and/or speak on behalf of civil society and publics as their spokespersons. Can such segments of lawyers be found in China, and, if so, how have they done so through formal legal settings, such as courts, or through the media? Most notably, does the emergence of the Internet and social media, despite the "Great Firewall" built by the Chinese state, open up a new terrain of struggle in Chinese lawyers' engagement with the civil society? This book seeks to provide a provisional answer to these questions.

In sum, political liberalism, as defined in this book and earlier political lawyering studies, is not equivalent to democracy or the rule of law, nor the economic neo-liberalism epitomized by the "free market" ideology and the Washington Consensus (Dezalay and Garth 2002); instead, it centers on the most fundamental citizen and political rights that many lawyers fight for, individually or collectively, in vastly different social and political contexts. It has three principal components: basic legal freedoms, the moderate state, and civil society. The three components of political liberalism are interrelated and together they form the legal, political, and social foundations for liberal political societies that many lawyers aspire and fight for, individually or collectively. Lawyers have the capacity to check arbitrary state power, pursue legal proceduralism, and call for judicial independence. Concomitantly, they can mobilize and form alliances with the media and other sectors of civil society to protect the basic legal rights of citizens. Politically liberal lawyers practice law to pursue justice and institutional change and, in their criminal defense work, they emphasize citizen and procedural rights more than substantive justice or crime control.

Yet not all lawyers are political liberals. In many times and places lawyers are silent and withdrawn in the face of attacks and repression of basic legal freedoms. Even more, lawyers may be complicit with repressive regimes that abrogate fundamental legal rights and oppose a liberal legal political order (Dezalay and Garth 2002; Ginsburg and Moustafa 2008). In practice, the shifting and sometimes antagonistic political connections between lawyers and other legal or political actors, including judges, prosecutors, legal scholars, and state officials, often shape the dynamics of the legal process in both lawmaking and the implementation of law (Michelson 2007; Liu and Halliday 2009; Liu 2011). Even those who possess liberal values and ideologies face structural constraints in pursuing political liberalism through their work, especially in authoritarian contexts such as China. These structural constraints are most evidently manifested in lawyers' formal or informal ties to the state through their career histories and social networks, which is termed "political embeddedness" by Michelson (2007).

Political embeddedness is a spatially bounded relational concept that emphasizes lawyers' proximity to the state as the way to get clients, facilitate their practice, and reduce difficulties in their everyday work. Politically embedded lawyers often (1) have previous work experience in the state justice system, and this leaves an imprint on their subsequent careers; and/or, (2) maintain strong institutional or personal ties with the state agencies and officials that hold power in the legal system. These lawyers have advantages in legal practice not only because they are "repeat players" (Galanter 1974) of the justice system, but also because of the symbiotic exchange of power and resources between lawyers and the state (Liu 2011, 2015). It is important to note, however, that political embeddedness has a spatial limit, that is, when lawyers practice outside of the "comfort zone" of their political connections (e.g., in another city or province), they may lose their embeddedness and face significantly more difficulties in their work.

While political liberalism is defined by lawyers' political values and choices, political embeddedness is defined by their social relations and structural constraints. These two meanings of politics constitute two dimensions for understanding lawyers' political mobilization. Accordingly, lawyers can be classified by their standing vis-à-vis those two dimensions. *Motivationally*, lawyers differ in accordance with whether or not their practice is motivated by or embodies values that are politically liberal. *Structurally*, lawyers differ as to whether they have had or currently have strong relationships with the state justice system. When we combine these two dimensions, four ideal types of lawyers emerge.

As Table 1.1 demonstrates, the quintessential politically embedded lawyers, *pragmatic brokers*, are those who are embedded in the state justice system but only use their embeddedness as brokerage to pursue economic gains rather than political ends. The quintessential politically liberal lawyers, *political activists*, are those who articulate liberal values and maintain some social distance in their careers and current practices from the state. *Progressive elites* are a mixed type. They comprise lawyers who are deeply embedded in the state

TABLE 1.1. *Four ideal types of lawyers in professional mobilization.*

	Politically liberal	Not politically liberal
Politically embedded	Progressive elites	Pragmatic brokers
Not politically embedded	Political activists	Routine practitioners

justice system but also possess highly liberal values and seek to promote political change within the state apparatus. These lawyers are often found at the top of the status hierarchy in the criminal defense bar. Finally, *routine practitioners* refer to the vast number of ordinary lawyers who are neither embedded in the state nor motivated by political liberalism, but merely practice law to meet the basic needs of survival.

By definition, progressive elites and political activists are more likely to mobilize for political liberalism than pragmatic brokers or routine practitioners. Nevertheless, these two groups of law practitioners adopt distinct strategies in their collective action. Progressive elites often advocate for an incremental approach to legal and political reforms and collaborate with the state in both lawmaking and implementation. For them, institutional changes are only possible if lawyers can protect themselves and win support from the liberal judges and officials inside the state apparatus. Political activists, in contrast, take a more radical approach and undertake bold, even heroic, lawyering in highly sensitive political cases. For them, the authoritarian regime is inherently corrupt and the only way for political change is to vehemently attack and overthrow it from the outside, even if it involves serious personal sacrifice. These two approaches may seem incompatible in theory, yet we find both simultaneously at work in the political mobilization of Chinese criminal defense lawyers.

Our last and most important theoretical proposition is that, in illiberal political societies, there is an inverse relationship between political liberalism and political embeddedness in professional mobilization. Political liberalism is a "push" factor for lawyers' mobilization, whereas political embeddedness is a "pull" factor. Politically embedded lawyers are less likely to take radical actions against the state or devote their careers to human rights work, even if they possess liberal values. Conversely, politically liberal lawyers are more likely to actively fight against arbitrary state power or participate in the construction of civil society if they are not deeply embedded in the state apparatus. Arguably, politically conservative lawyers might also mobilize collectively (e.g., Southworth 2008), but this is rarely seen in an authoritarian context such as China, because the interests of such lawyers are often in line with the interests of the state.

CRIMINAL DEFENSE LAWYERS IN THE CHINESE LEGAL COMPLEX

In theory, the application of the analytical framework that we propose in the previous section would result in a classification system of four ideal types of lawyer in any social context, namely, progressive elites, pragmatic brokers, political activists, and routine practitioners. For the case of Chinese criminal defense lawyers, however, the category of political activists needs to be further differentiated by location into two types: notable activists and grassroots activists. *Notable activists* refer to a small group of criminal defense lawyers concentrated in Beijing, but increasingly found nationwide, who often originate from humble professional and social backgrounds but proactively seek out politically sensitive cases and challenge arbitrary state power (Fu and Cullen 2008, 2011; Pils 2015). *Grassroots activists* refer to the ordinary lawyers all over China who possess politically liberal values and motivations but do not mobilize collectively due to unfavorable structural constraints. Instead, they only use their everyday criminal defense work to pursue substantive legal-political goals of protecting the basic legal rights of citizens through practices of proceduralism.

During our fieldwork of over a decade, we have met and interviewed all the five types of lawyers across the country, who together constitute a diverse and fascinating Chinese criminal defense bar. While their stories will be told with fine-grained data in later chapters, in this section we provide some brief sketches of the vastly different profiles of the five types of lawyers, as well as their relations to other legally trained occupations such as judges, procurators, and police officers. Arguably, these general sketches omit many nuanced variations within each type, but our goal is to present a broad picture of the landscape of lawyers and criminal justice in China in this introductory chapter and use it to guide the empirical analysis in the rest of the book.

Let us begin with routine practitioners, who account for the majority of Chinese criminal defense lawyers all over the country. Although a large number of Chinese lawyers prefer to avoid criminal cases, in order to survive in the increasingly severe competition in the legal services market (Liu 2011, 2015), many of them still have to take on criminal defense work in their practice (Michelson 2007). For these routine practitioners who are neither politically liberal nor politically embedded, criminal defense is merely another income source in addition to civil and commercial cases. They usually stay away from the risky parts of the criminal process, especially collecting evidence. Some lawyers even describe criminal defense work as "short, flat, and fast" (短平快) because they intentionally restrict their work to court arguments only and avoid any direct confrontation with procurators or judges during trial. As they are not politically embedded law practitioners, this is the safest way to handle cases, make money, and protect themselves from potential risks.

Pragmatic brokers have a different method of survival in China's criminal justice system. As many of them have previous work experience in the justice system and/or maintain a symbiotic exchange relationship with judges, procurators, and law enforcement officials (Michelson 2007; Liu 2011), they face less risk than routine practitioners in handling criminal cases. Nevertheless, pragmatic brokers use their connections for economic gains rather than political ends. Thanks to their political embeddedness, they face significantly less difficulty than routine practitioners and are often able to meet suspects, access case files, and collect evidence without much disturbance from the PPC. Furthermore, pragmatic brokers often collude with judges or procurators in the criminal process, which has earned some of them the reputation of "colluding-style lawyers" (勾兑派律师) in the Chinese legal community – a term in opposite to the "die-hard lawyers" (死磕派律师), who we will examine in detail later in the book. This instrumental orientation of criminal defense is particularly salient in their selection of case sources, which often exclude all politically sensitive or controversial cases from their practice.

Progressive elites are not scattered around the country, but concentrated in Beijing and other major cities. They are the most politically embedded Chinese criminal defense lawyers as many of them were once Party cadres who previously worked in the higher levels of the criminal justice system, such as provincial-level PPC or even the Supreme People's Court (SPC). Those who do not have previous work experience in the PPC are usually part-time lawyers who are also senior professors in elite law schools. These legal academics are politically embedded in criminal defense work because many of their students assume leadership positions in the local justice system. Paradoxically, the deep political embeddedness of progressive elites does not necessarily constrain their expression of liberal values and motivation. These elite lawyers are integral to the expansion of lawyers' procedural rights in China's criminal justice reforms and produce a large number of essays, speeches, and media interviews to reveal the plight of lawyers in criminal defense. Furthermore, most of the highest-profile corruption cases in China, such as the trials of Politburo members Bo Xilai and Zhou Yongkang, involve lawyers who are progressive elites, though these lawyers usually shy away from sensitive human rights cases because of their structural proximity to state power.

Not surprisingly, the vast majority of the most sensitive human rights cases in China are handled by notable activists, most of whom, until very recently, have residences in Beijing but take on cases throughout the country. This is a relatively small but fairly cohesive group of lawyers. With a few exceptions, most notable activists come from humble educational and social backgrounds and started their law practice in the provinces before moving to Beijing. A substantial number of them are Christians and thus they often represent freedom-of-religion cases. Other sensitive case types that notable activists handle include freedom of speech, tortured prisoners, forced abortion, and so on, most of which are too far out of the safety zone for ordinary Chinese lawyers. Notable activists display firm commitments to the elements of political liberalism and admirable courage in their defense work, but many of them have been disbarred, "disappeared," tortured, or suffered from other forms of state repression. They are marginalized and repressed inside China but often hailed as heroes in the international media.

Grassroots activists are perhaps the most neglected group of Chinese criminal defense lawyers. They exist at the local level widely across the country, but very little has been written on this obscure group of activist lawyers in both scholarly and popular writings. Because grassroots activists are not politically embedded and do not enjoy any international exposure (as notable activists do), their political mobilization is even riskier than the mobilization of notable activists or progressive elites. As a result, many grassroots activists choose to hide their liberal values and motivation in everyday practice and focus on legal proceduralism and rights defense in routine cases. A small number of them have gradually become "die-hard lawyers" in recent years and gained national fame, but the vast majority remain cautious and keep a low profile in their everyday struggles for political liberalism.

In sum, the Chinese criminal defense bar is differentiated into five types of lawyers according to their variations in commitment to political liberalism, political embeddedness to the state, and the locations where they regularly reside or practice: (1) routine practitioners, (2) pragmatic brokers, (3) progressive elites, (4) notable activists, and (5) grassroots activists. This typology of criminal defense lawyers will be applied and substantiated with empirical data throughout the book.

Besides the internal differentiation of the bar, Chinese criminal defense lawyers also work and live in a larger "legal complex" (Karpik and Halliday 2011) consisting of other legally trained and practicing occupations, including judges, procurators, police officers, legal scholars, and others (e.g., legal news reporters or law bloggers). Defined as "a cluster of legal actors related to each other in dynamic structures and constituted and reconstituted through a variety of processes" (Karpik and Halliday 2011: 220), the legal complex is a concept aimed at explaining the dynamics of legal mobilization across occupational boundaries. It recognizes that lawyers' politics and collective action are always intertwined with other legally trained occupations. These structural relationships can range from cooperative and coalitional to fractured and oppositional. The rapidly changing forms of criminal practice in China provide one such site to observe a legal complex in action.

In China, those relationships historically have been conflictual, as lawyers stand as weak actors in confrontation with the powerful, state-controlled PPC, with the police as a looming presence in both prosecution and adjudication, while the procuracy holds supervisory power over the court in addition to its role in criminal prosecution. With the increasing professionalization of judges and procurators since the 1990s, the social distances among the three legally trained occupations (lawyers, procurators, and judges) have been gradually reduced, whereas institutional conflicts within the PPC have been on the rise (Liu and Halliday 2009). However, a deep divide between lawyers and the PPC still exists in the Chinese criminal justice system (Liang, He, and Lu 2014).

Political mobilization by the legal complex can occur daily in ordinary practice. It also occurs periodically when the rules of practice are themselves being negotiated. This occurs at key moments of China's legal reform, such as the promulgation and revisions of the PRC Criminal Procedure Law (CPL) in 1979, 1996, and 2012, and in its conflicting interpretations by judicial and administrative agencies involved in the criminal justice system (Liu and Halliday 2009). Here the legal complex can manifest itself as segments of practicing legal occupations mobilizing for or against, agreeing or disagreeing with, the parameters of criminal procedure rules as they are being legislated and implemented. This book will show in the three cycles of China's criminal procedure reforms since 1979 where the lines of divide occurred as segments of the legal complex, including the PPC, lawyers, and legal scholars, sought to influence the lawmaking and law-implementing processes.

DATA AND METHODS

The data collection for this project was a long and exhausting journey over a hundred thousand miles that took ten years to complete, but it was also a journey full of excitement and serendipity. We made our first field trip to China in September 2005 and conducted twenty-four interviews with legal scholars, lawyers, judges, and procurators in Beijing and Xi'an, with a focus on the CPL reforms. From 2007 to 2015, we made eleven additional field trips and conducted 183 interviews across six major cities in China (Beijing, Chengdu, Chongqing, Hangzhou, Kunming, Shanghai) and two smaller cities in Sichuan Province. The vast majority of our informants were criminal defense lawyers, but we also interviewed some judges, procurators, justice bureau officials, bar association leaders, and law professors during the fieldwork. Furthermore, we conducted ten interviews in Hong Kong, New York, and London during 2009–2011 with program officers in international organizations specializing in human rights or rule-of-law projects in China. While the vast majority of the interviews were conducted with one informant in his or her workplace, some interviews included multiple informants and/or were conducted in restaurants or teahouses, where the interviewees felt most comfortable.

We adopted an inductive approach in the twelve rounds of fieldwork in China and shifted our emphasis over time. The first two rounds of interviews focused on progressive elites and experts on the CPL reforms. Then we expanded the scope of interviews to criminal defense lawyers all over the country, mainly pragmatic brokers, grassroots activists, and routine practitioners. During the most recent trips, we spent more time interviewing and observing notable activists in Beijing, seeking to gather some longitudinal data on how their ideologies and practice have changed over time. The core topics of the interviews include the CPL reforms and their consequences on lawyers' criminal defense practice; lawyers' coping tactics in their defense work; lawyers' political motivations and strategies for collective action; lawyers' involvements in other areas of coercive social control (e.g., the Party disciplinary system, re-education through labor, administrative detention, and state security); and so on. While organized systematically, most of our questions were open-ended and we adjusted the content of each interview according to the specific context of the conversation and the characteristics of the interviewee(s). It was not a process of affirming our presumptions, but a process of discovery.

While assembling a basic blueprint of the criminal defense work of Chinese lawyers through eight rounds of interviews that we conducted personally, we also collected more systematic data at sites less accessible to us. We trained sixteen law students from China University of Political Science and Law (CUPL) to conduct fully structured interviews with local criminal defense lawyers in their hometowns during May–July 2009. Among the sixteen research assistants, thirteen successfully completed their interviews strictly following our interview questionnaire and turned in 112 interviews with criminal defense lawyers in thirteen medium-sized and small cities across all major regions in China. Each research assistant interviewed five to ten lawyers from four to nine different law firms in the same locality. Given the fact that most Chinese lawyers in medium-sized and small cities are general practitioners (Michelson 2007; Liu 2011), when selecting interviewees, we asked the research assistants to prioritize lawyers who mainly specialize in criminal defense but also include lawyers who handle a larger variety of cases including criminal defense. For the sake of confidentiality and protection of the respondents, the names of the thirteen cities in which our CUPL research assistants conducted interviews are omitted from the book, but the nine provinces in which the cities are located are Anhui, Fujian, Guangdong, Henan, Hubei, Jiangsu, Liaoning, Shandong, and Sichuan.

We analyzed the 112 fully structured interviews both qualitatively and quantitatively. Among the 112 lawyers, seventeen are female (15 percent), nearly two-thirds were born in the same city where they practice, and 95 percent were born in the same province. The gender proportion and highly local character of our sample correspond well to the general demographic patterns of Chinese lawyers who practice in medium-sized and small cities found in national statistics and earlier surveys (Michelson 2003; Michelson and Liu 2010). The youngest lawyer in the sample was twenty-seven years old, while the oldest lawyer was seventy-two. Nearly 80 percent of our respondents were between thirty and forty-nine years old. Given the relatively recent history of the Chinese legal profession, the age distribution of our sample appears approximately representative.

Generally speaking, the educational level of the 112 lawyers in the sample is lower than that of lawyers in major Chinese cities where we personally conducted interviews. Half of the lawyers have at least one degree from "Project 211" universities in China, which are roughly similar to doctorate-granting universities in the United States. Only 5 percent of the respondents have a graduate degree. As the PRC Lawyers Law does not require a law degree to take the bar exam, only 71 percent of the respondents hold a law degree, and many acquired their degrees through self-study or distance learning. In terms of specialization in criminal defense, 25 percent of the respondents reported that at least half of their cases were criminal cases, while 37 percent reported that only less than 10 percent of their cases were criminal cases. Overall, our sample well represents ordinary criminal defense lawyers in smaller Chinese cities, many of whom are general practitioners with limited or low-quality legal education.

In the following text, we use two separate formats to number our own interviews and those of our research assistants. The interviews we personally conducted are coded as "B0501," in which "B" refers to the location of the interview ("B" for Beijing, "C" for Chengdu, "H" for Hangzhou, "K" for Kunming, "S" for Shanghai, "Q" for Chongqing, "X" for Xi'an, "G" and "M" for the two smaller cities in Sichuan Province, and "I" for interviews with international organizations or international media); "05" refers to the year of the interview; and "01" refers to the number of the interview in accordance with its time and location. The interviews conducted by the

CUPL research assistants are coded as "GDD0901," in which "GD" refers to the province (i.e., Guangdong), "D" refers to the city, and "0901" also refers to the year and interview number, as in our personal interviews.

The 329 interviews conducted by the two authors and thirteen research assistants constitute the core of our empirical data, but we also draw data from three additional sources: (1) archival materials on the historical development of the CPL in legislation and practice; (2) online ethnographic data from a nationwide Internet forum hosted by the official All China Lawyers Association; and, (3) a database of more than 10,000 articles related to lawyers and criminal defense in twenty-eight Chinese national and local newspapers.

First, we collected extensive archival materials that were available from each of the primary actors in the criminal justice system. While our identities as overseas researchers limited our direct access to police officers, procurators, or judges during the fieldwork, an indirect but effective way to learn about the opinions and experiences, agreements and disagreements of these actors is to analyze their exchanges with each other in their in-house organs. We systematically collected data from the newspapers and journals of the PPC and bar associations, including *Chinese Lawyers* (中国律师), *Beijing Lawyers* (北京律师), *Police Studies* (公安研究), *People's Police* (人民公安), *People's Procuratorial Daily* (检察日报), *People's Procuratorial Monthly* (人民检察), *People's Court News* (人民法院报), and *People's Judiciary* (人民司法), etc. We also collected the formal laws (e.g., statutes, judicial and administrative interpretations, notices, regulations) and government documents on criminal procedure and lawyer representation since 1979, as well as relevant declarations, covenants, and principles of the United Nations.

Second, based on Sida Liu's three-year online ethnographic work, we collected and analyzed a large number of written discussions from the official Internet forum of the All China Lawyers Association (ACLA; www.acla.org .cn) regarding the practice of Chinese criminal defense lawyers. The forum was established in August 2002 and has been developed into a large Internet community of lawyers, law students, and other legal professionals in China. By March 2005, it had over 34,000 registered users from every province of China (including Tibet and Inner Mongolia), who collectively had posted 271,925 messages on twenty-five discussion boards. Messages relating to criminal procedure law and the work of defense lawyers had been among the central topics and most heavily trafficked discussion sites since the beginning of the forum. As a long time participant and later a discussion board manager, Liu collected sixty threads of messages on lawyers' criminal defense work for data analysis from these online discussions. Among the sixty threads, there are nine threads (seventy-seven messages) on the difficulty in meeting criminal suspects, twelve threads (118 messages) on the difficulty in collecting evidence and cross-examining witnesses at trial, four threads (fifty-one messages) on the difficulty in getting access to case files, and twenty-two threads (382 messages) on the persecution of criminal defense lawyers. Through this unique data source we can observe, without contamination by outside researchers, the spontaneous exchanges among lawyers about their problems in criminal defense work as well as their political values. It also enables us to contrast the "public voice" of the bar association journals with the "private voices" of its members. The forum data are coded in the form of "F#431895," in which "F" refers to the ACLA forum, and "#431895" refers to the number of the first message in a discussion thread as it appears on the forum.

Third, with the assistance of our research collaborators Cheng-Tong Lir Wang, Hongqi Wu, Lily Liang, and six CUPL research assistants, we created a large database consisting of twenty-eight Chinese national and local newspapers targeting general or legal audiences. We used a combination of keywords to compile a comprehensive database of 9,486 newspaper articles relevant to lawyers and criminal defense. Pairing of the term "lawyer" with a variety of criminal justice-related keywords, the database has a particular advantage in that it captures a wide range of lawyers' activities in the criminal justice system. In addition to the Chinese media data, we also collected 282 articles from major international media including the *New York Times*, the BBC, and *South China Morning Post*, as well as eighty-one articles from Human Rights in China (HRIC), an international human rights organization that regularly reports on the work of notable activist lawyers in China. For the analysis of the Li Zhuang case in Chapter 6 and online networking in Chapter 7, we collected relevant media reports and legal documents, as well as online discussions among legal professionals from the blogosphere and social media. The media and Internet data are analyzed as primary data and coded in the form of "CQRB_20100226" in which "CQRB" (*Chongqing Daily*) is the abbreviated title of the newspaper, magazine, or website in Chinese pinyin or English, and "20100226" is the date of the publication (e.g., February 26, 2010).

In the rest of the book, we provide a comprehensive social science inquiry of the politics of lawyers in China's criminal justice system. This inquiry begins with a historical overview of the CPL reforms from 1979 to 2012 and its consequences for lawyers' criminal defense work (Chapter 2). We then proceed to analyze lawyers' difficulties and danger in criminal defense (Chapter 3), as well as their survival strategies in the unfavorable criminal justice system (Chapter 4). In Chapters 5–7, we focus on the multiple forms of political mobilization in the Chinese legal profession, including the fight of notable activists in human rights cases (Chapter 5), elite mobilization around the Li Zhuang case (Chapter 6), and the recent rise (and fall) of die-hard lawyering through online networking (Chapter 7).

The book concludes (Chapter 8) by circling back to the theoretical propositions and orienting questions in the Prologue and this chapter: Where are China's legal and political reforms going? And, how do lawyers fight for basic legal freedoms? We argue that China's contradictions are so deeply embedded in its ideologies, institutions, and law that its legal and political trajectories remain indeterminate. From the vantage point of lawyers' struggles, China's futures might conceivably be liberal-legal, despotic, or volatile, among others. Nevertheless, in China, as in many other illiberal political societies, past and present, there is empirical evidence of at least a small but discernible impulse by lawyers to construct a system of justice in which basic legal freedoms can be protected by a moderate state and an active civil society. China's lawyers display many forms of political action observed in earlier centuries and other histories, but they also exhibit distinctive creativity and innovative forms of mobilization that make China's unfolding history discernibly their own.

2

Recursivity in Criminal Procedure Reforms

Criminal procedure law is a vitally important weapon for criminal defense lawyers. It provides them with not only procedural tools for their everyday work, but also sources of protection against arbitrary state power. In authoritarian regimes such as China, criminal procedure law "on the books" is often twisted and compromised in practice, which makes the work of defense lawyers unpredictable and risky. Accordingly, in the three decades of China's legal reform following the Cultural Revolution, lawyers have been actively calling for the continuous revisions of the CPL, with more procedural constraints on the power of the PPC, as well as the institutionalization of basic legal rights for their clients and themselves. Nevertheless, China's CPL reforms have gone through a recursive process from 1979 to 2012, in which lawyers' procedural rights have been gradually expanded on paper but encountered strong resistance from the PPC in everyday work.

Cycles of domestic law reform in the contemporary world invariably are influenced to some degree by global contexts (Halliday and Osinsky 2006). Global norms frame the domestic debate because, since the late 1970s, China's leaders and lawmakers have been obliged to position themselves between their domestic challenges of social stability and China's presentation of self to the rest of the world. As a result, criminal procedure reforms, as in many other areas of Chinese law, have become experimental sites for this large project of state-led legal transplantation, which has often produced poorly implemented legal institutions (Liu 2006). The global influence on China's CPL lawmaking is realized through three major mechanisms (Braithwaite and Drahos 2000): (1) modelling, by which China conforms its CPL to the standards of the norms of the United Nations; (2) capacity building, by which international training and research programs shape the ideologies and practices of Chinese judges, lawyers, and academics; and (3) indirect coercion, by which powerful entities such as the United States or the

European Union frequently tackle China's human rights and procedural justice in front of the international community.

In our earlier work, we applied a recursivity theory of legal change (Halliday and Carruthers 2007; Halliday 2009) to examine the struggles of criminal defense lawyers in the lawmaking and implementation of the CPL during 1979–2008 (Liu and Halliday 2009). Recursivity theory maintains that legal change rarely occurs in a linear progressive manner, but more often cycles between the establishment of formal law in the books (statutes, regulations, cases, etc.) and the implementation of law in action until some level of settling occurs in legal meaning and practice. We argue that Chinese lawyers' difficulties in criminal defense had deep roots in the recursive nature of the criminal procedure reforms. In particular, those difficulties were produced by interactions of the four mechanisms of recursivity (i.e., indeterminacy of law, contradictions, diagnostic struggles, and actor mismatch) in both lawmaking and implementation. Only by conceiving of lawmaking and practice as intimately connected and mutually contingent processes can we fully explain the procedural reform of China's criminal justice system since the late 1970s and its consequences for lawyers' criminal defense work.

This chapter presents the core findings of our earlier research and complements it with updates on the 2012 CPL revision from our more recent fieldwork, without burdening readers with the technical details of recursivity theory (for this, see Liu and Halliday 2009). We begin with a brief historical overview of China's criminal justice system from 1949 to 1979 and discuss the global norms and national contexts that constitute the institutional environment for the CPL reforms. Then we analyze the recursive cycles of CPL lawmaking from 1979 to 1996 and from 1996 to 2012. In this ongoing process of legal change, the CPL has gradually become more effective in ordinary cases, yet in the politically sensitive cases where it is the most needed, the CPL is marginalized and sometimes rendered irrelevant. As a result, it remains to be seen whether lawyers can change the dynamics of recursivity and turn themselves from hapless victims to powerful actors in China's criminal justice system.

CHINESE CRIMINAL JUSTICE BEFORE 1979

The seeds of China's encounter with basic legal freedoms spring from very rocky soil. The legislative history of China's criminal law dates back to the Western Zhou Dynasty (ca. 1100–771 BCE) (Head and Wang 2005), but until a draft of the Great Qing Criminal Procedure Code was finished in 1910, there had never been a separate criminal procedure law in Imperial China.

Restraint on imperial executive power relied more upon the ethical behavior of the enlightened ruler rather than the check and balance of power through legal procedures. Public law was an instrument for guiding society and "indisputably a tool to serve the interests of the state" (Peerenboom 2002: 41). Criminal law and penal codes were retributive and relied heavily on punishment. A primitive legal profession, often called "litigation masters"(讼师), not only was never established as a major player in politics, but was often suppressed and fragmented by the government (Macauley 1998; Dang 2005).

Following the collapse of the Qing Dynasty in 1911, a brief window of legal reform opened up in the Republican period (1912–1949) with the establishment of a nascent legal profession, the opening of law departments and training institutes, and the founding of Western-style courts following the Continental legal tradition (Xu 2000). The Criminal Procedure Law was promulgated twice in this period (by the Beiyang government in 1912 and the Kuomintang government in 1935, respectively), though after the PRC was established in 1949 all Republican laws were abolished (Cai 1999). Yet these initiatives sprouted mostly in major urban centers (e.g., Shanghai) where they had too short a time to become institutionalized, and the fractiousness of wars and internal conflicts in Republican China never permitted a full flowering of the seeds planted by the legal reformers.

The dislocations that the Communist Revolution brought in 1949 carried over into the criminal justice system. Driven by the principle of "leniency for confession, harshness for resistance" (坦白从宽，抗拒从严), the criminal process in the early years of the PRC was characterized by long, informal, and secret interrogations and a lack of defense for criminal suspects (Cohen 1968: 48–49). Lubman (1999) argues that the PRC criminal law has swung between two rival conceptions that arguably have continued to the present: (1) the *mass line*, a largely arbitrary criminal process that relied on shifting Party priorities and local cadre discretion; and (2) the *bureaucratic model*, the Soviet model of criminal justice in which a professionalized staff (i.e., police officers, procurators, and judges) administer a somewhat orderly and predictable rule-governed system. The "alternation and competition" between these two models from 1949 to the Cultural Revolution (1966–1976) were played out in the relationships among the "iron triangle" of the PPC. However, in either model the process had no place for independent actors who might defend the accused against abuses committed by those who administered it (Cohen 1968), though lawyers were formally tolerated and briefly cultivated in certain periods.

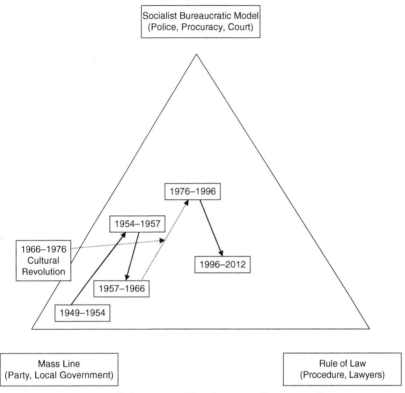

FIGURE 2.1 Temporal changes in China's criminal justice policy since 1949.

As Figure 2.1 illustrates, following this logic, from 1949 to 1954 the mass line dominated and most legally trained personnel held over from the Republican era were purged. However, beginning in 1954, the pendulum swung towards regularization, including the passage of legislation to organize the procuracy and courts, statutes to set some guidelines for criminal procedure, policies to differentiate functions among the PPC, and tentative steps towards creating a defense bar. This brief turn towards what was essentially a Soviet model of criminal justice was reversed sharply in 1957, when mounting criticism of the Party provoked it to strike back through the Anti-Rightist Campaign that reverted to the mass line and called upon the PPC to act as a unified force to implement Party policy, like "three workshops in one factory" (Lubman 1999: 84). Meanwhile, the Soviet-style offices for lawyers that had been founded in the previous three years were largely dismantled in this period. The Cultural Revolution (1966–1976) swept away even the mass line: the formal criminal process ceased to exist and the activities of the PPC were variously suspended, reorganized, and disbanded, depending on the location and time (Hurst 2015). Lawyers disappeared altogether.

But the Cultural Revolution left a powerful residue. Its destructive and pervasive effects for the breakdown in law enforcement, collapse of public order, and the abandonment of any kind of regularized institutions of social control led many leaders in subsequent years (e.g., Peng Zhen and Deng Xiaoping) to value rational legal administration and restraints on arbitrary power so that such devastations might never recur. The rise of Deng Xiaoping to power in the late 1970s signified a revival of law, lawyers, and legal institutions. But much began *de novo*. The bar needed to be "invented as a profession without any guidance from Chinese tradition or China's recent history" (Lubman 1999: 158). Taking effect in 1982, the Interim Regulation on Lawyers defined lawyers as "state legal workers" whose work was to "serve the cause of socialism" and protect "the legitimate rights and interests of citizens" (Lubman 1999: 154). The 1997 Lawyers Law reflected the progressive expansion of civil and commercial legal practice and signaled some "unhooking" of the profession from the state (Michelson 2003). Licensed lawyers today are directly regulated by the All China Lawyers Association (ACLA), which is under close control of the Ministry of Justice (MOJ). Thus a revived legal profession has emerged, although it remains highly fragmented and its quality varies greatly (Michelson 2006, 2007; Liu 2011, 2015).

Interwoven with the transformation of the legal profession have been cycles of criminal justice reforms that directly affect the capacity of defense lawyers to present restraint on law enforcement agencies. Over the past thirty-five years, China has enacted legislation that registers a sharp turn from its criminal law practice in history by intimating at prospects of state moderation and basic legal rights for its citizens. These ideals are most progressively advanced through the 1979 CPL enactment and its revisions in 1996 and 2012, with numerous judicial interpretations and administrative regulations in between. While both the 1996 and 2012 CPL revisions are comprehensive in nature, this chapter focuses more specifically on issues related to lawyer representation, which is a key indicator of the struggles over basic legal freedoms in the Chinese criminal justice system.

THE 1979 CRIMINAL PROCEDURE LAW: BEGINNING OF A REFORM EPISODE

Since the People's Republic of China was established in 1949, no formal criminal procedure code or criminal code was adopted in its first thirty years, except for a number of criminal law–related statutes issued by various judicial and administrative agencies and Party organs. From 1979, a CPL lawmaking reform episode began in China, which lasted until the promulgation of the 2012 CPL. Since the 1996 CPL was put into practice, lawmaking activities by the National People's Congress (NPC), Supreme People's Court (SPC), Supreme People's Procuracy (SPP), Ministry of Public Security (MPS), Ministry of State Security (MSS), and Ministry of Justice (MOJ) have become much more frequent. To explain the dynamics of CPL lawmaking in this episode, we divide it into three major legislative cycles, namely, the 1979 CPL legislation, the 1996 CPL revision, and the 2012 CPL revision, complemented by smaller regulatory cycles in between. In this section, we provide a brief overview of the lawmaking and implementation of the 1979 CPL as a historical background for more detailed analysis of the two later cycles.

The 1979 CPL, together with the 1979 Criminal Law, was among the first major laws promulgated by the NPC after the Cultural Revolution. This round of lawmaking was the direct result of a deep lesson from the social and political turmoil during the Cultural Revolution (B0515; Folsom, Minan, and Otto 1992; Lo 1995; Cai 1999; Potter 2001). In reaction to the unlimited flexibility and discretion of the administration of justice in earlier periods, during the groundbreaking Third Meeting of the Eleventh Congress of the Chinese Communist Party (CCP) in late 1978, Deng Xiaoping, Peng Zhen, and other central leaders decided to build a legal system that had the capacity of maintaining social order and promoting economic development (Cui 1996). As part of this effort, the 1979 CPL laid down the basic framework of an inquisitorial system of criminal justice following the civil law and Soviet law traditions that informed the PRC's formal legal system.

The 1979 law was primarily based on an earlier draft in 1956 (Cui 1996), which drew upon both the Soviet law and some experiences from the old Communist areas before 1949 (B0504). From the CCP meeting in December 1978 to the promulgation of the law in July 1979, the whole lawmaking process lasted a mere seven months. Due to the special circumstances of its enactment, the 1979 CPL contained only 164 articles in total; many specific procedures were left to the discretion of the PPC. Although the NPC drafting committee consisted of a number of widely recognized national legal experts, few legal scholars specializing in criminal procedure participated in the 1979 CPL lawmaking process because many of them were expelled to the provinces during the Cultural Revolution (B0504). The exclusion of legal scholars led to a potential mismatch between those who drafted the law and those who taught future generations of practitioners who would implement it.

The 1979 CPL divided the criminal process into three separate phases: the police were in charge of the investigation phase, including investigation, detention, and pretrial; the procuracy was in charge of the prosecution phase, including arrest approval, prosecution, and some investigation; and the court was in charge of the trial phase (Article 3). Although the procuracy also had the procedural power of supervision over the whole process, in each phase only one of the three agencies was in control of its respective area of responsibility. In other words, the relationship among the three agencies was more sequential and coordinative rather than checking and balancing one another (Article 5). Defense lawyers obtained access to the defendants only when a case reached the trial phase, and they were given no more than seven days before trial to prepare the case (Article 110).

This unbalanced structure of the criminal process made the role of criminal defense lawyers very limited in practice. The defense lawyer, as a state employee, was expected to "act on the basis of facts, take the law as the criterion, and be loyal to the interest of the socialist cause and the people" – he was not an agent of the defendant in a criminal proceeding, but an independent party who must carry out his activities within the legal framework without fabricating evidence or distorting facts for the interest of his clients (Leng 1985: 93). During the no more than seven days between appointment and trial, the defense lawyer was allowed to visit the defendant and review the case files transferred from the procuracy at the relevant court (LCHR 1993; Fu 1998). However, the effect of the lawyer's defense on the case outcome was kept to the minimum – the great majority of defendants remained unrepresented by lawyers and, for those who did get legal representation, lawyers' plea for innocence was rarely offered (LCHR 1993; Fu 1998).

The limited role of defense lawyers, coupled with the huge discretionary power of the police and the procuracy, made it difficult to protect the rights of defendants. In 1983, the NPC Standing Committee promulgated the Decision Regarding the Procedure for the Swift Trial of Criminals Who severely Endanger Social Security, or the so-called September 2 Decision, which abolished the trial notification period in death penalty cases and thus stripped the defendant's *de facto* right to legal counsel – this provided the legal basis for the several "strike hard" (严打) campaigns on crimes all through the 1980 and 1990s (Cui 1996: 208–215). During these campaigns, the procedures enacted in the 1979 CPL were largely replaced by the "severe and swift" (从重从快) principle and by the unrestricted discretion of the PPC (Dutton 1992; Tanner 1999; Bakken 2005; Trevaskes 2007). Among all the various procedural problems in the criminal process, two measures frequently used by the police and the procuracy in practice aroused most attention by both Chinese legal scholars and foreign observers, i.e. shelter for investigation (收容审查) and exemption from prosecution (免予起诉). While shelter for investigation allowed the police to detain and investigate a person in the police office without any approval from the procuracy or the court, exemption from prosecution allowed the procuracy to convict a criminal suspect and withhold his punishment without court trial (B0515; Clarke and Feinerman 1995; Lubman 1999; Luo 2000; Chen 2002). Such procedural measures enabled the rights of defendants to be easily abused by the PPC.

In sum, when the 1979 CPL was drafted, there was no formal legal profession in China; most legal scholars had been exiled to the provinces; the procuracy and the judiciary were newly revived – the whole criminal justice system was still in an embryonic stage. After the law was put into practice, lawyers and defendants were almost completely lost in struggles over how the law actually worked and how it should work. The "iron triangle" of the PPC closely cooperated with one another and tightly controlled the criminal process in the 1980s.

By the early 1990s, however, the NPC's institutional power had significantly increased (O'Brien 1990; Cai 1999; M. Tanner 1999; Ngok 2002; Paler 2005); lawyers as a profession had been revived and their privatization had begun; legal academics became more active participants in the lawmaking process (Ngok 2002); and both the procuracy and the judiciary had grown into large bureaucratic organizations that had the capacity to challenge the police from time to time. Externally, although the Chinese legal system still mainly followed the Continental and Soviet legal traditions, ideas and practices of Anglo-American law already entered China through the diffusion of global norms as well as increasing scholarly and professional exchanges between China and the West, particularly the United States. All these situations implicitly called for a major redistribution of power in the criminal justice system (B0504) and led to a comprehensive revision of the CPL in 1996.

LAWMAKING PROCESS OF THE 1996 CRIMINAL PROCEDURE LAW

The legislative process of the 1996 CPL revision started in January 1991 and ended in March 1996, five years in total. In appearance, this revision, with its goals of expanding adversarial proceedings, increasing rights of defendants, and widening the role of defense lawyers, seemed a great step forward (Chen 1995). Yet the reality of criminal defense practice in the next fifteen years indicated that several provisions in the legislation might in fact have been regressive. In this cycle of legal change, a wider range of actors with conflicting interests were involved than in the cycle of the 1979 CPL and, accordingly, power struggles and conflicts of interest in lawmaking became much more salient.

The preparation for the 1996 CPL revision began with a small-scale symposium held at China University of Political Science and Law (CUPL) in January 1991, organized by the Criminal Law Office of the NPC Legal Work Commission (Cui 1996). After this symposium, legal scholars began extensively to discuss many specific issues in the CPL through research papers and academic conferences. In September 1993, the NPC Legal Work Commission held a two-day symposium with the SPC, the SPP, the MPS, the MSS, the MOJ, and several legal scholars in Beijing to discuss how to revise the CPL. Soon afterwards, the NPC Legal Work Commission appointed Professor Chen Guangzhong to lead a research group at CUPL to draft a preliminary version of the 1996 CPL (B0503; B0504; Chen 1996; Cui 1996). Based upon research on the UN covenants and the criminal procedure codes in other countries, the scholarly draft of the CPL completed in 1994 contains 329 articles, twice as many as the number of articles in the 1979 CPL (Chen and Yan 1995; Cui 1996). Academic discussions on the CPL through conferences continued after the scholarly draft was submitted to the NPC, including with foreign experts and scholars from Taiwan (B0504; Cui 1996).

Yet legal scholars were by no means the only active players in the 1996 CPL lawmaking process. As early as 1992–1993, some NPC representatives proposed bills for the CPL revision, and the MPS, the SPP, and the SPC all put forward their ideas for the revision (Chen 1996). At the local level, in 1993 a judge in Zhejiang Province wrote an entire book on the CPL revision and proposed a complete CPL draft with 212 articles (Cui 1996). On the other hand, lawyers were almost completely excluded from the 1996 CPL revision – they could only make indirect opinions through the MOJ and a few prominent legal scholars (B0502; B0507; B0508; B0510; X0505; H0701; S0703).

In June 1995, the NPC Legal Work Commission held another five-day symposium with leaders and research staff of the MPS, the SPP, the SPC, and the MOJ, as well as some legal scholars in Beijing, in which twenty-four major issues on the CPL revision were comprehensively debated (Chen 1996; Cui 1996). Based on all these discussions, the NPC's Legal Work Commission made a revised draft CPL in October 1995 and distributed it nationwide for comments and suggestions – a standard practice also observed in the 2012 CPL revision. In January 1996, two meetings with high-ranking officials from the SPC, the SPP, the MPS, the MOJ, and the MSS were held by the NPC Standing Committee and the Central Political-Legal Committee of the CCP to coordinate the divergent opinions on several key issues in the revised draft, including shelter for investigation and exemption from prosecution (Chen 1996; Cui 1996). Finally, through a series of routine legislative procedures, the 1996 CPL was passed by the Fourth Meeting of the Eighth NPC in March 1996 and became effective on January 1, 1997.

The final version of the 1996 CPL contains 225 articles, 61 articles more than the 1979 CPL but 104 articles less than the scholarly version. According to the estimation of a distinguished law professor who participated in the entire 1996 lawmaking process, only about 65 percent of the content of the scholarly draft was finally incorporated into the 1996 CPL (B0504). The significant reduction of articles during the lawmaking process indicates the divergent opinions between legal scholars and other actors (esp. the PPC) over many issues. The four most heavily debated issues in the five years of revision were the presumption of innocence, shelter for investigation, exemption from prosecution, and the adversarial trial system (ZGFX_199405; Cui 1995). Both legal scholars and the SPC representatives proposed to add the presumption of innocence as a general principle of the CPL, whereas the SPP and MPS representatives strongly opposed it (ZGFX_199405). On the police's power of shelter for investigation and the procuracy's power of exemption from prosecution, there had also been intense debates between legal scholars and the SPP/MPS representatives before they were abolished. The movement of trial reform toward an adversarial system encountered strong oppositions of the SPC and the SPP representatives.

Lawyers were largely excluded from the 1996 lawmaking process, but their interests were indirectly represented by the MOJ representatives and a few legal scholars. For example, a MOJ representative proposed that, in order to fully protect the procedural rights of the criminal suspects and defendants, lawyers should be allowed to intervene in the criminal process from the phase of investigation and they should be able to meet their clients and collect their own evidence (ZGFX_199405). Not surprisingly, representatives of the police strongly opposed these proposals (B0504). Although the power of the MOJ was weak compared to that of the MPS, legal scholars were able to exert their influence through the scholarly draft and later discussions.

As a result of all these debates, compromises were built into in the final version of the 1996 CPL. In so doing, the law incorporated contradictory concepts and ideologies. A law professor who directly participated in the lawmaking process identified four interrelated ideological contradictions inherent in the CPL: (1) striking crimes vs. protecting human rights; (2) substantive law vs. procedural law; (3) efficiency vs. justice; and (4) rights of the victim vs. rights of the defendant (B0513). These ideological cleavages in lawmaking led to many conflicting measures in the 1996 CPL. For example, both striking crimes and protecting rights were written in the 1996 CPL as basic principles (Articles 1 and 2); the lawyer was allowed to meet the suspects in the phase of investigation, but they were not given the status of a defender (Article 96); lawyers could collect their own evidence but they needed the witness's consent and, for testimony from the victim's witnesses, the approval from the procuracy or the court (Article 37); etc. All these tensions in the law reflect the ideological contradictions and struggles between different actors in the lawmaking process over what was wrong with the system and how it should be corrected.

Furthermore, structural contradictions in the criminal justice system were also built into the 1996 CPL. The structural position of the procuracy is a good case in point. The procuracy has two basic functions, namely, to prosecute cases and to supervise the work of the police and the court. However, as each of the PPC controls one phase of the criminal process (i.e., investigation, prosecution, and trial), the procuracy's supervision of the police and the court cannot be a substantive supervision, therefore the 1996 CPL only gives a procedural power to the procuracy, i.e., when a decision of the police (e.g., case filing) or the court (e.g., court procedure) is not in accordance with the law, the procuracy can issue a "correcting opinion" (纠正意见), to which the police or the court must respond (Article 87; Article 169). However, if the police or the court decides to stick to their original decision, there is no sanction that the procuracy could exercise (B0509; X0505; X0508; F#431895).

These ideological and structural contradictions produced ambiguities and inconsistencies in the 1996 CPL. Many of our interviewees, particularly lawyers and scholars, expressed the view that the 1996 revision was made "in a hurry" (B0503; B0504; B0507; B0508; B0511; etc.). By this they did not mean that the lawmaking period was too short, but that many important issues were not clarified in the law. For example, under the 1996 CPL, the defense lawyer could intervene in the criminal process from the investigation phase, much earlier than under the 1979 CPL, but the 1996 law did not provide enough complementary measures or sanctions to guarantee the lawyer's procedural rights. The supervisory power of the procuracy discussed above is another example.

All these indeterminacies of law quickly generated conflicting regulations and interpretations by the implementing agencies. After the 1996 CPL was promulgated, in less than a year the SPC, the SPP, and the MPS all made their own interpretative regulations and notices on how to implement the new CPL in practice. These include the MPS's 1996 Notice on Issues Related to the Implementation of the Criminal Procedure Law and 1996 Regulation on the

Lawyer's Involvement of the Criminal Process in the Phase of Investigation, the SPP's 1996 Notice on Guaranteeing the Smooth Implementation of the Criminal Procedure Law and 1997 People's Procuracy's Rules for Criminal Procedure (Interim), and the SPC's 1996 Interpretation on Several Issues in the Implementation of the Criminal Procedure Law (Interim). Numerous rules and notices at the provincial and municipal levels were also promulgated during this period.

A notable feature of these early interpretations is that they are often in conflict with the 1996 CPL or contradict one another over many issues, particularly issues related to lawyers' criminal defense work. For instance, a September 1996 notice of the SPP emphasizes the importance of sticking to the "severe and swift" and "severe and strict" principles of "strike hard" campaigns in the implementation of the new CPL; a December 1996 regulation of the MPS sets the time and place of the lawyer's meeting with suspects and allows the police to be present during the meeting; the three interim CPL interpretations by the SPC, the SPP, and the MPS made during December 1996–January 1997 provide contradictory prescriptions on a variety of issues. As a law professor commented:

> Our current CPL has 225 articles. This is too few for a large country like China. It is not satisfactory. In the implementation the PPC have made all kinds of interpretations for implementation. Altogether there are approximately 1,440 articles from interpretations. In China the procuracy and the court could be considered judicial agencies. But the MPS is an administrative agency and it is inappropriate for it to put together an interpretation like the court. All three contradict each other and each has its own rule and all try to check and constrain the power of other agencies. Also there are situations where the interpretations may directly violate the law. So the result of this in practice is that all the agencies when they deal with a case they use their own interpretations and this reduces the efficiency of the process.
>
> (B0511, Beijing)

To solve the conflicts among those interpretations and guarantee the smooth implementation of the 1996 CPL, the NPC Legal Work Commission organized the SPC, the SPP, the MPS, the MSS, and the MOJ and made a Joint Regulation in January 1998. The Joint Regulation emphasizes that, unless the case involves state secrets, the lawyer's meeting with criminal suspects needs no approval from the investigating agency and should be arranged within forty-eight hours (Article 11), and the scope of "state secrets" should be restricted to the content of the case (Article 9). Both the SPC and the SPP adjusted their interpretations in accordance to this Joint Regulation, but the MPS

Regulation remained intact – the police could still set the time and place for the lawyer's meeting and be present at the meeting if necessary (Articles 11 and 12). Meanwhile, the MOJ and the ACLA also promulgated their regulations to protect lawyers' rights in criminal cases, but these regulations have no binding effect on the behavior of the police or the judicial agencies. Conflicts of interpretations persisted in practice and they made the work of defense lawyers extremely difficult.

IMPLEMENTING THE 1996 CRIMINAL PROCEDURE LAW

When the 1996 CPL was initially passed by the NPC, many of the new prescriptions in the law were highly acclaimed by criminal defense lawyers (e.g., BJLS_199603) and overseas observers. By contrast, the police and the procuracy expressed concerns about the law's restriction on their power and discretion (B0501; B0509; RMJC_199708; GAYJ_199801), while many legal scholars registered disappointment as the stipulations in the law on several key issues were still far behind "international standards" (ZGFX_199603). However, soon after the law was put into practice, procurators and police officers were much relieved because they discovered that in practice they could still control the criminal process almost the same as they had previously (B0501; B0515; C0708), whereas lawyers found that they were facing even greater difficulties and personal danger in practice.

According to the official statistics of the ACLA, in the five years after the 1996 CPL became effective (1997–2001), 142 criminal defense lawyers were arrested by the police and procuracy, among which 77 lawyers were illegally detained or even beaten, and 27 cases were directly concerned with Article 38 of the 1996 CPL, which, together with Article 306 of the 1997 Criminal Law, established the crime of lawyer's perjury (Wang 2001, 2003; ACLA 2002; Fang 2005). Those numbers continued to grow in later years, but the ACLA stopped publishing the statistics. These lawyer persecution cases, though relatively few in number, had a powerful signaling and chilling effect on the entire Chinese legal profession. More and more Chinese lawyers, particularly those working in economically developed areas, were staying away from criminal defense work in the early 2000s (Yu 2002; Sheng 2003, 2004). In 2000, for example, all 5,495 Beijing lawyers collectively only handled around 4,300 criminal cases, which amounts to an average of 0.78 cases per lawyer (ZGLS_200207). In their public discussions on the ACLA forum, lawyers also expressed serious concerns about the various problems in criminal defense (Halliday and Liu 2007). Together, the difficulties in meeting suspects, collecting evidence, and accessing case files, as well as the threat of the crime of lawyer's perjury, heavily restrained lawyers from mounting an active defense and indeed compelled them to adopt defensive strategies to protect themselves at the expense of protecting their clients (see Chapter 3 for details).

These unintended consequences were the result of both the conflicting interpretations of the CPL and the everyday struggles among different actors in the workplace. Take lawyers' difficulty in meeting suspects. The 1996 CPL and the 1998 Joint Regulation prescribed that the lawyer's meeting should be arranged within forty-eight hours and did not require the approval of the police, but the 1996 MPS Regulation prescribed that the time and place for the lawyer's meeting should be decided by the police and police officers could choose to be present during the meeting. These conflicts in the law led to serious conflicts between lawyers and police officers in practice: lawyers believed that their meeting applications did not need approval and the meeting should be arranged within 48 hours, whereas the police insisted on their power to approve and be present during the meeting.

In their workplaces, the police had various strategies for rejecting the lawyer's meeting or setting obstacles during the meeting. Although the 1998 Joint Regulation restricted the meaning of "state secret," police officers still often broadly interpreted the scope of "state secret" to reject the lawyer's meeting application (B0510; B0515). A law professor who trained a large number of police officers explained this and other techniques that the police used to reject or postpone the lawyer's meeting:

> When the lawyer wants to meet the suspect they have all kinds of reasons to reject you: first, now the suspect is in the investigation phase and the investigation itself is a state secret, so you cannot interfere; second, they will postpone the meeting with all kinds of methods, for example, the lawyer comes and the police officer says I have to report to the superior but my superior is out of town, so two days later the lawyer is back and [the police officer says] I have to report to the division chief and he is in a meeting now. This is a very prevalent phenomenon. So the consequence is that it is extremely difficult for the lawyer to meet.
>
> (B0515, Beijing)

Even if a meeting were arranged (often long exceeding the forty-eight-hour requirement by the 1998 Joint Regulation), the police officer was almost always present, and the officer sometimes intimidated the criminal suspect not to reveal information to the lawyer. Some lawyers ironically described this as "not the lawyer's meeting with the criminal suspect, but the police officer's investigation with the assistance of the lawyer" (F#618182). Some detention centers also had informal rules for the lawyer's meeting; for instance, the meeting should not exceed half an hour (B0508). An experienced female defense lawyer in Beijing recounted:

> Earlier last year I went to meet a suspect in Suzhou and the procuracy led me to meet the suspect and after five minutes they wanted to take him away. I shouted for more time and they gave me another five minutes. Then I procrastinated for another two minutes. I got twelve minutes altogether. This was only a few days after the SPP Regulation on Lawyers was passed. So the SPP think they did an excellent thing for lawyers – they want us to say good things about it and held a symposium with a lot of media there. So I told this case at the meeting and it was reported on the *Legal Daily* the next day. They were pretty upset about it.
>
> (B0510, Beijing)

This quote not only shows the severe difficulties in conducting the lawyer's meeting (even for a famous Beijing lawyer), but also lawyers' strategies for fighting back. It is only one of many cases in which lawyers turned to the media as potential allies in their bid to fix in the minds of public audiences their particular diagnosis of wrongs in the criminal justice system (e.g., H0701; S0703; Halliday and Liu 2007).

Besides the media, some lawyers relied on legal scholars – their natural allies, most of whom firmly believed in legal proceduralism – to promote changes (B0508; C0709; C0710). Many law professors discussed lawyers' problems in their articles and speeches, and sometimes these were even published in the police's and the procuracy's newspapers and journals. Furthermore, some defense lawyers with previous work experience in the PPC were also able to use their connections to reduce the difficulties in practice (B0508; B0516; X0505; C0708; H0703; Michelson 2007). Therefore, although in their direct confrontations with the state judicial and law enforcement agencies lawyers were almost completely powerless, they could find means and mobilize resources to indirectly change the power equilibrium in the implementation of the CPL.

Similarly, struggles over what is the new distribution of power in the criminal process were prevalent within the "iron triangle" of the PPC. The 1996 CPL restricted the power of the police and the procuracy by abolishing some discretionary measures (e.g., shelter for investigation, exemption from prosecution) and partially changed the trial mode from the inquisitorial system to the adversarial system. However, in implementation the police and the procuracy quickly developed a series of countermeasures to rebalance the power structure in the criminal process. A former vice-chief

procurator in a local procuracy in Beijing in the late 1990s described the
experience of procurators after 1996:

> Immediately after the 1996 revision a lot of procurators were nervous. Then
> they found that the new provisions were not practical. For example, after
> 1996, the procuracy only transferred the major case files to the court but not
> all of them, so procuracies could make a restrictive interpretation of this
> regulation to keep evidence that is advantageous to the defendant away from
> the lawyer who doesn't get access before the proceedings. . . . Also, the 1996
> CPL stipulated that the procurators needed to xerox the case files and transfer
> them to the court. But in some areas the procuracies are very poor and they
> could not afford to make photocopies, so it is not practical.
>
> (B0501, Beijing)

The prescription in the 1996 CPL on transferring the procuracy's evidence is
ambiguous, that is, after the case is prosecuted the procuracy should transfer
the photocopies of "major evidence" in the case files to the court (Article 150).
This indeterminacy in the law generated conflicting interpretations in implementation – judges and lawyers wanted to see as much evidence as possible in
the case files, whereas procurators preferred to keep all important evidence by
themselves until the court proceeding to give the defense lawyer a sudden
attack. The result was that the procuracy would only transfer the evidence
adverse to the defendant and keep all the evidence advantageous to
the defendant out of the case files (B0510; B0512; H0702; S0703). This struggle
between the procuracy and the court was an underlying reason for the
difficulty lawyers experienced when examining case files.

Similar conflicts were also found in tensions between the police/procuracy
and the court over the exclusion of illegal evidence. As confession by torture
was still prevalent in the investigation phase, the prosecutor's evidence was
often obtained through illegal means. If the defender could find evidence for
confession by torture and argued for the exclusion of illegal evidence in the
court proceeding, the judges would face a dilemma – if the defender's argument was adopted and the case was dismissed, then the procuracy's work
record would be damaged and the defendant could request state compensation from the police and the procuracy; if the argument was rejected, then if
the defendant appealed to the higher level court and the verdict was reversed,
the trial record of the court would be stained. A judge at a basic-level court in
Xi'an explained what would usually happen in this situation:

> If the defense lawyer can show confession by torture, what is the result?
> The rule of evidence in China is not comprehensive. In practice when this
> occurs we will request the procuracy to investigate in three days. If it is

confirmed and illegal evidence is involved, you cannot really declare the person innocent but we request the procuracy to withdraw the case and "digest" it in the system. The police, the procuracy, and the court are not independent from one another. They have equal positions under the guidance of the Party, so we will try to avoid state compensation.

(Xo503, Shaanxi Province)

This phenomenon of withdrawing wrong prosecutions to avoid state compensation was not unique to this court; it was prevalent all over the country (Bo510; Bo514; Xo504; Ho701). It indicated the bargaining between the court and the police/procuracy to reduce the mutual risks to the minimum. Apparently, the victims of this informal rule in judicial decision-making were lawyers and defendants – it became extremely difficult for lawyers to get verdicts of innocence for their defendants (Bo507; Bo510; Bo514).

Yet the PPC do not always reach consensus after bargaining over controversial issues in the criminal process. The procuracy's supervisory power over the police and the court, as a procedural rather than substantive power prescribed in the 1996 CPL, generated conflicts and struggles in the work of the three agencies. The irony of this struggle was that each agency diagnoses its own situation so as to require remedies in its favor. Each considered its power to be too weak and called for restrictions on the power of the other agencies. Compare the following three paragraphs from our interviews concerning the procuracy's supervisory power:

The power of the procuracy was strengthened. . . . For example, if the police arrest someone and then release him, in the past no one could control this, but now they need to get approval from the procuracy . . . if you should file a case and did not, the procuracy will supervise.

(First-rank police supervisor and law professor, Bo515, Beijing)

If the procuracy prosecutes a case and we think it should be fifteen years and the judge says three years and we think it is wrong, we can do nothing about it. So in the procuracy if we find something is wrong with a case, if the court wants to listen it does, otherwise not. And also with police, if we need some evidence from them and we send them a letter, they look at it and [if they] agree they will, if [they] disagree they won't listen to us. The most important thing is to restrict the power of the court.

(Procurator at a high-level procuracy, Xo505, Shaanxi Province)

The supervisory power of the procuracy is getting bigger and bigger. Now the supervision of the procuracy is not only for criminal issues, it can make objections in criminal cases and now also civil and administrative cases.

It has supervisory power over the court and more power over the police than before. For example, for the supervision over the police, the procuracy has an office in the detention center and has supervisory power from the arrest through the trial phase … If the court wants a police officer to come and discuss a case, nothing happens; but if the procuracy asks the police officer, they run faster than rabbits.

(Judge at a basic-level court, X0503, Shaanxi Province)

The sharp contrast among the three quotes suggests that, on the supervisory power of the procuracy, police officers, procurators, and judges often hold conflicting views, which were strengthened in their day-to-day workplace interactions.

Given the fact that defense lawyers faced tremendous difficulties in the criminal process, it is not surprising that the basic procedural rights of criminal suspects and defendants were also poorly protected. According to the statistics collected by Chen Xingliang, a distinguished criminal law professor at Peking University, over 70 percent of all criminal cases in China were tried without lawyer representation even after the 1996 CPL revision (ZGLS_200207). Extended detention and confession by torture still widely existed in spite of the frequent notices made by the SPP and the MPS to control the problem. The acquittal rates in criminal cases remained insignificant and the lawyer's presence in criminal proceedings had little effect on case outcome (Lu and Miethe 2002; Michelson 2003: 100).

FROM POST-1996 IMPLEMENTATION TO 2012 LAWMAKING

While the implementation of the 1996 CPL and its subsequent interpretations displayed many regressive and contradictory elements, on the international front China had taken significant formal steps to conform with global norms on the protection of citizen rights since the 1990s. In 1997 and 1998, China signed the United Nations' International Covenant on Economic, Social and Cultural Rights (ICESCR) and the International Covenant on Civil and Political Rights (ICCPR), respectively. In particular, as a major global standard for protecting human rights and restricting government power, the ICCPR strongly infuses criminal procedure law reforms in national contexts. In the process of ratifying the ICCPR, the Tenth NPC (2003–2008) put another round of CPL revision into its five-year legislation agenda, which initiated the third legislative cycle of China's CPL reform.

In the 1996 CPL revision, all actors but lawyers who participated in the implementation of the 1979 CPL played their roles in lawmaking, but the initial drafting was completed by legal scholars, who had little experience with implementation. In the 2012 CPL revision, lawyers finally appeared in the lawmaking process, and the NPC Legal Work Commission controlled this round of CPL revision much more closely (B0503; B0504; B0511; C0703; S0702). Although symposiums with legal scholars and representatives from the relevant state agencies were still held regularly, the NPC did not appoint any outside legal scholar or other CPL expert to draft the law.

Among all actors in the criminal justice system, lawyers encountered the most serious problems in the implementation of the CPL and had the strongest incentives to change the status quo. However, during the first two legislative cycles of the CPL, lawyers' input in the lawmaking process was almost negligible: in 1979 the legal profession had not yet been revived, and in 1996 lawyers could only express their opinions through the MOJ and legal scholars. After 1996, the intensification of the difficulties and risks in their work made Chinese criminal defense lawyers realize that participation in lawmaking was crucial for their practice, and some progressive elite lawyers in Beijing began actively to seek opportunities to directly represent the profession in the NPC symposiums and other discussions in the 2012 CPL revision (B0507; B0514).

In the 2000s, much of the regulatory power on the Chinese legal profession (e.g., membership fees, disciplinary measures, training, etc.) was transferred or delegated from justice bureaus to bar associations, and many special committees, including the Criminal Law Committee, were established in the ACLA and some urban bar associations (B0507; B0508; S0701). Accordingly, progressive elites were able to use their professional associations to mobilize lawyers from all over the country to participate in the current lawmaking process. During the 2012 CPL revision, all major provincial bar associations held conferences on the CPL revision and proposed suggestions to the ACLA Criminal Law Committee (B0508; B0510), and the ACLA made a partial CPL draft on issues related to lawyer representation based on all these suggestions and its own meetings with prominent defense lawyers in Beijing and some legal scholars (B0507). Furthermore, perhaps for the first time, three lawyer representatives from the ACLA Criminal Law Committee appeared in a NPC symposium on the CPL revision in 2003 (F#431895). The director of the ACLA Criminal Law Committee, also a nationally renowned criminal defense lawyer, stated to the NPC Symposium (excerpt posted on the ACLA lawyer forum):

> Let me say something about the obstacles in my business. ... Regarding investigations, first of all we must make it certain what the lawyer's role is.

I propose that the lawyer is the defender of the criminal suspect since the very beginning of his authorization. The defense is an integrated process from the beginning to the end, and it is not only embodied in the court proceedings. The second problem is that the witness can reject the lawyers' investigation. It must be made clear whether the witness can reject the lawyers' investigation. Thirdly, the lawyers cannot carry on the investigation in the phase of investigation. In practice, the public security officers made the investigation first and, in almost in all cases, the lawyers did their investigation after the police. Fourthly, there is a restriction on the lawyers' investigation to the victims that it must be approved by the court or the procuracy. I think this restriction must be deleted. . . . The remedy measures for the violations on the right of defense are too weak. Now all parties are used to go to their superiors, but this is not a legal procedure. They should not go to the superior in their own agencies, but need an organization to solve this problem, need a procedure. Meanwhile, we should consider the legal consequences after the lawyers' rights are violated. If these issues could not be clearly specified, the problem of protecting lawyers' rights would not be fundamentally solved.

(F#431895, April 1, 2004, 8:51pm, location unknown)

This strong call for restricting the power of the police and expanding lawyer's rights was a reflection of the struggles between the two in their daily interactions in the workplace. In the meantime, the lawyer-spokesman also proposed to reduce indeterminacy in the law by specifying the consequences for procedural violations and abolishing the opaque and murky internal supervision process within the PPC. Similarly, the vice-director of the ACLA Criminal Law Committee stated to the Symposium (excerpt):

The construction of the legal system of China in the early 1980s was relatively good, and now it has lagged behind compared to the situation then. We have two issues to consider for this revision: (1) what is the status of the lawyer in the investigation phase? The revision this time cannot continue with such a bizarre conception; (2) Article 36 of the CPL about the responsibility of the defender is actually on substantive defense, not procedural defense. The defense is not simply that the lawyers bring forward materials and opinions – a large part of it is the defense for procedural issues. Therefore, in order to penetrate into the procedures of investigation and so on, the lawyers must participate in some procedures, for example, appraisals, interrogations, identifications, etc. That is defense. Does China really need the system of defense or just pretending to need it, or half of both? My impression is that the answer is the last. The design of a system cannot be ambivalent, so we need to make up our minds.

(F#431895, April 1, 2004, 8:51pm, location unknown)

The propositions of this lawyer were even more radical than his colleague's because he not only called for the defender status of lawyers in the investigation phase, but also for the participation of defense lawyers in police interrogation. And he trenchantly pointed out that the role of defense lawyers in the actual criminal process was merely half substantive and half symbolic, a weakness stemming from the structural contradictions in the criminal justice system. Such radical proposals by lawyers were likely to generate new conflicts in the lawmaking process. For instance, with regard to the procuracy's supervisory power, lawyers and procurators presented completely opposite judgments about the state of affairs in practice. Compare the following two excerpts:

> The supervisory power of the procuracy made by Lenin is actually the distrust of the trial power of the court. But it is not the truth anymore under the present conditions. The combination of the power of supervision and the power of prosecution would easily cause confusion in role orientation.
> (ACLA representative, F#431895, April 1, 2004, 8:51pm, location unknown)

> The principle of supervision by the procuracy is a run-through principle that should be maintained. This is determined by China's social situation. In China we do not carry out the principle of separation of the three powers. Under the current structure of the state system, we need a supervisory agency of the law. The procuracy's supervisory power embodies the idea of the check and balance of power. . . . The real problem in China nowadays is not that the procuracy's supervision is too powerful, but it is too weak. The supervisory power of the procuracy is not the main reason for the obstacles on judicial justice.
> (SPP representative, F#431895, April 1, 2004, 8:51pm, location unknown)

The message from the procurator's speech was very clear: the supervisory power of the procuracy should be further strengthened in the new CPL; the procurator could never be equal to the lawyer-defender. Although lawyers and some legal scholars (e.g., B0511) strongly resisted this point of view, the procuracy's supervisory power was prescribed by the Constitutional Law and could not be abolished in the CPL revision (B0505). A few scholars even pointed out at the symposium that the only way to change the procuracy's supervisory power and the relationship among the three agencies was through constitutional reform (F#431895).

Practice also affected differences in statutory recommendations by lawyers and legal scholars. The proposals of most legal scholars in the 2012 CPL revision were much less radical than lawyers' proposals. Because the 1996 CPL left out many articles in their initial draft and generated conflicting interpretations, scholars' focus in the 2012 revision was principally upon reducing indeterminacy and contradictions by adding more articles and specifying the CPL more precisely (F#431895).

Yet legal scholars themselves did not share a consensus on how much the 2012 revision should change the 1996 CPL. As many of them assumed adjunct positions in the PPC in recent years, their diagnoses sometimes also reflected the interests of these agencies. A law professor in Shanghai, for example, declared that the procedure law annual meeting had become a battleground for the PPC to win scholarly support (S0702). Whereas some scholars made radical proposals such as abolishing the procuracy's supervisory power or purging socialist ideological language out of the law (F#431895; B0511), others argued that the CPL reform should keep a steady pace to maintain the authority and stability of the law. A senior law professor who played a crucial role in the 1996 revision stated in 2005:

> The term of the current NPC has three years remaining so the law will need to be revised within three years. But for many issues people do not have the same understanding yet. For example, do we make a big, medium or small change? If a big change, we will make a very comprehensive revision. If a medium change, only a portion of it. If a small change, we will only revise some articles. So friends from different places hold different opinions. I think that now the situation is not mature. If we make a big change it will be an incomprehensive law. So after five to eight years it may need another round of revision. I do not want this situation to happen. Because the law needs to be stable – you cannot make it in the morning and change it in the evening. So my argument is that we should make a comprehensive revision when the time is right. But for some articles where the problem is really serious, we can change several articles using the method of amendment.
>
> (B0515, Beijing)

His phase "the situation is not mature" reminds us that China's lawmakers and scholars find themselves constantly caught between domestic exigencies and international pressures. Accordingly, some legal academics adapted by changing their strategy. For instance, a research group at Renmin University of China, led by Chen Weidong and supported by an aid program of the American Bar Association, created a "Model Criminal Procedure Code" that claimed to have incorporated the most "advanced" experiences of CPL legislation in other countries (B0505; B0511). This tactic deliberately created a "model" that was far in excess of what was enactable in contemporary China, but it was intended to pull the NPC drafting committee further towards international practices and global standards than it might otherwise be inclined to do.

While the 2012 CPL revision was going through fierce diagnostic struggles among various actors in the criminal justice system, on another front lawyers and scholars made some significant achievements. When the PRC Lawyers Law was revised in 2007, several articles beyond the scope of the 1996 CPL were added to protect lawyers' procedural rights in criminal defense. For example, Article 33 stipulates that lawyers' meetings with criminal suspects and defendants should not be monitored by the police, Article 34 expands lawyers' access to case files to "all relevant files" of the case, and Article 37 exempts lawyer's speech and opinions during the court proceeding from being investigated by the procuracy. In August 2008, the NPC Legal Work Commission made an official reply regarding the potential conflicts of law and gave the new Lawyers Law priority over the 1996 CPL in practice. According to a law professor who attended the internal discussion of the NPC on this reply, the final decision was made under the direct guidance of a member of the CCP Politburo, and progressive elites from the ACLA played a significant role in the process (B1310). Unlike the CPL revision in which the MPS, SPP, and SPC were all vital players, the revision of the Lawyers Law was mainly undertaken by the MOJ and therefore lawyers were able to input their opinions into the draft more easily than in the CPL revision.

Despite the breakthroughs made in the Lawyers Law, the Tenth NPC did not finish its task of CPL revision by 2008. It took the Eleventh NPC another four years to complete the legislative process of the 2012 CPL. In the final stages of the process, the NPC made great efforts to reduce actor mismatch by holding several major symposiums that included lawyer representatives and then distributing the draft CPL for comments from the public in 2011 (B1303; B1304; B1309; B1310). Meanwhile, the CCP leadership also produced an important Party document on the major tasks of the legal reform in 2008, a significant proportion of which were related to the CPL reform, such as preventing wrongful convictions and confession by torture (B1309; B1312). This Party document became the policy guidelines of the 2012 CPL revision. On March 14, 2012, the revised CPL was finally passed by the Eleventh NPC during its fifth meeting.

The 2012 CPL contains 290 articles in total, sixty-five articles more than the 1996 CPL. The law on the books expands lawyers' intervention in the criminal process by giving lawyers the status of defender in the investigation phase (Article 33). This enables defense lawyers to collect evidence for their clients during police investigation. With a few exceptions (i.e., state security cases, terrorism cases, or extraordinarily significant bribery cases), a lawyer's meeting with a criminal suspect no longer needs the police's approval and the meeting shall be arranged within forty-eight hours without being monitored by the police (Article 37). The crime of lawyer's perjury remains in the 2012 CPL (Article 42), but a new procedural restriction is added, that is, a lawyer suspected of the crime shall be handled by an investigation agency other than the one handling the case in which the lawyer provides representation. Some lawyers considered this new restriction a response to the serious abuse of police power in the nationally renowned Li Zhuang case (see Chapter 6). In general, the 2012 CPL substantially strengthens lawyers' procedural rights and reduces the indeterminacy of the 1996 CPL regarding lawyers' participation in the criminal process.

Furthermore, the 2012 CPL adds important general principles of human rights and legal proceduralism such as "respecting and protecting human rights" (Article 2) and "no person shall be found guilty without a verdict by a people's court in accordance with law" (Article 12). It also establishes specific procedural rules for the exclusion of illegal evidence (Lewis 2011), including evidence collected through torture (Articles 50–59). However, the 2012 CPL gives the police and the procuracy new powers, such as the controversial expansion of residential surveillance (监视居住) to residences designated by the investigating agency (Article 73). Many foreign observers criticized this article as the legalization of the Party disciplinary procedure on corrupt officials, commonly known as *shuanggui* (双规) (Sapio 2008), as well as a new repressive tool for "disappearing" political dissidents (McConville 2011; Pils 2015).

IMPLEMENTING THE 2012 CRIMINAL PROCEDURE LAW: A NEW RECURSIVE CYCLE?

It is still too early to fully observe or assess the implementation of the 2012 CPL and its consequences for the practice of criminal defense lawyers, yet our recent interviews suggest that the recursivity of legal change continues to drive the dynamics of CPL implementation. While the CPL may have reduced the professional difficulties for routine practitioners, a determination that has not yet been verified by cross-sectional empirical research, it has not improved the practice conditions of political activists in the most sensitive cases where protections by law are most critically needed (B1318; B1319; B1323; B1415; B1519; B1522). Even progressive elites continue to encounter difficulties in the workplace when they handle high-profile or sensitive cases (B1506). The procedural restriction on the crime of lawyer's perjury in Article 42, however, seems to be effective in reducing lawyer perjury cases. Thanks to the change in jurisdiction over Article 306 cases, it has become less convenient for the police or the procuracy to take revenge on defense lawyers in the same case after 2012 (B1506; B1507).

The recursive nature of CPL implementation can be well observed from the new struggles over lawyer's rights of meeting suspects, collecting evidence, and accessing case files. Most of our interviewees acknowledged the improvement of the 2012 CPL in these three aspects, but some also expressed the frustration in practice, particularly in politically sensitive cases or large-sum bribery cases. For instance, the anti-corruption authorities sometimes interpret "extraordinarily significant bribery cases" loosely to prevent lawyers from meeting the suspects until the phase of investigation is nearly over (B1506; B1509). When lawyers try to videotape the conversation with their clients, police officers often present practical obstacles (e.g., not to videotape the detention facilities) or request that criminal suspects apply in writing (B1507). A notable activist in Beijing pointed out that, despite the improvement of lawyer's rights in meeting suspects in the CPL, "there are no sanctions for non-compliance by the police" (B1311). Another lawyer complained that they had no control of "secret audio or videotaping" by the police when meetings with their clients and "in sensitive cases they will do whatever they want to do" (B1321). "Now these technologies are so advanced, how would you know if they had been recording your conversation in the room?" (B1302)

Furthermore, although the 2012 CPL permits lawyers to collect evidence during police investigations, many lawyers told us that they would not take any evidence until they see the police's evidence in the case file because earlier evidence collection would be inefficient and risky (B1304; B1320; B1506). Or, as a lawyer bluntly put it, "It could become a new minefield for lawyers" (B1302) given the continuing threat of "Big Stick 306." Even the less controversial right of accessing and using the procuracy's case files generated serious struggles when the five state agencies (MPS, SPP, SPC, MOJ, and MSS) made a Joint Regulation on the interpretation of the CPL. According to a progressive elite lawyer who participated in the making of the Joint Regulation, the MPS and SPP representatives advocated for procedural limits on the lawyer's ability to share information in the case files with criminal suspects, which lawyer representatives strongly opposed. Eventually, the Joint Regulation left this issue indeterminate (B1535). As a result of such indeterminacy and contradictions in lawmaking, the procedural rights granted to lawyers by the 2012 CPL are often compromised in practice by the resistance of the police and the procuracy, especially in important or sensitive cases. This is reminiscent of the 1996 CPL implementation discussed earlier in the chapter and it confirms the recursive nature of legal change that we have observed and analyzed in earlier work (Liu and Halliday 2009).

Another good example of recursivity is on the exclusion of illegal evidence. When we interviewed some Chinese legal scholars and progressive elite lawyers in 2013, most applauded the addition of exclusionary rules in the 2012 CPL (Lewis 2011) and dismissed the potential risk of Article 73 on designated residential surveillance, as they believed it would be used cautiously in practice (B1304; B1309; B1312). Two years later, however, designated residential surveillance is widely used in bribery cases involving corrupt officials, as well as state security cases, and some procuracies even set up their own facilities for it (B1508; B1509). Article 73 has become, as a defense lawyer put it, "a synonym for confession by torture" (B1506). Although the 2012 CPL requires the investigating agency to provide written or oral testimonies on potentially illegal evidence, in practice some police officers would simply appear in court and read a written document of denial without cross-examination (B1507). As a result, little illegal evidence is excluded in criminal trials except for cases with apparent injuries from torture (B1506). Even when exclusion does occur, it is often partial and insignificant to the case outcome (B1509). A notable activist expressed his pessimism on the persistence of torture in the criminal justice system, "We cannot rely on the law only. It is only a piece of paper. We have to rely on a system. But the Chinese system allows torture to exist." (B1311) Another lawyer made the same point using an analogy: "The judicial system is a rock. The new CPL is just a tiny brick on the rock for the exclusion of illegal evidence." (B1401)

From this brief discussion on the initial implementation of the 2012 CPL, it is evident that the deep ideological and structural contradictions between the PPC and defense lawyers remain resilient (Liang, He, and Lu 2014). Everyday struggles in the workplaces of the criminal justice system, such as detention centers and the proliferating sites of designated residential surveillance, continue to drive the recursive process of CPL implementation. Lawyers remain a weak actor in the criminal justice system and the PPC can still take advantage of the indeterminacies in the 2012 CPL to further weaken the role of defense counsel in the criminal process. Although the text of the 2012 CPL is likely to last for a relatively long time before the next revision, the recursive process of China's CPL lawmaking has not fully settled. Despite the improvement in its efficacy in ordinary criminal cases, in the politically sensitive cases where it is the most needed, the CPL is often marginalized and sometimes rendered irrelevant, while criminal defense lawyers encounter significantly more difficulties and risks (see Chapter 5).

CONCLUSION

In spite of some persisting criticisms from observers of China's criminal justice system, it is clear that a vast distance has been traversed since 1979. China's legal rhetoric and much practice are qualitatively different than that which existed at any time between 1949 and 1979, when the first CPL was promulgated. The convergence has been strongest at the level of norms: both the 1996 and 2012 CPLs were hailed as breakthroughs in China's conformity with United Nations norms by commentators inside the country and overseas. But this evaluation rested on a primitive understanding of formal law – that it resided only or principally in statutes – and in an ante-sociolegal concept of law – that law on the books was a reasonable indication of law in action. Similarly, an overemphasis on lawyers' difficulties and problems in practice masks their deep social, structural, and political roots, some of which may be traced back to the dynamics of lawmaking that long antedates struggles in the workplace.

We have argued that China's CPL reforms have followed a recursive trajectory. The entire episode of reforms began in 1979 and has gone through three statutory lawmaking cycles. Within the statutory cycles have been cycles of administrative and judicial lawmaking, most particularly in the wake of the 1996 CPL. By focusing on criminal procedure law, and more precisely, lawyers' capacity to provide an effective representation of criminal defendants, we have a particular indicator of China's move towards political liberalism (Halliday, Karpik, and Feeley 2007). To accomplish either a moderate state or basic legal freedoms, however, requires a limiting of authoritarian power and a reconstitution of the structure of the state. Since this would constitute a fundamental reorientation of Chinese politics and law, it is not surprising that the struggle continues with no clear direction in sight. Awareness of the structural configurations of power that underlie criminal procedure law in China helps avoid naïve notions that more precise formal law, more training of lawyers and judges, and more refinement of purely legal institutions will suffice to produce a criminal procedure law consistent with global norms without reconstruction of the state.

3

Difficulties and Danger in Lawyers' Workplaces

The criminal procedure reforms discussed in Chapter 2 provide the historical and institutional background for the practice of Chinese criminal defense lawyers. To fully understand their everyday work, in this chapter we closely examine the social interactions in lawyers' workplaces, particularly their interactions with police officers, procurators, and judges. Until the 2012 CPL revision, when meeting criminal suspects, lawyers needed to get approval from the detention center, and police officers were almost always present at the meeting. When collecting evidence from witnesses, lawyers often needed approval or assistance from the court or the procuracy, otherwise many witnesses would not cooperate. Even if lawyers gave up the right of meeting suspects in the investigation phase and did not obtain their own evidence, they would still need to get access to the procuracy's case files, argue against procurators, and try to persuade judges in court proceedings. The relationship between lawyers and the PPC, therefore, is not only prescribed in the CPL, but also constructed in their workplace interactions.

Anyone unfamiliar with the Chinese criminal justice system would be surprised by the daunting difficulties and danger that defense lawyers faced in their everyday practice. While both the 1996 and 2012 CPLs granted lawyers procedural rights in the three consecutive phases of investigation, prosecution, and trial, in reality lawyers complained vehemently about their difficulties in all three phases of the criminal process. The term "Three Difficulties" (三难), originally referring to the difficulties in meeting suspects, collecting evidence, and accessing the procuracy's case files, has become a popular term in the lawyer community to characterize all the procedural problems that they encounter in criminal defense work. Furthermore, the crime of lawyer's perjury, often labeled "Big Stick 306" (306大棒) because of its origin in Article 306 of the 1997 PRC Criminal Law, presents a "Sword of Damocles" (B0507) constantly hanging above the heads of all criminal defense lawyers in

China. Since 1997, hundreds of Chinese lawyers have been detained, prose-cuted, or sentenced to prison for allegedly committing this crime in their work (Wang 2001; Fang 2005; Halliday and Liu 2007).

This chapter documents the workplace manifestations of "Three Difficulties" and "Big Stick 306" using our interview data from 2005 to 2015 as well as earlier online ethnographic data from the ACLA lawyer forum. We begin with three cases of lawyer persecution reported on the ACLA forum which illustrate the seriousness of those problems.

DEFENSE LAWYERS IN DANGER: THREE CASES OF LAWYER PERSECUTION

Three case stories captured the vulnerability of Chinese lawyers in criminal defense work in the early 2000s. These were reported on the ACLA forum during 2003–2004 and aroused heated discussions among the forum users. One case (the Ma Guangjun case) was also widely reported in mainstream public media, while the other two cases were a subject of debate within legal circles only. Although a decade has passed since these case stories first appeared online, the professional risks that they represent remain substantial in today's criminal defense practice.

The Lawyer SOS Case

No case had been more passionately and thoroughly discussed on the ACLA forum than the case of a defense lawyer from Anhui Province who fled from the police and posted an SOS message on the forum on April 8, 2004. The message generated 134 responses by ninety-nine distinct users from at least twenty-one provinces. Here is the full text of the original message:

> I am a lawyer in Anhui Runtian Law Firm (Lawyer License Number: 12890110309). On February 15, 2004, my colleague Lawyer Yu Huakun and I were appointed by the law firm to provide legal help to the criminal suspect of a case of death by malicious injury which was investigated by the police of the Changping section of the Dongguan City Police Department of Guangdong Province. Lawyer Yu Huakun was already detained by the Dongguan City Police Department for obstructing testimony, and now I am fleeing and cannot go home.
>
> On reflection of the process in this case, we did not violate Article 306 or 307 of the Criminal Law on the crime of obstructing testimony at all. If we indeed violated the law and committed a crime, we would have nothing to say about this situation. In fact, during the process of the case, we strictly obeyed

the relevant laws, rules, and regulations, not even taking half a step to the bombing area, but now the result is that one of us is in jail and the other is fleeing. I must say this is a huge grievance in the Chinese legal profession! Although this might only be an exceptional phenomenon, it clearly happened in reality. If we let things like this go, won't China's lawyers and legal system be trashed by anyone? The tragedy that happened to me and Lawyer Yu Huakun today might also happen to other lawyer colleagues tomorrow.

The role of lawyers in the development of the socialist legal system cannot be substituted. Lawyers provide legal service to criminal suspects, defending their legal rights, which is the responsibility and right that the law endows to lawyers. If lawyers' right to practice according to the law could be violated, then how could the legal rights of the represented party be guaranteed? Therefore, protecting lawyers' right to practice according to the law and increasing lawyers' status in criminal cases are urgent matters.

Now the ACLA is holding a conference in Huangshan, Anhui Province. I, also representing Lawyer Yu Huakun, send this message for help to all of you, please save us save yourselves, and save China's lawyers and legal system. SOS, SOS, SOS . . .

The person crying for help: a lawyer at Anhui Runtian Law Firm (anonymous).

April 8, 2004.

(F#440419, April 8, 2004, 10:56pm, Anhui Province)

The last reply to this SOS message was posted in January 2005, nine months after the original message was posted. However, the fate of the fleeing lawyer remains unknown.

The Wen Zhicheng Case

The second case concerns the persecution of Wen Zhicheng, a 61-year-old defense lawyer in Ruijin City, Jiangxi Province, by the local police and procuracy. The message was posted by a lawyer from Sichuan Province in December 2004. The message started with a long case description said to be written by Wen Zhicheng himself. Here is an excerpt:

I am a licensed lawyer in Huarui Law Office in Jiangxi Province, my name is Wen Zhicheng, and I am 61 years old this year. I was appointed by our law office to defend Zeng Hailin, the defendant of a suspected corruption case. . . . Zeng Hailin was set free on September 11 this year, but I, the defender, have still been obtaining guarantor pending trial (取保候审) as a criminal suspect. . . .

Zhu Dexin, the section chief of the Bureau of Anti-corruption of Ruijin Procurator's Office, invited me to have a talk in the law office at 5pm on June 5 (Saturday). But at that time he promptly detained me in the name of the Ruijin City Bureau of Public Security, and then made a search of my body and my office desk . . . The alarm of the police car resounded before I walked to the police car, so the crowd built up of thousands of people . . . Yang Xiaoshan, the deputy section chief of the Anti-Corruption Bureau, ordered the driver to put down all the windows of the police car. And then the police car drove me slowly to the Procuracy with the alarm resounding. It was actually to use a police car to make a parade and pillory of a lawyer under escort.

Arriving at the procuracy, two police officers and four officers of the Anti-Corruption Bureau used torture to coerce a statement from me for a period of up to 8 hours, in the "Interrogation Room" of the Procurator's Office. . . . I asked to pee for three or four times. They said: "You may pee. But you cannot be allowed to do it until you confess the crime." . . . They forced me to confess the criminal facts of forging evidence and obstructing testimony for Zeng Hailin in the process of the Zeng Hailin corruption case. I said: "I have practiced as a lawyer for more than twenty years, and have never forged any evidence or obstructed testimony for any client. And similarly I have not forged any evidence or obstructed any testimony for Zeng Hailin this time. On the contrary, it is you the procuracy who detained Zhu Jingfu, the defending party's witness on the court day of Zeng Hailin case, and detained Yang Haiping, the defending party's witness on the following day. And now you are detaining and extorting a confession by torture from the defender [me]. Your actions will be accused by the law sooner or later." . . . They afflicted me bodily, insulted me personally, and frightened me mentally, in order to compel the lawyer to surrender to their orders.

This detention and interrogation lasted from 6pm, June 5 to 2:40am, June 6 . . .

At 7am I was committed into No.17 prison room of the Ruijin City Detention Center and began a life living with the criminal suspects of intentional homicide, robbery, rape, theft and racketeering. . . . From 9am to 11am on June 7, the Deputy Chief Procurator, Zou Yuansheng, picked me out of the prison room . . . He said, "For a bad guy rotten from head to feet, why would you defend him? What you antagonize is against the nation, the laws of the nation, and the powerful state judicial agencies. If you had cooperated with the procuracy in the evening of June 5, maybe you could have gone back home to sleep that night. But you had a hard head so you are still here today. Now if you cooperate with our procuracy, maybe you can go back this afternoon." I said, "What is the responsibility of the lawyer as a defender for the criminal suspect? Do you know? This lawyer [me] practiced according to the law, but you detained lawyers. Have you estimated the outcome of this behavior?" The talk ended unpleasantly.

The Public Security Bureau stated that my criminal detention was extended to June 13. ... At 5pm of June 20, the Public Security proclaimed to me the decision of obtaining guarantor pending trial ... Thus I had been detained for 15 days altogether.

(F#620344, December 4, 2004, 11:07am, Jiangxi Province)

There was no further information on whether the lawyer was later prosecuted or not.

The Ma Guangjun Case

In the two preceding cases, the defense lawyer was either chased by the police or detained for interrogation, but neither of them was reported to be arrested or prosecuted. In Ma Guangjun's case, the lawyer was prosecuted and detained for 210 days before finally being acquitted by the court. After the acquittal, the case was widely reported in local and national media. Three of these media reports were posted on the ACLA forum, including two newspaper articles from the *Southern Metropolitan News* (南方都市报) and the *Inner Mongolia Legal System News* (内蒙古法制报), as well as a long interview with Ma Guangjun by the CCTV, the official central television station in China.

Ma Guangjun was a fifty-year-old lawyer in Ningcheng County, Inner Mongolia, who defended Xu Wensheng, an impotent patient, in a rape case in 2003. On May 23, the next day after the court proceedings, seven key witnesses who testified in court were detained and coerced to confess that the defense lawyer advised them to commit perjury. Soon after, Ma Guangjun, the defense lawyer, was arrested for the crime of obstructing testimony and detained in the local detention center from August 22, 2003, to March 20, 2004 (F#536452). During his trial process, the Inner Mongolia Lawyers Association investigated the case and appointed two prominent lawyers in the province to defend Ma Guangjun (F#536448).

After being released, Ma was interviewed by CCTV and the program was broadcast internationally. During the interview, Ma described the difficult situation he faced when handling the rape case:

> He [the defendant] said he had confessed three times, but all were against his will. I asked him, why did you confess against your will? He said that every time he confessed it was because the policemen had made him confess through torture for more than twenty hours. He could not put up with the torture. In order to preserve himself he had no choice but to confess. ...
> I didn't believe him entirely at the beginning. ... I knew that if I, as a lawyer, obtained the most crucial evidence in order to reverse the testimony in this

case, I would take the risk of being caught up for committing perjury, so I decided not to collect evidence by myself. ... I think that was my habit. At present it is the situation in my area that you cannot see anything, and the procuracy does not allow you to see. It only tells you that this case involves the crime of rape. ... You can only wait until the case files are transferred to the court, then you can go and see it. We have no ability, and no other means.

(F#536452, July 12, 2004, 01:22am, Inner Mongolia)

He then proceeded to talk about his experience as a subject of the charge of perjury, starting from the moment he heard from a villager that seven witnesses had been detained by the procuracy on June 23, the second day of the court proceedings:

I was shocked at that moment, and I told him that the procuracy had the power to check the evidence, but if it captured someone without releasing them, at that time I absolutely would not believe it was true, because the procuracy was not only the agency for implementing the law, but also the supervisory agency. How could it do such an illegal thing? I could not believe then so I said that you had to wait in patience, they would surely be released in the evening. But in the end they had not been released by the evening of the 24th. He called me the same night and then I had the hunch that the procuracy had put its hand on the witnesses and the purpose was not only the witnesses, but also pointing at me. ... Because when we were in the court, the prosecutor and I debated very harshly. I was very aggressive and consolidated my argument step by step. So in terms of the effect in court, I think I did quite well and the prosecutor from the procuracy was placed in a very passive position. ... If the witnesses did not appear in court, nothing would happen. ... I had a feeling that, although I was clear in my mind where the trap was, I had no choice but to jump into it. ... Because I had to maintain my dignity, I am a lawyer, so I could not escape. ... I was very ill treated in the detention center, and my every word and action was watched out every day. ... I got rheumatoid arthritis when I was young, and my disease was quite severe. The heating was not good in my room so my legs began to jerk when I was in bed at night. Also I was not permitted to have two cotton-padded mattresses, only one was permitted and the cotton clothes sent by my family I was not permitted to wear. ...

(F#536452, July 12, 2004, 01:22am, Inner Mongolia)

At the moment of his own defense he wept. Here he describes the moment he saw the two defense lawyers appointed by the Inner Mongolia Lawyers Association to represent him in the detention center:

I was very sad then. So I cried, really. As the defense lawyer for Xu Wensheng, I was sitting outside to meet with Xu Wensheng half a year ago, hoping to defend his innocence. I didn't expect that, half a year later, I would be sitting in the position of Xu and the Inner Mongolia Lawyers Association would have appointed two lawyers to defend my innocence. I was changed from the defense lawyer into the defendant. This kind of feeling was impossible for anyone to accept. But in the face of the facts, you had no choice but to accept it.

(F#536452, July 12, 2004, 01:22am, Inner Mongolia)

The case ended with a verdict of not guilty and Ma Guangjun's story was widely disseminated across the country. His account vividly expresses the ultimate fears of all criminal defense lawyers in China.

"THREE DIFFICULTIES" IN CRIMINAL DEFENSE WORK

The three cases presented in the previous section, albeit extreme, nevertheless symbolize the yawning gap that exists between the aspirational norms promulgated in the statutes and the murky practices of everyday criminal defense. The "iron triangle" among the PPC that has existed for decades has proved immensely difficult to fracture and to rebalance in practice, even with the notable progress of the CPL reforms (see Chapter 2). As a result, Chinese criminal defense lawyers faced great difficulties in almost every step of the criminal process. Lawyers complained most vigorously about their difficulties in meeting criminal suspects, getting access to case files, and collecting evidence – the well-known "Three Difficulties" in criminal defense work. Moreover, our interviews over a decade suggest repeatedly that persuading judges to adopt their defense opinions in court proceedings is at least as difficult as the other three difficulties for most lawyers. These problems are not only widely discussed within the lawyer community (e.g., on the ACLA forum and, more recently, on Weibo and WeChat), but also frequently observed by legal scholars and media reports.

In 112 fully structured interviews conducted in thirteen medium-size and small cities in 2009, we asked lawyers to identify the most serious problem(s) among the four major difficulties in their practice, namely, meeting suspects, accessing case files, collecting evidence, and persuading judges in court. As Figure 3.1 shows, meeting criminal suspects during police investigation remained the most problematic issue in the criminal process – nearly 70% of the respondents reported it as one of the most difficult issues. Meanwhile, 57% reported the difficulty in collecting evidence and 48% reported the difficulty

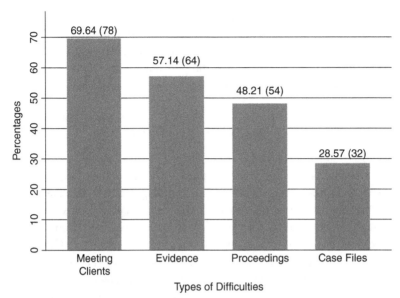

FIGURE 3.1 Percentages of lawyers' assessment of the four major types of difficulties in their criminal defense work.

in persuading judges. In contrast, only 29% of the respondents selected accessing case files as one of the most difficult issues in the process. A lawyer from Shandong Province provided a good overview of the situation:

Meeting [suspects] is very difficult. In the investigation phase usually the lawyer can only meet [the suspect] once and is not allowed to ask about the content of the case, just telling the suspect some legal rights. In the phase of the procuracy's prosecution, the lawyer can see the case files, but usually only the procedural evidence and materials. Only when the case reaches the trial phase is it possible for the lawyer to touch on the substantive evidence and materials. Moreover, in terms of collecting evidence, the lawyer's rights cannot be guaranteed. So to protect ourselves and to prevent additional problems, lawyers often do not collect evidence. Also, the lawyer's defense opinions are not useful. After the police and the procuracy have gone through the case, it is more or less decided, and the role of the lawyer is limited, only providing some opinions on the reduction of the sentence. . . . I usually do not collect evidence, perhaps I only do so in one percent of my cases.

(SDY0901, Shandong Province)

Among the 112 respondents, only three lawyers reported that none of the four issues was difficult for them. Two of them (in Hubei and Sichuan Provinces, respectively) had previous work experiences in the judiciary and less than

10 percent of their cases were criminal cases. The third lawyer was a middle-aged female lawyer in Hunan Province specializing in juvenile delinquency cases. But even she complained that in her cases collecting evidence was "none of the lawyer's business" and the police often postponed the meeting with suspects until they had completed the interrogation process (HNY0907).

Difficulty in Meeting Suspects

With regard to lawyers meeting with criminal suspects, Article 96 of the 1996 CPL broadened the scope of legal representation from the trial phase to the investigation phase. Article 11 of the 1998 Joint Regulation by six state agencies (see Chapter 2) required that, except for some special occasions (e.g., involving state secrets), the lawyer's application for meeting the criminal suspect should be arranged within forty-eight hours. Article 37 of the 2012 CPL further stipulates that, except for three exceptional case types (i.e., state security, terrorism, or extraordinarily significant bribery), a lawyer's meeting with a criminal suspect no longer needs the police's approval and the meeting shall be arranged within forty-eight hours without being monitored by the police. In reality, however, lawyers complained vociferously that delay was the order of things as "lawyers' right of meeting is often restricted 'layer by layer'" (F#556167). As a defense lawyer from Chongqing remarked on the ACLA forum in 2004:

> According to my own experience, this Article [Article 11] is equal to nothing. It often happens that after the lawyer's application, the police officer would make all kinds of excuses. Forty-eight hours is impossible, and you are a lucky dog if you can make it within 480 hours. Even if the lawyer is really pushy and can finally get the meeting settled, the officer is still reluctant.
> (F#618182, November 27, 2004, 11:13am, Chongqing)

Another indicated that "this regulation promulgated and implemented by the six agencies of authority has become a mere scrap of paper: three days, five days, ten days, a hundred days . . . the agencies for investigation find all kinds of reasons to refuse the lawyer's meeting" (F#256600).

One tactic was to broaden the exception that exists in the law and regulations: "Some police agencies willfully expand the meaning and scope of 'state secret', often by rejecting the lawyer's meeting on grounds of involving state secrets" (F#556167). Or the police would "postpone the meeting with all kinds of methods, e.g., the lawyer comes and the police officer says 'I have to report to my superior but my superior is out of town,' [and then] two days later he is back and the police officer says, 'I have to report to the division chief and he is in a meeting'" (B0515). If a meeting did take place it might be restricted to a single occasion and for only a few minutes, frequently in spaces that make conversation difficult (F#555662). The Chongqing lawyer quoted above gave an example:

> During the meeting, the police officer is not just "present at the meeting," but sometimes "intimidates" the criminal suspect [by saying things] like "What did you say in the police office? Why say such confusing words to the lawyer?" This is not the lawyer's meeting with the criminal suspect, but the police officer's investigation with the assistance of the lawyer.
> (F#618182, November 27, 2004, 11:13am, Chongqing)

After the 1996 CPL revision, lawyers commonly reported that in meetings they might do no more than provide emotional support for the detainee and possibly inform the detainee of the suspected offence and some relevant statutes. For lawyers who were more aggressive during the meetings, such as Li Zhuang (see Chapter 6), police retaliations were prevalent and sometimes severe. Lawyers across China complained that these facts on the ground nullified the 1996 CPL. In a lawyer's words, agents of criminal investigation used "illegal behaviors to deal with lawyers who obey and loyally implement the law" (F#256602).

Even after the 2012 CPL revision, which strengthened lawyers' procedural rights in the investigation phase, in practice the meeting of lawyers with detainees remains a site of police resistance, especially in politically sensitive cases (B1311; B1317; B1323; B1506; B1507). For instance, a progressive elite lawyer in Beijing reported that, when she tried to meet a suspect in Guangdong Province in 2014, the local police changed the location of the suspect's detention three times and even used three pseudonyms to prevent the lawyer from getting access to her client (B1512). Although police presence has become the exception rather than the rule, most lawyer–suspect meetings are video-recorded either openly or in secret (B1507; B1512). In bribery cases involving state officials, the procuracy often intentionally raised the amount of bribes under investigation to 500,000 yuan to qualify for "extraordinarily significant bribery" and prevent lawyers from meeting their clients, and then later charge the defendants with a smaller amount (B1506; B1509). The definition of "state security cases" in practice was also ambiguous and often expanded deliberately to prevent lawyers' meetings (B1507).

Difficulty in Accessing Case Files

Getting access to the procuracy's case files could also be a challenging task, sometimes a mission impossible. To change the prevalent practice of "judgment before trial" (先定后审) and make the court proceeding more substantive, the 1996 CPL partially changed the trial system from the Continental inquisitorial system to the Anglo-American adversarial system, in which all evidence must be presented and cross-examined during the court proceeding. As a result, the procuracy did not transfer its entire case files to the court before the proceeding for review, but only a list of evidence and witnesses with photocopies of "major evidence" (Article 150). In practice, this left huge discretion to the procuracy's file preparation. To gain a better position in the court argument, the procurators rarely provided a comprehensive set of case files for judges and lawyers to review before the trial. Instead, many would simply transfer only evidence that was adverse to the defendants (B0510; B0512). Some procurators even concealed a few pieces of crucial evidence to surprise defense lawyers with a "sudden attack" in court. Since the evidence in these files effectively amounted to the totality of evidence available to defense lawyers, they found themselves actually in a worse situation after the legislation than before (B0501; B0503; B0510). In the Ma Guangjun case, for instance, Ma claimed that no information at all was in the case file from the police interrogation of Xu Wensheng, the defendant (F#536452). A progressive elite lawyer in Beijing described the difference in the procuracy's case files before and after 1996:

> There were some backward movements. Not as good as before. In the past, when the procuracy transferred the file to the court all the documents were transferred, but now [they] only transfer the evidence list and copies of major evidence, not everything. So in the past lawyers could get access to all the case files but now can only read what the procuracy wants you to see and they are selected to be negative to the defendant. So if [there were] ten testimonies from the suspect, then [they] would only transfer the only negative one to the defender. And for a lot of material evidence, in the past they needed to bring the actual material to court (a knife, for example) and show it to the defendant, but now [they] only [need to] show a photo of the knife.
>
> (B0510, Beijing)

Access to case files is also a matter of practicality. A lawyer reported that he was denied such access in a criminal case merely because the court charged a high price for xeroxing case files before and was criticized by the higher-level court, so it decided not to let lawyers xerox case files any more – i.e., lawyers had no choice but to take notes of several volumes of files, even if they got the access to them (F#619075). A report of the NPC's investigation on the implementation of the 1996 CPL in 2000 indicates that both the time and extent of the defense lawyers' access to case files were highly restricted in practice (ZGLS_200103).

Nevertheless, the 1996 CPL reform also produced a useful by-product. Since lawyers faced significant dangers in relying on any evidence other than case files (see below), they were becoming increasingly artful in examining written materials. As a distinguished criminal defense lawyer in Beijing picturesquely commented, "the cross-examination in court is living people examining dead papers" (B0507). Some progressive elite lawyers reported success in inducing the procuracy to withdraw charges or in persuading the court to impose lighter sentences by demonstrating inadequacies, contradictions, missing information, and fabrication in the case files. Some even argued that this close scrutiny of police and procuracy evidence might be producing compelling investigation agencies to obtain better quality evidence (B0507; B0508; B0510).

Given the unintended negative consequences to lawyers' access to case files, the 2012 CPL revision reversed the 1996 revision and allows defense lawyers to read and copy the procuracy's case files from the date of prosecution (Article 38). If the defender considers the case file to be incomplete and missing evidence conducive to the defendant, the defender shall have the right to apply to the procuracy or the court for submission of such evidence (Article 39). Nevertheless, a law professor in Beijing expressed his disappointment about this revision because Article 34 of the 2007 Lawyers Law went one step further by giving defense lawyers access to all materials related to the case since the date the court accepts the case, including materials outside the case file, yet the 2012 CPL retracted this article and made it easier for the prosecutor to hide evidence from the defense lawyer before trial (B1310). The Lawyers Law was also revised accordingly in 2012.

While most of our lawyer interviewees acknowledged the positive effect of the 2012 CPL in reducing their difficulty in accessing case files, nuanced obstacles remain in their workplaces. Some procuracies would simply give lawyers an electronic copy of the case file, which is carefully selected and often incomplete (B1512). A local procuracy in Beijing requires lawyers to make reservations to get access to case files, which could take as long as twenty days (B1512). The most prevalent problem is lawyers' access to the audio and video records of the police interrogation. In most situations, such records are deliberately made unavailable to defense lawyers to conceal inconsistencies in the testimonies or evidence of torture; even when lawyers have obtained access to the CDs from the court or the procuracy in rare occasions, their contents are often broken or made unreadable (B1506; B1507; B1512). As a result, it remains difficult for defense lawyers to exclude illegal evidence from the case file during trial.

Difficulty in Collecting Evidence

The 1996 CPL gave lawyers limited rights to collect evidence. Lawyers could not easily gather their own evidence because they needed to obtain the consent of witnesses and the permission of the procuracy or the court in order to collect evidence from witnesses on the victims' side (Article 37); and they had insufficient powers to compel the provision of evidence (Yu 2002; Sheng, 2003, 2004). Witnesses were easily intimidated by authorities and were usually loath to appear in court and contradict official testimony. Consequently, collecting evidence from witnesses was a difficult and dangerous practice for Chinese criminal defense lawyers.

The Ma Guangjun case vividly illustrates the extremes of witness coercion by the police and the procuracy. As Xu Wensheng's defense lawyer, Ma managed to persuade several witnesses to give their testimonies in support of Xu in court. When those testimonies contradicted the police account, the witnesses were detained by the police soon after they left the court; some were beaten, tortured, and compelled to retract their testimony (F#536452). Witnesses might even be used to compel self-incrimination for forging evidence by defense lawyers, as the Wen Zhicheng case suggests (F#620344). Because witnesses were rarely present in court proceedings, the defense lawyer had almost no chance to cross-examine on the evidence collected by the police and the procuracy (F#572387). It is not surprising, therefore, that the lawyer's presence in criminal proceedings had little effect on case outcome (Lu and Miethe 2002).

The difficulty of collecting evidence comes partly from the traditional conception in Chinese society that only public officials are entitled to collect testimonies from witnesses. But even public officials are rarely able to bring a witness in court, because litigation, and criminal cases in particular, is widely detested in Chinese traditional culture. As a criminal law professor and part-time lawyer in Xi'an explained:

> We don't have any statistics, but the witness presence rate is very low. ... The reasons are so complicated. First, cultural and historical [reasons] – the Chinese believe in harmony and detest litigation. This is the main cultural reason. Second, social reasons – this relates to living conditions – China is a society where everyone knows everyone else and this has a deeper influence in the rural area. These people have been familiar with each other for hundreds of years, not just a friend for several years or a lifetime, so because of this people are not willing to become a witness at trial, to speak against a familiar person.
>
> (B0518, Shaanxi Province)

Besides the constraint of traditional culture, a major institutional reason for the difficulty of collecting evidence is the presence of "Big Stick 306" (see the next section). Although the 2012 CPL revision gives defense lawyers the status of defender in the investigation phase, it also presents new risks for them. A progressive elite lawyer in Beijing expressed his concern of the new risks of collecting evidence during police investigations with an interesting analogy: "Imagine the police investigation is a car and the lawyer's investigation is a bike. The car is ahead of the bike and the bike follows it. But imagine if the bike was before the car, it would be extremely dangerous" (B1304). This is to say, if the defense lawyer began to collect evidence before the police investigation was completed, the police could easily accuse the lawyer of committing the crime of lawyer's perjury. The Li Zhuang case (see Chapter 6) is a good example here. Li was arrested and charged by the Chongqing police precisely because he actively prepared to collect evidence during a police investigation. Accordingly, many lawyers would wait until they have obtained access to the case files before beginning to collect any evidence (B1506; B1512).

"BIG STICK 306": DANCING HANDCUFFED IN A MINE FIELD

Chinese lawyers experience considerable risk as they conduct criminal defense work – their personal safety, their liberty, their careers, and their finances are frequently at jeopardy. These risks arise from a combination of provisions in the law. The 1996 CPL gave lawyers increased powers to protect their clients in the investigation and prosecution phases of a criminal case. As a political tradeoff intended to meet objections of the police and the procuracy (B0507; B0512; B1512), the CPL prohibited lawyers from assisting their clients by concealing or destroying or forging evidence or allowing defendants to collude with each other; it further prohibited counsel from threatening witnesses or getting witnesses to commit perjury (Article 38). A year later the NPC yielded to intense law enforcement pressure by incorporating Article 306 of the Criminal Law, which provides that lawyers are subject to criminal penalties if they destroy or falsify evidence, or threaten or induce witnesses to lie, change testimony, or make false testimony. While these provisions seem consistent with many rule-of-law norms, in practice they opened up avenues for abuse. The law itself inadequately clarifies what constitute this crime of lawyer's perjury and thus its meaning can be stretched to suit the interests of the police and procurators.

Chinese lawyers label this crime "Big Stick 306" (Michelson 2003: 99–111), as it puts a "Sword of Damocles" (B0507) above the head of every criminal defense lawyer. A widely known saying within the lawyer community goes like this:

> If you want to practice law, don't become a lawyer; if you want to become a lawyer, don't do criminal work; if you want to do criminal work, don't collect evidence; if you want to collect evidence, don't collect testimonies from witnesses. If you fail to follow all these, just go to the detention center to register.
>
> (F#268, October 3, 2002, 6:15pm, Beijing)

Why does the crime of lawyer's perjury become an intimidating "big stick" for lawyers' evidence collection? The problem lies in the dual identities of the procuracy in China's criminal process as both the prosecutor and the supervisor. On the one hand, the procuracy prosecutes the case against the defendant and thus its work is in direct conflict with the work of defense lawyers; on the other hand, the CPL also gives the procuracy supervisory power over the entire criminal process (Article 8 of both the 1996 and 2012 CPLs); therefore it could easily file a lawsuit against the defense lawyer using Article 306 of the Criminal Law if the lawyer dared to present evidence different from or contradictory to its own evidence. In this sense, the procuracy is both a strong player and a backstage referee in the criminal process, whereas the defense lawyer is a weak and vulnerable player fighting against this powerful opponent.

This huge imbalance of power between procurators and defense lawyers led to the abusive use of Article 306 in practice as the procuracy's tool of revenge on uncooperative lawyers in the criminal process. Shortly after Article 306 was added to the 1997 Criminal Law, a police chief in Beijing even told one of our lawyer interviewees that "the trap has already been set up and now it just awaits you to jump into it" (B1512). According to the statistics published by the ACLA, in merely five years from 1997 to 2001, there had been 142 cases in which defense lawyers were arrested, illegally detained, or even beaten (Wang 2001; Fang 2005). Although the majority of these lawyers were finally declared innocent by the court (F#556167), the process of detention and prosecution was already a substantive punishment (Feeley 1979). A few well-known early Article 306 cases in which defense lawyers were detained for a long time include: (1) Li Kuisheng, a Henan lawyer, detained for twenty-six months before receiving a not-guilty verdict; (2) Huang Yabin, a Fujian lawyer, similarly wrongly detained for more than a year; (3) Wang Yibing, a Yunnan lawyer, wrongly detained and tortured for two years and became a monk after his release; and, (4) Zhang Jianzhong, a nationally renowned Beijing lawyer, who was found guilty and spent two years in prison (ZGLS_200207; F#368312).

This cold reality had the chilling effect of "killing one, intimidating a hundred" (杀一儆百) for the entire lawyer community in China. In 2002, the national lawyer representation rate for criminal cases was merely 27.8% (Fang 2005). And the average number of criminal cases that lawyers represented significantly fell in major cities such as Beijing and Shenzhen (ZGLS_200207; Fang 2005). Meanwhile, even fewer lawyers were willing to collect evidence from witnesses or present any extra evidence than the procurator's evidence in court. Instead, most lawyers simply chose to examine the procurator's case files and try to find problems in them in order to support their own arguments.

Not surprisingly, discussion on the persecution of defense lawyers was one of the hottest topics on the ACLA forum when it launched in 2002. A message posted on October 3, 2002, on "Big Stick 306" generated seventy-three responses from sixty users in the following five months (F#268). This message was one of the earliest messages on the forum. The contrast between the relatively small number of users at the time and the large number of responses suggests the wide and deep concerns about this problem that existed among Chinese lawyers at the time. Many cases were cited in the forum discussions as first-hand testimony of its immediacy and pervasiveness:

> Last week, during the court proceeding of a criminal case at the Gansu Province Jingtai County People's Court, the defendant overthrew a confession. ... But the prosecutor immediately left his seat and made a phone call outside the courtroom. During the adjournment, two policemen held up Lawyer Hu and had him handcuffed, announcing detention for the crime of perjury.
>
> (F#39466, January 15, 2003, 1:29pm, Gansu Province)

No case has been more passionately and thoroughly discussed on the ACLA forum than the lawyer SOS case reported above. In view of the fact that his lawyer-colleague had already been detained by the police for obstructing testimony, this lawyer rejected the charge that he had violated the same law, and fled his city (F#440419).

The logic of "Big Stick 306" is straightforward. A witness gives testimony to the police. When questioned by the lawyer, the witness changes his testimony. Police allege that the change in testimony shows that the lawyer induced the witnesses to lie or present false testimony, and as a result it follows that the lawyer is obstructing justice. Or, as a prominent defense lawyer put it, when a lawyer brings evidence rebutting the police or the procuracy, they may collect further evidence that leads witnesses to retract their statements on grounds that "'it was the lawyer who let me say this,' or 'I didn't say this, the lawyer wrote it himself'" (F#256602).

It is for this reason that Ma Guangjun, the defense lawyer in the Ningcheng County rape case, refused to take statements from his illiterate witnesses on behalf of the defendant. He insisted that they come to court and give oral testimony. "If I made notes and signed them, then two [witnesses] who were not able to write could break their words and say that [the statement] was written by me the lawyer. ... So I chose not to take any notes and let witnesses appear in court ... " (F#536452). Even then, as we have seen, Ma did not escape "Big Stick 306" because the police forced the witnesses to retract their in-court statements and this opened the way to detention and charges of perjury and obstruction. In the nationally renowned Li Zhuang case in 2009 (see Chapter 6), the Chongqing police pushed the boundary of Article 306 even further and charged the lawyer who had not even collected any evidence but merely met with the suspect and witnesses a few times.

Although many lawyers had been strongly advocating for the abolition of "Big Stick 306" for more than a decade, the 2012 CPL revision only added a modest restriction on this crime, that is, a lawyer suspected of the crime of perjury shall be handled by an investigation agency other than the one handling the case in which the lawyer provides representation (Article 42). The objective of this revision is to prevent the local police or procuracy from taking direct revenge on defense lawyers who present different evidence in court, as happened in several cases discussed in this chapter. Furthermore, as Chapter 6 will demonstrate, the professional and media uproars around the Li Zhuang case also served an important educational function, namely, they made the Chinese public as well as the PPC more aware of the serious risks that criminal defense lawyers face in their everyday work. Our recent interviews suggest that the tooth of "Big Stick 306" has become less sharp in criminal defense practice since 2013, yet many lawyers still shy away from collecting evidence because of the potential threat it poses (B1506; B1512).

POLITICAL EMBEDDEDNESS AND PROFESSIONAL DIFFICULTIES

In his pioneering study on Chinese lawyers, Michelson (2003, 2007) argues that political embeddedness (i.e., lawyers' previous work experience in the PPC or personal connections with state officials) has a significant effect in reducing their professional difficulties. In our fieldwork, we also find much evidence to test this argument as well as the theoretical framework that we have proposed in Chapter 1. This section presents data from the 112 interviews that our CUPL research assistants conducted in thirteen medium-sized and small cities in 2009 to examine the relationship between political embeddedness and lawyers' difficulties in criminal defense work, including the effect of "Big Stick 306." Chapter 4 will provide a more comprehensive analysis of Chinese lawyers' survival strategies in the criminal justice system.

To investigate what kinds of lawyers face fewer difficulties in their criminal defense work, we ran cross tabulations between the four types of professional difficulty and other social and legal characteristics of the respondents, including gender, age, education, years of practice, case types, and political connections. The difficulties do not seem to vary much with the lawyer's gender, age, or years of practice, except that female lawyers (41 percent) were significantly less likely to report the difficulty in meeting suspects than male lawyers (75 percent). In our fieldwork in a medium-size city in Sichuan Province, a local lawyer told us that one female lawyer in his firm even specialized in meeting suspects – she had an office right outside the local detention center and established a good relationship with the officers there by giving them cigarettes and small gifts (M0904).

Both education and case types seem to have some effects on criminal defense lawyers' professional difficulties. Lawyers with at least one degree from "Project 211" universities are less likely to report on difficulties in all the four categories than lawyers without a "Project 211" education. Lawyers who specialize in economic or white-collar crimes face more difficulties in accessing case files and collecting evidence than lawyers who mainly handle violent crimes. Because economic and white-collar crimes often involve higher-status defendants (e.g., government officials or business executives) and sometimes contain a higher degree of political sensitivity, the PPC are more cautious toward defense lawyers. Interestingly, for the difficulty in persuading judges, lawyers who specialize in economic and white-collar crimes reported less difficulty than other lawyers. This is because lawyers who have access to these profitable cases are usually lawyers who are more experienced as well as more embedded with the state apparatus.

Based on our typology of lawyers in Chapter 1, it should follow that politically embedded lawyers who signal they are close to the PPC by indicating that they would go to them for help when facing problems in their criminal defense work will be less likely to face difficulties in their everyday practice with justice system officials. Table 3.1 provides support for this hypothesis: lawyers seeking help from the PPC report less difficulty in all problem areas. Most notably, the number of well-connected lawyers who reported difficulty in persuading judges is half that of lawyers without connections. In other words, lawyers who are more politically embedded in their everyday practice

TABLE 3.1.   *The association between lawyers' professional difficulties and their*
ability to seek help from the PPC.

| PPC | Most serious difficulties encountered | | | | |
Help	Meeting	Case files	Evidence	Proceedings	N
Yes	26 (65.00%)	8 (20.00%)	20 (50.00%)	11 (27.50%)	40
No	52 (73.24%)	24 (33.80%)	44 (61.97%)	42 (59.15%)	71

Note: The percentages in the table are row percentages. The row percentages do not add to 100 percent because respondents can choose multiple categories.

appear to have advantages in criminal defense work over other lawyers. This finding confirms Michelson's (2007) argument that political embeddedness reduces professional difficulties in Chinese lawyers' work. Meanwhile, in the 2009 China Legal Environment Survey, Michelson and Liu (2010) find that Chinese lawyers with high degrees of vulnerability in their work possess significantly more liberal values on political rights and democracy than lawyers with low degrees of vulnerability. Taken together, these preliminary results suggest that Chinese lawyers' professional difficulties are negatively associated with political embeddedness, but positively associated with political liberalism.

When asked about "Big Stick 306," which specifically targets defense lawyers, 62% of our respondents knew of cases of local lawyers who were detained or charged for violating Article 306 of the Criminal Law, and 31% felt that the Article substantially affected their criminal defense work. Another 42% reported that the Article had a modest impact on their work. For example, a lawyer in Liaoning Province said that he suspended his practice from 1996 to 2000 precisely because a senior lawyer in his firm was charged with violating Article 306 and he felt that the risk of legal practice was too high (LNP0903). Another lawyer from Shandong Province elaborated on the negative effects of this Article on lawyers' defense work, particularly in collecting evidence:

> Yes, [because of Article 306] now many lawyers do not dare to collect evidence. In many criminal cases, there are no witnesses present at the court proceeding. To be honest, those testimonies are all unstable, the prosecutors often just casually bring some paperwork, which you cannot question or refute, and the court would confirm them directly. In criminal cases, the power of the lawyer is too weak. The state agencies sometimes do not care about you at all, and they won't even look at the stuff you got after so much trouble. You go to the witnesses and they do not want to appear in court

either. So it is not only useless, but also dangerous, and smart lawyers would not do any work in this area.

(SDZ0902, Shandong Province)

Not surprisingly, the most significant factor in reducing the impact of Article 306 is previous work experience in the PPC. Of the lawyers in our sample, 22 percent used to work in these three agencies in their earlier career. Among them, only 12.5 percent reported that Article 306 had a major impact on their work, 50 percent felt it had a modest impact, and 37.5 percent said the Article had no impact on their work at all. This is in sharp contrast to the opinions of lawyers without such experience, 35 percent of whom felt a major impact of Article 306. Similarly, 46 percent of the lawyers who used to work in the PPC reported difficulty in collecting evidence, compared to 61 percent of the lawyers without such experience. Evidently, earlier careers in the criminal justice system, which is the most direct source of political embeddedness, provides defense lawyer with substantial protection from retaliation and persecution in the system, as a lawyer in Anhui Province who used to work in the municipal procuracy commented:

> With my experience I do not worry about this. Because I have work experience in the procuracy, at least in this city, I don't worry about my ability in self protection and in making personal connections. Actually it is good to have some limit, but it cannot be used as a means to strike [on lawyers]. I don't think Article 306 should necessarily be abolished. Everything needs supervision, but now this [Article] is improperly used in some places.
>
> (AHH0904, Anhui Province)

The advantage of the politically embedded lawyers who either worked in one of the three justice agencies or have close connections with them is not limited to collecting evidence and protecting themselves from potential official retribution, but is found in most areas of the criminal process. When asked to what extent previous work experience in the PPC is helpful to a lawyer's criminal defense work, 45 percent of our respondents selected "very helpful," 50 percent selected "somewhat helpful," and only five percent selected "not helpful at all." When asked about a similar question on previous work experience in other Party or government agencies, only 16 percent of the respondents selected "very helpful," while 61 percent selected "somewhat helpful." This suggests that, although career history in the state sector is generally helpful for criminal defense work, direct work experience in the criminal justice system is considered the most valuable asset for criminal defense lawyers.

CONCLUSION

Criminal defense lawyers in China work in a minefield filled with trenches and bombs, sometimes with their hands cuffed. The "Three Difficulties" and "Big Stick 306" discussed in this chapter have demonstrated the great professional risks and personal danger involved in the work of criminal defense lawyers. As they stumble forward, these lawyers realize that the only actors that hold the decisive power to reduce their professional difficulties and change case outcomes are the public officials in the criminal justice system. Some of those actors dug the trenches and imbedded the bombs, some holding the handcuffs in their hands. The lawyers' best weapon, ironically, is their political embeddedness with these somewhat hostile state agencies and officials. To survive in this unfavorable criminal justice system, Chinese lawyers (with or without such embeddedness) have developed complex coping strategies in their everyday work, which is the focus of the next chapter.

4

Survival Strategies and Political Values

In a criminal justice system that is heavily weighted against criminal defense lawyers, how do they survive? Lawyers might adopt personal tactics, adapted to their personal tolerance for risk and their locations, backgrounds or experiences. They might also seek allies and resources in order to reduce the difficulties and danger of law practice. The potential channels lawyers could use include other lawyer colleagues, bar associations, the media, personal connections, and contacts inside the PPC. The issues of survival are in turn compounded by self-understanding of their vocation. If lawyers seek only to protect their job status and to ensure a satisfactory income, then tactics and alliances might take one form. If, on the other hand, lawyers imagine their everyday practice as a means to advance their professional skills, or, even more, as transformative of China's justice system so that it will protect basic legal freedoms, then tactics and alliances might take another form. The issue of survival in everyday work is inextricably interwoven with the types of orientations and values that drive their practices.

This chapter explores complexities and nuances of adaptive strategies by examining patterns and associations of criminal practice in a small but evocative sample of 112 lawyers in thirteen medium-sized and small cities (see Chapter 1 for a description of the methodology used), complemented by interview data from our own fieldwork and discussions on lawyers' political values. In our 2009 interview questionnaire, we asked lawyers to identify which methods they used to solve problems in their criminal defense work. Figure 4.1 summarizes their responses. Nearly two-thirds of our 112 respondents, most of whom were ordinary practitioners, reported that they mainly relied on themselves when facing problems in the criminal process. This is not surprising given the fact that the vast majority of Chinese lawyers work individually (Michelson 2003; Michelson and Liu 2010; Liu 2011), although until the 2007 revision of the Lawyers Law all lawyers were required to join a

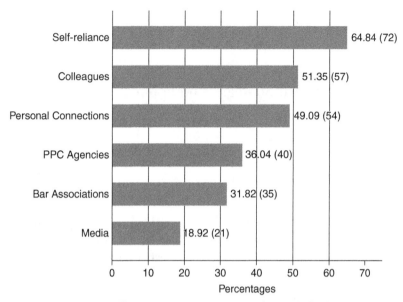

FIGURE 4.1   Varieties of lawyers' coping tactics when facing difficulties and danger in criminal defense work.

law firm. There are few case referrals or substantive cooperation even among lawyers from the same firm. Lawyers doing criminal defense work, especially in smaller cities, are no exception (JXN0903; SCL0907). Compared with other legal fields, criminal defense in particular is a solo field for Chinese lawyers because of its difficulties and risks.

Yet the high degree of self-reliance does not mean that other coping tactics are not important. As we demonstrate in this chapter, while all the channels identified in Figure 4.1 can be useful in certain cases or situations, political embeddedness within the state is often more effective than the other channels for lawyers to protect themselves and defend their clients. We also find that the five types of lawyers discussed in Chapter 1 (i.e., progressive elites, pragmatic brokers, notable activists, grassroots activists, and routine practitioners) differ in the ways they protect themselves as well as in their motivations and political values.

LAWYER COLLEAGUES AND BAR ASSOCIATIONS

Half of the respondents reported that they would seek help from their lawyer colleagues in moments of difficulty. Such collegial help among lawyers mainly works in three ways. First, until the 2012 CPL revision, many law firms and local bar associations required two lawyers to work together when meeting suspects or collecting evidence for mutual protection (e.g., AHH0903; GDD0901; HNZ0905; JSD0905; SDY0904). Second, for important and difficult cases, some lawyers, particularly those who are younger and less experienced, would seek advice from their senior colleagues (e.g., AHH0910; GDD0907; JXN0905; JSD0901; SDZ0902). Some well-managed law firms would also organize informal discussions among lawyers handling such cases (C0709; LNP0904; LNP0910). Finally, lawyers sometimes ask their colleagues who have connections in the PPC for help in contacting the relevant agencies (HNZ0901; JXN0905). For example, a Shandong lawyer said that once he faced potential procuratorial investigation because the evidence he collected was different from the police evidence, but another lawyer in the firm had close connections with the local procuracy and persuaded the procurators to give up the Article 306 charge (SDY0902).

Lawyers were particularly likely to seek help from one another when collecting evidence, for which two lawyers were generally required by Article 49 of the 1999 ACLA Regulation on Lawyers' Handling of Criminal Cases. In practice, this requirement was often fulfilled by a senior lawyer and his/her associate (B0510). Meanwhile, for politically sensitive cases such as those involving social stability issues or white-collar crimes, some local bar associations or law firms would suggest that two lawyers collaborate in order to reduce difficulties and protect each other (C0710; S0705). In some law firms, there were also informal discussions among lawyers regarding important or complicated cases. As an example, here is how a progressive elite lawyer in Chengdu described his experience in the firm:

> If it were an important case, our law firm would hold a discussion of the case by many lawyers. A one-person defense might involve only two lawyers, but if a case were really complicated, many lawyers would discuss it together. For example, recently I had a big case. I first collected the case materials and made my own judgment about how to defend it. Then I asked the law firm to hold a meeting with other lawyers. We examined the case files and discussed the weaknesses and whether or not to take evidence, etc. The formal discussion was within the law firm, but privately I discussed cases with former friends in law school or professors. But if there were two or more defendants and they all had lawyers, we would not communicate because it could become a form of tallying confessions.
>
> (C0709, Sichuan Province)

This lawyer was able to use resources from both the law firm and his previous law school connections in his cases because he was a well-known criminal defense lawyer with a doctoral degree from a premier law school in Sichuan Province. For many less well-connected lawyers, assistance from the firm or former colleagues was much less common (C0707; S0705). In particular, when a lawyer got into trouble with "Big Stick 306" or other difficulties, the law firm could rarely provide any substantive protection.

Meanwhile, almost one-third of the respondents indicated that they would seek help from bar associations and justice bureaus when facing difficulties in criminal defense work. Although bar associations in China were often considered merely an extension of justice bureaus and mainly serve regulatory functions, both the ACLA and local bar associations were active on several occasions in protecting lawyers from persecution in the 2000s. After "Big Stick 306" was established in 1997, the ACLA made consistent efforts to publicize the serious problems in criminal defense and try to rescue lawyers all over the country from the crime of perjury. Provincial and municipal bar associations also provided substantive assistance to criminal defense lawyers, particularly those prosecuted by the local procuracies (B0507; S0703). In the Ma Guangjun case discussed in Chapter 3, the Inner Mongolia Lawyers Association (IMLA) organized nearly a hundred lawyers from all over the city of Chifeng to attend Ma's trial (F#536448). Ma was finally declared innocent by the court. When being interviewed by the media, the secretary-general of the IMLA regarded this case as one "concerning the practice environment and right of criminal defense for all lawyers" and, according to their statistics, in Inner Mongolia the percentage of lawyer representation in criminal cases had dropped from 40 percent in 2002 to 35 percent in 2003 (F#536448).

Yet bar associations were not as powerful in other cases of lawyer persecution. In 2007, for example, Ma Kedong, a renowned criminal defense lawyer in Guangdong Province, suddenly was arrested by police officers from Liaoning Province for the crime of fraud for charging a one-million-yuan lawyer fee to two mafia leaders in Shenyang, whose illegal activities caused the fall of a number of high-ranking officials in the local public security system. After the case was exposed in the media, it was widely perceived in the legal circle as the Shenyang police's revenge for Ma's successful legal services for the mafia leaders in 2001. A judge in Liaoning told a journalist that, without Ma's background operation, the mafia leaders would have already been in jail in 2001 and thus the "earthquake" in the Shenyang police system would not have happened later (MZYFZSB_20071007).

Because of Ma Kedong's prestige in the lawyer community, the ACLA, the Guangdong Provincial Lawyers Association, and the Guangzhou Municipal Lawyers Association were all actively involved in the case to support the defendant. The ACLA held two symposiums of legal experts to analyze the case before the trial, and the three bar associations all sent representatives to attend the court proceeding in September 2007 (MZYFZSB_20071007). One month after the trial, while waiting for the judicial decision, the ACLA even published an "expert opinion" signed by fifteen prominent law professors and other legal experts in Beijing, arguing that Ma Kedong's behavior did not constitute the crime of fraud and should only receive administrative sanctions (XKB_20071110). However, Ma Kedong was still sentenced to eleven years in prison by the Liaoning court in May 2008.

Comparing the Ma Kedong case with the Ma Guangjun case, it is striking that the bar associations' intervention in lawyer persecution cases was more effective when the counterpart was a lower-level state agency and when the case did not contain any political sensitivity. In the Ma Guangjun case, the provincial bar association could easily mobilize lawyers and other relevant agencies to support the defendant and fight against the county procuracy. In contrast, after the ACLA's symposiums raised doubts about the Liaoning court's jurisdiction over the Ma Kedong case, the court was able to obtain a document from the SPC, which appointed the district court to try this case. Confronting the powerful Shenyang police, the bar associations' effort did not make a difference in the final case outcome. In fact, the "expert opinion" that the ACLA issued after the trial already indicated their pessimistic expectation about the judicial decision.

Indeed, the higher the political stakes and the more powerful the counterpart state agency, the less likely that the bar association's support of defense lawyers will influence the outcomes of lawyer persecution cases. Another case in point here is that of the Beijing lawyer, Zhang Jianzhong, who was once one of the "ten best lawyers" in China but was prosecuted by the crime of lawyer's perjury in 2002. Before his arrest, Zhang defended vigorously several corrupt high-ranking officials such as Cheng Kejie and Li Jizhou, and his prosecution was regarded by many criminal defense lawyers in Beijing as a political retribution by the central Party leaders rather than a purely legal action by the local procuracy (B0508; B0510). During the whole criminal process, over five hundred lawyers signed a petition to the government in Zhang's support, and the ACLA also published legal analyses to help his defense (Human Rights Watch 2008: 56–57). Nevertheless, because the political stakes were too high, none of these measures worked and Zhang served two years in prison. After all, as a criminal defense lawyer in Shanghai commented, "the bar association is also a weak party in China" (So705). It is not an official part of the state apparatus and only has indirect influence on case outcomes through the justice bureau, which is a much weaker agency than the PPC in China's legal system (HBXo901; SDYo902). In smaller cities, the role of the local bar association is weaker still. Several respondents in our interviews indicated that the main task of the local bar association was to collect fees from lawyers (HNYo902; SDYo907) and it would only offer assistance when lawyers were facing Article 306 charges or other forms of serious persecution (AHHo901; AHHo906; SDYo908).

It is also important to note that, in recent years, bar associations in China have become less active in helping lawyers in perjury cases than before. In the Li Zhuang case in 2009–2011 (see Chapter 6), for instance, the ACLA kept silent during the entire trial due to the high political sensitivity of the case. Although the Chongqing Lawyers Association refused to cooperate with the local PPC in accusing Li Zhuang of ethical problems during his first trial, it did not make any active effort to help him either. The Beijing Lawyers Association (BLA) sent a work team to Chongqing to observe the case in its early stage but did little more than lip service. In Li's second trial in 2011, some local bar associations even issued notices to lawyers to prevent them from going to Chongqing to support Li or spreading rumors about the case. In some other recent cases, such as the Beihai case or the Xiaohe case (see Chapter 7), bar associations also made similar warnings to lawyers. For notable activist lawyers in Beijing, the local bar association appeared even more repressive (see Chapter 5). Even their law firms presented more obstacles than support to their practice, such as refusing to issue the letter granting the lawyers' meeting with suspects or threatening to not renew their licenses (B1522; B1526).

Why have bar associations' recent attitudes toward lawyer persecution cases changed from earlier years? One obvious reason is the rising activism among Chinese lawyers in both politically sensitive cases and other cases in which their procedural rights are severely violated. In addition to the growing population of notable activists, both the emergence of a network of "die-hard" lawyers and the conversion of some progressive elites to activist lawyering have put the justice bureaus in Beijing and other major cities on high alert (see Chapter 7). As bar associations in China are not autonomous professional associations, but tightly controlled by the justice bureaus, it is not surprising that they have become more repressive on lawyers' political activities, particularly in criminal cases. Another reason is that some of Chinese lawyers' collective actions in the late 2000s were directed towards bar associations (e.g., the 2008 Beijing Lawyers Association election movement, see Chapter 5), particularly the exorbitant amount of mandatory membership fees that they charged every lawyer. As a result, bar associations have begun to use their regulatory power to make sanctions on these political activists in the legal profession.

THE MEDIA

Lawyers are controversial figures in the popular media. They can be portrayed as charismatic, justice-assuring heroes in court trials, or greedy, law-bending villains in accordance with to public opinion (Galanter 2006). In an analysis based on 669 case reports from our newspaper media data (Wang, Liu, and Halliday 2015), we find that, in addition to the common image of advocates, lawyers are also presented in Chinese media reports as legal experts and criminal suspects. Even when they are presented as advocates, their roles frequently are characterized vaguely and their indispensability for a just outcome is left in doubt. The characterizations in turn rely less on their legal skills or commitment to procedural justice and more on presumptions of guilt or innocence. Lawyers seldom are characterized in fully rounded portraits because their contribution to criminal justice is only fully recognized when the media's substantive judgment about the case favors them.

Despite the media's frequent neglect or distortion of their image, as weak actors in China's political and legal systems, both individual lawyers and bar associations sometimes rely on the media to expose lawyer persecution cases. Even in ordinary cases, some lawyers would go to the media to seek public support of their defense work. This is particularly common for progressive elites and notable activists. Nevertheless, the media in different regions of China vary markedly in their coverage of lawyers' criminal defense. In Beijing, Shanghai, and other major cities along the east coast, it is relatively easy for defense lawyers to get access to the media. In smaller cities and the western provinces, by contrast, it is uncommon for defense lawyers to get media exposure, and the effect of media reports on case outcomes is minimal, if not negative. As Figure 4.1 shows, among our respondents from thirteen medium-sized and smaller cities, only 19 percent reported that they would use the media to help solve problems in their practice, and many were doubtful of the media's impact on case outcomes.

Like the legal profession, the Chinese media operate between the state and the market. Although the state still exercises tight control and censorship on newspapers, TV programs, and even the Internet, in the past three decades there has been a notable trend of commercialization in the Chinese media (Lin 2012). Consequently, legal news, as well as other social news, has become a popular section for many newspapers and TV programs. Reports on criminal cases constitute a large proportion of the legal columns and programs in the popular Chinese media, yet among them only a small proportion are concerned with lawyers' defense work. A progressive elite lawyer in Shanghai described his view of the media as follows:

> Of course, [using the media is] the first option that comes to my mind. But our media is a broadcasting machine, and the outlet is not working very well. To make an analogy, if the media is a throat, then it is blocked by something. It is a good channel but very often you cannot go through it. So my personal view is that I really hope that we have the freedom of media in China. Also, lawyers can use the media to report cases to the public, a kind of check on the people who have power. We can make appointments with the media. And a new thing is the Internet that we use – lawyers post cases to the Internet, to forums. I am not sure I would use it, but if other lawyers post a message I would be interested in responding.
>
> (S0704, Shanghai)

Because of the political sensitivity involved in many criminal cases, the Chinese media are usually cautious when reporting on the plight of defense lawyers, especially when the case is related to local leaders or powerful state agencies. To publicize their cases, therefore, lawyers would use the media from localities outside the case's jurisdiction, e.g., another province, or another city in the same province (H0703; S0705; B1003). This is often the case when progressive elites and notable activists in Beijing and other major cities handle cases in other provinces. If there was trouble at the local level, they would be able to use the national media to expose their problems with local judges and law enforcement officers, which could lead to inspections from higher-level state agencies (B0510; S0704). In the meantime, the media are also a good outlet to influence public opinions and, in a sense, to restore the defendant's reputation in society. A progressive elite lawyer in Hangzhou explained this special function of the Chinese media:

> We will disclose to the media some facts of the cases, especially when the police or the Party Disciplinary Committee has done something wrong. From my experience the media exposure doesn't make a big difference. It can only make the public know some of the facts of the case, but it will not influence the outcome of the case, because our judicial decisions are made by the will of the officials, by the will of man. The main purpose is to let society know, to restore the social reputation of the defendant. I did a case in a mountain area in the province when someone went to the police to report corruption of local officials. When he returned home he was arrested. So after he was back [to the police station] the police and the procuracy made four accusations, I made a defense of not guilty. Eventually the procuracy

withdrew the case. According to Chinese law, without new evidence they could not prosecute him again. But some powerful local people requested they prosecute again. And the defendant was sentenced for eleven years. So after this case I went to the national media. During the proceedings 500 local residents appeared in the court. Although I could not change his fate, at least his social reputation was restored.

(H0701, Zhejiang Province)

Besides restoring the defendant's social reputation, a more important function of the media is to generate potential intervention from local leaders or higher-level state agencies. In each level of the Party-state apparatus, there is a research office in charge of collecting media reports and writing briefs for the government leaders. Then the leaders give their opinions back to the relevant state agencies, including the courts (S0703). If the case is significant enough, this official mechanism of media reporting could go all the way to the central leadership. For many lawyers, getting the leadership's attention on a case is far more important and effective than winning public support, as the PPC are all subordinates to the local or provincial leaders. A pragmatic broker in Zhejiang Province described the relationship between media reports and political intervention in his cases:

> For example, in certain locations there are local leaders who influence the verdicts and make unfair decisions. In this situation we would use the media to just arouse public concern for the case. Usually the local media is useless, [so we] have to use the media from other places. There are two aspects: locally, if a case is reported in the media, some black boxes are opened, so they cannot act in certain ways anymore; also, if it reaches the upper-level leaders they will have opinions that could influence the outcome. It also happens that for some cases, local lawyers won't accept the case but go to lawyers in other places, maybe more famous, so that they will not offend local leaders. I often handle cases from other counties. For example, for county-level corruption cases they come to the provincial capital for a lawyer. . . . In fact, the media cannot directly influence the case, but [they] can shape [public] opinions. In China the circumstances are different – my strategy is that if I don't need the media, I don't use them. Because media exposure could make the lawyer famous but it is not for the good of the case.

(H0703, Zhejiang Province)

Here the media were used by the lawyer as merely an intermediary for accessing political power and constraining the behavior of local judicial agencies. Yet this intermediary is not always effective – in some western provinces where local political control is stronger and exposure to international norms is more limited, the media are far less useful for criminal defense lawyers than are the urban media on the east coast. In Sichuan Province, for example, although the media are relatively developed compared to adjacent provinces and they report on many criminal cases (C0707), few criminal defense lawyers used newspapers or TV programs to publicize their cases. Many lawyers believed that media intervention during case trials might have a negative effect on their defense work, because it could irritate procurators and judges (C0704; C0706; C0709). As a progressive elite lawyer in Chengdu explained:

> There are several reasons [why I do not use the media]. First, the media are not autonomous in China. For some cases, you can say that the media apply certain pressures to the judiciary, but they are not cases of concern to the government. For those really important cases, if the government had already made the decision on how to deal with the case, the media would not dare to report it. Or before they report they would consult the government on how to report it. And sometimes the involvement of the media would have a counter effect. For example, there was a case reported on the Internet where a scientist killed his wife and he was sentenced to death. He was famous. So after he was sentenced many people wrote to the court to plea for a lower sentence. That aroused the attention of the media. Then the public had a lively discussion. Where is the justice in this? If someone was a famous scientist, could he escape punishment? From my perspective, in the second trial, the court had no option but to sentence him to death because of the media pressure. It is very difficult to predict the reactions of the public. In some cases, if a lawyer contacted the media and aroused public attention, the government would hate this. They don't want a problem to be made public. Then the lawyer would be at great risk. Another reason is that most cases that I handle are white-collar crimes, and in these cases you have to be very, very careful in using the media.
>
> (C0709, Sichuan Province)

It is evident that state control on both the media and law practice is tighter in Chengdu than in east coast cities such as Hangzhou or Shanghai. In smaller cities, pragmatic brokers, routine practitioners, and even grassroots activists are all cautious about using the media because they do not want to offend the local justice agencies whom they must maintain a good relationship with for the sake of their work (AHH0908; FJN0904; JSD0902; SDZ0902). In contrast, for highly sensitive cases (e.g., Falun Gong cases, freedom of speech cases) on which no official Chinese media would report, some notable activists in Beijing sometimes use Internet blogs and microblogs or go directly to the international media (B1003; B1005; also see Chapter 5). WeChat groups, which are more private than blogs and microblogs, have also become a popular tool for activist lawyers to provide support for like-minded colleagues in recent years (B1515; B1520).

Nonetheless, a consensus across different regions is that the state holds the ultimate power in deciding case outcomes as well as the effectiveness of other means of protection. Therefore, using the media becomes a political process too, and lawyers must walk a fine line between the state and the public when they make an alliance with the media. This is a particularly subtle issue for notable activists, who have developed sophisticated tactics in using the Internet and the international media to mobilize support without being disbarred or heavily sanctioned by the Chinese government (B0901; B1001; B1003). As using the official media are often ineffective and risky, many politically liberal lawyers have switched to the Internet and social media to reach the Chinese public directly, without having to use heavily censored newspaper or TV reports as an intermediary. Chapter 7 will discuss the rise of lawyers' online networking in detail.

POLITICAL EMBEDDEDNESS WITHIN STATE AGENCIES

When the media and bar associations are not very helpful, lawyers may go directly to the relevant judicial agencies for support. Thirty-six percent of our respondents in smaller cities reported that they would seek help from the PPC to solve problems in criminal defense work, and 49 percent reported that they would rely on personal connections – these lawyers are mostly pragmatic brokers who are embedded in the local justice system but not politically liberal. The irony here, however, is that the agencies lawyers often rely on for protection are precisely the ones they are supposed to challenge in the criminal process.

If researchers were able to conduct a comprehensive biographical analysis of well-known criminal defense lawyers in China, they would be surprised to discover just how many of these lawyers had previous work experiences in the PPC. Due to the tremendous professional difficulties and personal danger faced by criminal defense lawyers, the majority of Chinese lawyers try to stay away from criminal defense work as much as they can. Even some successful lawyers in this field switch to civil and commercial cases after they have gained a certain reputation from defending in criminal cases. Not incidentally, most lawyers who persist and thrive in criminal defense work rely heavily on political embeddedness (Michelson 2007) with the PPC. The most straightfor-ward type of political embeddedness is previous work experience in one of the three agencies. The higher level of the agency, the more advantage and less difficulty the lawyer would enjoy in practice. For example, the senior progressive elite lawyer in Hangzhou quoted above gave the following answer when asked how he dealt with the "Three Difficulties" and "Big Stick 306":

> I am different from ordinary small lawyers. I am a member of the Legal Expert Committee of the Zhejiang Provincial Public Security Bureau. I used to work in the Provincial High Court as a secretary for the court president, so police officers do not dare to cause me trouble. That is the first reason. . . . Once when I went to a detention center to meet a suspect, the police put a glass window between us. I protested. I cannot meet a suspect that way. I went to their leaders and finally they removed the window. I solved the problem for defense lawyers that had existed for twenty years. After that the glass window was removed, and the local lawyers were very grateful. This is because of my prestige, reputation, and social status. I just went to the head of the local bureau because I am a provincial-level supervisor of the Public Security Bureau.
>
> (H0701, Zhejiang Province)

Arguably, former and present connections with the provincial state agencies made a significant difference to this lawyer's practice. While local lawyers struggled with the glass window issue for two decades without any success, this elite lawyer solved the problem at once by going directly to local leaders, whose administrative rank was lower than both his former rank in court and his present supervisory position in the provincial police. For such a well-embedded lawyer, his contacts in the police and in court could help him solve almost any work-related problem within the province. Going forward, as long as he practices according to the law and within his "comfort zone" (i.e., Zhejiang Province), "Big Stick 306" would never fall upon his head.

This pattern of political embeddedness is also observed in the work of progressive elites in other regions. For instance, in contrast to the negative responses from most of our interviewees regarding the "Three Difficulties," two prominent defense lawyers in Beijing and Xi'an, respectively, gave quite positive answers (B0508; X0505). They claimed that they had little problem in meeting suspects, collecting evidence, or even calling witnesses to court trials. The reason is simple: the Beijing lawyer worked in the municipal public security bureau for ten years before becoming a lawyer, and the Xi'an lawyer also had very close connections with the provincial procuracy – in fact, even his office was located near the provincial procuratorial building. They both admitted that their connections with the police and the procuracy significantly reduced the difficulties in their work.

Besides previous work experience, another increasingly important type of connection between lawyers and state officials is through legal education.

Since the vast expansion of legal education in China in the late 1990s (Minzner 2013), a large number of Chinese judges and procurators went back to law school for part-time study in order to get a bachelor or master's degree in law. Meanwhile, law professors were also frequently invited to hold adjunct positions in local courts and procuracies (B0501; C0702; S0703). These new developments substantially strengthened the connections between law professors and the PPC. This gave criminal law professors who practice as part-time lawyers great advantages in their work, because many judges and procurators, including some leaders of local courts and procuracies, had been their students. A criminal law professor in Chengdu gave an example of the advantage he enjoyed in his part-time practice:

> Being a law professor brings me a lot of advantages in law practice. For example, at a trial I found the procurator was one of my students. The procurator told me afterward that usually he would be much more critical of the sneaky defendant, but because I, his professor, was there, the procurator showed more respect. I think this is a good way of achieving judicial justice.
>
> (C0708, Sichuan Province)

Law professors are not the sole beneficiaries of the increase in legal education for judges and procurators. Sometimes defense lawyers with master's or doctoral degrees from major local law schools also benefit from their academic advisors' connections (C0709; C0710). Yet such political embeddedness has a limit; that is, it only works well within the local political context. If a well-connected lawyer handled a case in another city or another province, then his or her political embeddedness would significantly diminish and the work would become almost as difficult as the defense work of other ordinary practitioners. The law professor quoted above described his experience in a case in Yunnan, an adjacent province of Sichuan:

> One of the cases was in Yunnan Province. . . . The suspect was detained for eight months. The result was that the procuracy decided not to prosecute the case. In this case, I spent half a month [trying] to meet the client. I brought an assistant, went to the provincial public security bureau and the provincial political-legal committee, and finally the mayor of the city made an order for the police to give access. I have more difficulties outside my own province. You know much fewer people there. I have colleagues in the academia and the profession and that helps.
>
> (C0708, Sichuan Province)

Not incidentally, several progressive elite lawyers in Beijing also complained ferociously about the difficulties in handling out-of-town cases (B0502; B0510;

B0515). Although in many situations they still could mobilize their political resources to complete their tasks, just as the Sichuan lawyer did in the Yunnan case, it was far more complicated than doing work in their local territories. Consequently, even some nationally renowned criminal defense lawyers in Beijing would advise their out-of-town clients to use local lawyers in the phases of investigation and prosecution, where local connections are most important (B0515).

Even if a lawyer had no work experience or law school connection with judges and procurators, he or she could still gain certain political embeddedness through the exchange of resources with these state officials, or what Liu (2011) terms "symbiotic exchange," such as gift giving or kickbacks for case referrals. When the symbiotic exchange between defense lawyers and state officials had become relatively stable, some procurators and judges would even refer cases to lawyers in order to get kickbacks.

Therefore, among all the coping tactics for Chinese criminal defense lawyers, political embeddedness with state agencies is the most effective means and, in a sense, the ultimate source of protection. In the political context of China, the influence of bar associations, the media, or even public opinion has to work through the political system to have any substantive effect on the criminal justice system. It should follow from the logic of our typology in Chapter 1 that lawyers with different motivations and different structural locations would have recourse to different tactics of self-defense in their everyday practice. Our extensive interviews provide support for this hypothesis. Among the five types of lawyers, progressive elites and pragmatic brokers are politically embedded and therefore more likely to use their connections with the justice system to cope with problems in criminal defense work. In contrast, notable activists usually do not have the embeddedness but mainly rely on the media, Internet, and international community for self-protection. And routine practitioners who have no direct access to the media or the justice system mostly rely on themselves or their colleagues when handling criminal cases.

Finally, as Table 4.1 shows, if we contrast grassroots activists – those lawyers who are not politically embedded but express politically liberal motivation – with other lawyers in the medium-sized and small city sample, we find some corroboration of the results of our qualitative field-work that activist lawyers must use alternative tactics to defend themselves and their clients. These grassroots activists tend to rely less on colleagues and personal connections, but use the media more often than pragmatic brokers and routine practitioners. In other words, they appear to be more isolated from other lawyers and are compelled to pursue strategies outside

TABLE 4.1. *The association between lawyers' politically liberal motivation and their coping tactics in criminal defense work.*

Politically liberal motivation	Coping tactics						
	Self	Colleagues	Media	PPC	Bar association	Personal connection	N
Yes	13 (72.22%)	6 (33.33%)	5 (27.78%)	7 (38.89%)	6 (33.33%)	6 (33.33%)	18
No	58 (63.74%)	49 (54.44%)	16 (17.58%)	32 (35.56%)	29 (31.87%)	48 (53.33%)	91

Note: The percentages in the table are row percentages. The row percentages do not add to 100 percent because respondents can choose multiple categories.

the state in their work, most notably by employing the media and thereby, indirectly, engaging civil society or the public. On using the PPC or bar associations, however, there is no significant difference between grassroots activists and other lawyers.

MOTIVATIONS AND POLITICAL VALUES

The importance of political embeddedness in criminal defense work poses a challenging question for the politics of Chinese lawyers: how could lawyers effectively push for institutionalization of the values of political liberalism if their own survival is dependent on the system that they seek to change? This section sheds light on this question by first examining the political values and motivations of criminal defense lawyers in medium-size and small cities, most of whom are pragmatic brokers, grassroots activists, or routine practitioners. The analysis will show that there is an inverse relationship between political liberalism and political embeddedness in ordinary Chinese lawyers' political orientations. Following that, we shall proceed to discuss the different patterns of political motivation for progressive elites and notable activists in major cities.

In our 112 structured interviews in thirteen medium-sized and small cities we asked the open-ended question: Why do you still do criminal defense work despite all the difficulties and danger? We coded the responses into four categories: (1) economic motivation; (2) professional motivation; (3) political liberalism; and, (4) political embeddedness. The four categories are not mutually exclusive, and the answers of some respondents fall into multiple categories. Figure 4.2 presents the descriptive results of this analysis.

More than three quarters (78 percent) of our respondents indicated that they practiced criminal defense work because of economic reasons and self-

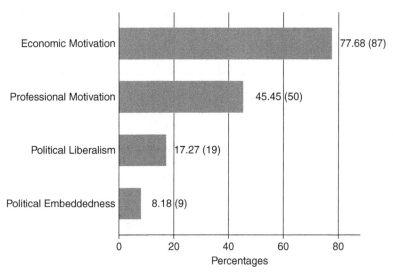

FIGURE 4.2 Percentages of lawyers' motivations in doing criminal defense work.

interests. Of this group, many indicated that they could not pick and choose cases. Work was thrust upon them as a condition of practice and survival. This is not surprising given the fact that all respondents practice in medium-sized and small cities where the degree of specialization is relatively low. Meanwhile, some respondents said they did criminal cases because of the referrals and requests from their friends and old clients. In smaller cities, where social connections are important and often intimate, it is hard for law practitioners to refuse help to close friends or old clients. In addition, some respondents admitted that making a profit was a major concern in doing criminal defense work, or they considered criminal cases conducive to developing professional and social reputation.

But economic considerations are not the only driving force behind lawyers' motivations in doing criminal defense work. One striking result in our respondents' answers to the motivation question is that 45 percent reported that they worked in the field of criminal defense because criminal cases were professionally challenging. By "professionally challenging" the lawyers mean that criminal cases often involve more rigorous procedures than civil or administrative litigation, so they feel a strong sense of achievement when they win a case against the powerful police and procuracy. A lawyer in Hubei Province explained why criminal defense work was particularly challenging and valuable for lawyers:

Doing criminal cases is the best test for the lawyer's ability in using the law to solve practical problems. Its requirements for understanding the law, using statutes, oral skills, and comprehensive quality all exceed those in civil litigation. It trains the lawyer's legal reasoning better than civil cases do. And the lawyer must also have passion. . . . Your understanding of civil law could be ambiguous, but it would not be a problem for you to handle a civil case well. But the understanding of criminal law is very strict. It is not only related to the defendant's rights, but it is also required that the lawyer supervises [the implementation of] the law. Sometimes your understanding of a principle or value could determine whether a person is guilty or innocent. (HBX0901, Hubei Province)

While nearly half of the respondents emphasized the rigorous procedural training and strong sense of satisfaction that lawyers can get from their criminal defense work, professional challenge as a motivation for doing criminal cases seems to diminish with a lawyer's years of practice. In our sample, more experienced lawyers are significantly less likely to emphasize the professionally challenging aspect of criminal defense. As a matter of fact, many Chinese lawyers who used to practice criminal law in their early career switch to civil and commercial cases after they have established a professional reputation and reached a certain income level. For them, criminal defense is merely an interim exercise in professional training and reputation building. As a lawyer in Sichuan Province commented:

[Doing criminal defense work] is particularly helpful for new lawyers. . . . Criminal cases can reflect the lawyer's professional ability. You did well in one criminal case, and the client highly praised your work, then he would naturally introduce you to other people. This is a good opportunity for new lawyers to develop a clientele. That's why many senior lawyers would tell young lawyers to do more criminal cases. It can expand your social network. (SCN0902, Sichuan Province)

But this is not to say more experienced criminal defense lawyers do not care about the law and legal rights. On the contrary, lawyers' motivation in pursuing justice and constraining state power increases with years of practice. Our analysis shows that lawyers who had practiced for more than twenty years were significantly more likely to identify justice, proceduralism, and constraint on state power as their motivation for doing criminal cases than less experienced lawyers. This finding not only shows the attrition of the less politically motivated lawyers from the criminal defense bar, but also suggests that lawyers' liberal political motivation is partially the product of their legal practice: the longer they practice criminal defense and the more difficulties and problems they have experienced, the more salient their political motivation. In contrast to the large number of lawyers who switch to commercial cases after establishing themselves professionally, those lawyers who work on criminal cases for a long time are the real vanguards of political liberalism in China.

Altogether, 17 percent of our respondents suggested that they persisted in criminal defense work because they wanted to pursue justice, reform the legal system, and constrain the power of the law enforcement agencies. In comparison, 8 percent of our respondents admitted that they practiced criminal defense because of their political embeddedness with the criminal justice system – previous work experience or current connections with the PPC not only reduced their professional difficulties, but also gave them more case sources and better means to achieve favorable outcomes in their cases. It is not surprising that the percentages in these two categories are much smaller than economic and professional motivations – on the one hand, politically motivated lawyers are always the minority in the legal profession, in China and elsewhere; on the other hand, even if a larger percentage of lawyers benefit from political embeddedness in their work, not all of them would explicitly attribute their motivations for practicing law to such connections to the state apparatus.

Furthermore, a striking result from the analysis of motivations is that none of the eighteen lawyers who were motivated by politically liberal values had any previous work experience in the criminal justice system (see Table 4.2). In other words, none of the lawyers with previous work experience in the PPC reported that they did criminal cases to pursue justice and reform the legal system. This contrast reinforces the difference in practice orientations between pragmatic brokers and grassroots activists. The former are well connected to the justice system, where they usually have started their career, and thereby have little inclination to reform it. The latter are motivated by legal-liberal ideals to practice criminal defense and pursue justice despite the personal dangers that their dealings with the state agencies may pose. For instance, a lawyer in Sichuan Province said he only did criminal cases that involve "serious injustice" (SCL0907); another Sichuan lawyer in a different city said criminal cases "let lawyers develop a strong sense of justice" (SCN0909); a lawyer in Liaoning Province said he hoped to do criminal cases to "improve the [practice] environment" (LNP0907); and a veteran lawyer in Hubei Province only said one short sentence when asked his motivation for doing criminal defense: "Because I believe evil cannot crush justice!" (HBX0903) Another middle-aged lawyer in the same city explained his motivation in more detail:

TABLE 4.2. *The association between lawyers' politically liberal motivation and their previous work experience in the PPC.*

PPC experience	Politically liberal motivation	No politically liberal motivation	N
Yes	0 (0.00%)	24 (100.00%)	24
No	18 (21.18%)	67 (78.82%)	85

Note: The percentages in the table are row percentages.

Only by doing criminal defense can lawyers learn legal reasoning and show our expertise in the competition with the three agencies, to make them improve too. You do criminal defense, do your best to write the defense opinion, and if the opinion is adopted, the client would also appreciate our work. This helps the PPC to improve their work, to enhance their qualities. It is also helpful for the progress of the rule of law in our nation.

(HBX0907, Hubei Province)

The approach that this and many other ordinary criminal defense lawyers adopted is different from the "heroic lawyering" approach of the small number of notable activists in Beijing who often appear in the Western media (see Chapter 5). Instead of openly confronting the Party-state and its judicial agencies, these grassroots activists seek to reform the system through everyday defense work, by incrementally improving the work of the PPC and spreading the ideas of the rule of law, locality by locality, across the vastness of China. For instance, when we interviewed a Chongqing lawyer in March 2009 (Q0910), he insisted on giving us a copy of his defense opinion for a murder case in 2007. We were perplexed at first because the defendant in that case had already been executed and there could be no possible legal remedy. But the lawyer said emotionally that he still hoped to restore justice for his deceased client someday, because he firmly believed that it was the wrong verdict. This strong sense and persistent pursuit of justice in ordinary cases is the essence of "everyday political lawyering" in the Chinese criminal justice system.

This leads us to our analysis of Chinese lawyers' political values, particularly values on basic legal rights and procedural justice. In the interview question-naire, we asked each respondent to evaluate the relative importance of two goals of the CPL which are in tension, namely, "striking crimes" versus "protecting citizens' legal rights." As Table 4.3 shows, lawyers who used to work in the PPC were significantly less likely to prioritize protecting legal rights over striking crimes than other respondents; instead, the majority of them gave the official answer in Article 2 of the 1996 CPL, i.e., both are equally

TABLE 4.3. *The associations between lawyers' political values and their previous work experience in the PPC.*

	Priorities of criminal procedure law				Importance of justice			
PPC exp.	Strike crimes	Both	Protect rights	N	Substantive	Both	Procedural	N
Yes	1 (4.17%)	16 (66.67%)	7 (29.17%)	24	6 (25.00%)	12 (50.00%)	6 (25.00%)	24
No	17 (19.54%)	24 (27.59%)	44 (50.57%)	87	19 (21.84%)	29 (33.33%)	39 (44.83%)	87

Note: The percentages in the table are row percentages.

important. Similarly, these politically embedded lawyers were more likely to emphasize the importance of substantive justice than that of procedural justice. These results strongly suggest an inverse relationship between political liberalism and political embeddedness, i.e., previous work experience in the criminal justice system has negative effects on lawyers' political motivations and liberal values, at least in smaller cities. An earlier career in the PPC reduces the likelihood that criminal defense lawyers will adopt legal and constitutional values that restrain the institutions of social control in which they previously worked.

In Beijing and other major cities, however, lawyers' political values appear to display some different patterns. While pragmatic brokers, grassroots activist and routine practitioners still constitute the vast majority of lawyers in the metropolitan areas, there are two small anomalous groups, namely, progressive elites and notable activists. The politically liberal motivations of these two types of lawyers is evidently stronger than ordinary practitioners. The former adopt two distinct strategies in their criminal defense work to pursue political change in China.

The first anomaly occurs at the very top of the criminal defense bar among those we call progressive elites. All leading criminal defense lawyers that we interviewed in the seven major cities are politically embedded: most of them hold important positions in bar associations, many had previous work experience in high-level agencies of the PPC, and some are even part-time law professors who teach a large number of judges, procurators, and police officers. Nevertheless, these prestigious lawyers disproportionately displayed highly liberal values and motivation in their work. For example, a senior criminal defense lawyer in Hangzhou told us the following in a 2007 interview:

> There are two types of lawyers in China. The first type is career-driven. They want to survive and make money. The second type is lawyers with conscience, they want the rule of law, democracy, want China to change. To some extent I belong to the second type. Because I had been a public official in the police, court, and provincial government, my choice in becoming a lawyer is to promote social justice, to pursue the highest level of human beings, of humanity, social justice and equality. I had been a judge for eight years. But then finally I left the court because as a judge I could not make decisions in my own cases. Within this system if you have a strong sense of justice and equality you cannot be a judge. Only if you are very loyal, [and] listen to others, can you be a good judge and you can rise to the division head, become court president, etc., and, within this bureaucratic judiciary, lawyers cannot play a big role. Their priority is to protect the interests of the state machinery

like the police and procuracy. But they do not have to consider the preference of the public, the facts of the case, or the truth of the law. . . . In China we have a saying: public justice lies in people's hearts (公理自在人心). I think I maintained the essence of the law, that is, social justice. But for Chinese lawyers, to stick to their sense of justice has a limit. Some lawyers like Gao Zhisheng, Guo Guoting, stuck to their sense of justice too much and destroyed themselves. They are lawyers with conscience. But within the Chinese system you cannot rely on your personal will alone. You must tolerate some imperfections of the society. Only if we can protect ourselves can we make a difference.

(H0701, Zhejiang Province)

The complexity of politics for Chinese criminal defense lawyers is well embodied in this quote and in the approach that this senior lawyer adopts in promoting institutional change. Unlike the two activist lawyers he mentioned who bravely fought against state power in politically sensitive cases and then were persecuted by the Chinese government, this lawyer sought to use his high political status in the criminal justice system to change the system from within. He was an external expert for the Zhejiang Provincial Public Security Bureau and held a high position in the municipal bar association. Hence he was able to exert influence on the provincial justice system from both inside and outside of the criminal process. For him, the only feasible path to change in China is to work inside the system and promote the rule of law from within the Party-state (H0701). Accordingly, he wrote frequent essays both on the Internet and in the official media, which include the official newspaper of the Central Party School that trains high-level Party cadres, seeking to change Chinese people's conceptions of the law and justice.

This Hangzhou lawyer is not alone. Across China, bar association leaders and distinguished criminal defense lawyers write extensively and speak openly about their problems in criminal defense. For instance, the Criminal Law Committee of the ACLA, composed of several prominent defense lawyers in Beijing, Shanghai, and other cities, has organized many conferences related to the "Three Difficulties" and Article 306 in recent years and proposed its own draft when the Lawyers Law was being revised in 2007 (see Chapter 2). Even in the provinces, we often find leading criminal defense lawyers to be more liberal, taking stronger stands on the problems in the criminal procedure than ordinary practitioners (X0505; C0708; C0709; S0703; M0901; Q0911).

But how could these leading lawyers be so liberal in their values and motivations if they are so politically embedded in the criminal justice system? One plausible reason is that many of these lawyers graduated from elite Chinese law schools and received a more liberal legal education and training in their early career. Yet a more important reason we find in our fieldwork is that these progressive elites usually practice beyond their local cities; therefore they have encountered more difficulties in the criminal process than other practitioners who mostly practice locally. This suggests again that political embeddedness is a spatial and relational concept – it only works well in the local context. It is not incidental that several distinguished criminal defense lawyers in Beijing complained bitterly about the difficulties in handling out-of-town cases (B0502; B0510; B0515). Even a nationally renowned criminal defense lawyer would advise his out-of-town clients to use local lawyers in the phases of investigation and prosecution, where local connections are the most important (B0515). The wider scope of practice only aggravated the professional difficulties of these prestigious defense lawyers and, in turn, strengthened their liberal values and motivations.

In contrast to this "inside" strategy of pursuing political liberalism adopted by progressive elites, the small group of notable activists in Beijing uses a more confrontational "outside" strategy to defend for the basic legal rights of Chinese citizens and constrain the arbitrary power of the state. Their main strategy for pursuing political change is to defend politically sensitive cases concerning the basic legal rights of marginalized population in China in order to get the attention of the international media, foreign donors, and human rights organizations (B0901; B0902; B0906; B1005). Besides everyday criminal defense work, whenever there is an influential legal case, they speak collectively through the Internet using social media to voice their opinions to the public sphere (B1002; B1003; B1515; B1520; B1522). By resorting to forces in Chinese civil society and the international community, these notable activists seek to build an alternative path to political reform from the incremental road paved by the Chinese government and the bar leaders. Chapter 5 will discuss their motivations and collective action in greater detail.

CONCLUSION

"Trembling with fear, like standing by the abyss, like walking on thin ice" (战战兢兢，如临深渊，如履薄冰). This old Chinese saying is often adapted to characterize the risky practice of Chinese criminal defense lawyers (e.g., Human Rights Watch 2008). For those lawyers who persist in doing criminal defense work, however, they have no choice but to make this professional "minefield" habitable. In this chapter, we have discussed and compared the various survival strategies that lawyers adopt when navigating the criminal justice system. Although political embeddedness is the ultimate source of protection, not all lawyers have equal access to it. Progressive elites and pragmatic brokers are able to use the PPC to solve their problems in criminal defense work more easily than the other three types of lawyers. In the meantime, politically liberal lawyers, including progressive elites and notable activists, are more likely to use the media than pragmatic brokers and routine practitioners. Law firms and bar associations can provide some support to criminal defense lawyers when they face difficulties and danger, but the extent of the support is often limited and contingent upon the nature of the case.

Overall, no lawyer is perfectly safe in the Chinese criminal justice system, because even the most politically embedded lawyers need to travel to other cities or provinces to handle cases and, as we have discussed in Chapter 1, their embeddedness has a spatial limit. This is precisely why some prominent criminal defense lawyers in Beijing have become progressive elites. When these lawyers experience or witness the abuse of power by the local PPCs in other provinces, their liberal values and motivations are also strengthened. Progressive elites seek a more pragmatic strategy to reform the authoritarian state from within, by strategically turning judges, procurators and even police officers from their enemies to their allies in their everyday work. Notable activists, by contrast, often display sophisticated networking techniques and extraordinary bravery, yet their blunt opposition to the authoritarian state sometimes results in relentless repression against both their clients and themselves, as Chapter 5 will demonstrate. For the vast number of ordinary law practitioners, the contingent relationship between political liberalism and political embeddedness is manifested in even more complex and nuanced ways in their everyday struggles for the rights of their clients and themselves. Using everyday work as a starting point, the next three chapters will analyze varieties of lawyer mobilization in the Chinese criminal justice system.

5

The Courage of Notable Activists

A very small number of notable activist lawyers have emerged over the last decade to take on the most controversial and even dangerous cases across China. These lawyers were once located principally in Beijing, but more recently they have been distributed throughout the country. Their names are rarely known to the Chinese public, but often appear in the international media. They can be found standing in solidarity with the parents of poisoned children or peasants unfairly deprived of land. They appear in cases of late-term abortions or environmental disasters. They represent the believers of Falun Gong (a banned religious group), or champion the causes of tortured prisoners, or express solidarity with persecuted house church leaders. Their networks include lawyers, barefoot lawyers, and other activists incarcerated in past years, such as Gao Zhisheng, Ni Yulan, and Chen Guangcheng, and prominent lawyers arrested or "disappeared" in 2014 and 2015, most notably, Pu Zhiqiang, Wang Yu, and Li Heping. They take great risks and live with the consequences, experiencing fraught lives where they can lose their livelihoods and practices at any time, and periodically suffer from surveillance, disappearances, torture, and imprisonment (Pils 2015).

What motivates these Chinese activist lawyers to take such great risks? What gives them the courage to persist in the face of such intimidating repression? Despite the proliferating media reports and scholarly writings on this small group of Chinese lawyers, this important question of motivation remains a puzzle. Fu and Cullen's (2008, 2011) path-breaking studies, now joined by Pil's (2015) incisive book, provide by far the most compelling scholarly account of this unique lawyer population. Fu and Cullen argue that activist lawyers, or what they call "weiquan (维权, right-protection) lawyers," can be divided into three categories (i.e., moderate, critical, and radical) and constitute a pyramid in which a radicalizing process often occurs and defines their motivation and behavior.

While this theoretical framework is analytically strong and compelling, it has two notable limitations. First, *"weiquan* lawyers" are defined by Fu and Cullen (2008: 112) as those lawyers who "accept the legitimacy of the existing political system and seek to protect and improve the rights of citizens within the constitutional constraints and legal framework of the PRC" – a definition that is not only imprecise because some activist lawyers are clearly against the existing political system, but also potentially problematic because it could include a large proportion of Chinese lawyers. In fact, Michelson and Liu's 2009 China Legal Environment Survey finds that about half of the 1,511 lawyer respondents identified themselves as *weiquan* lawyers (Liu 2013), but few of them would fall into the category of notable activists in our theoretical typology. Second, Fu and Cullen's "climb the *weiquan* ladder" argument is made without establishing a solid foundation for the "ladder climbing" because the key question of "where does the activism come from" is inadequately answered. Although several factors such as life history or client radicalism are mentioned in the study, they do not constitute a systematic framework for explaining the complex motivations of these lawyers.

In this chapter, we use "activist lawyers" to replace the ambiguous and confusing concept of *"weiquan* lawyers." Following the typology of criminal defense lawyers that we have proposed in Chapter 1, we define activist lawyers as those lawyers who are not politically embedded in the justice system, but are committed to ideals of political liberalism and actively fight against the Party-state. The empirical data are drawn principally from repeated interviews with twenty-nine notable activist lawyers in Beijing conducted since 2009. We have followed many of those activists closely across six years; others talked earlier but preferred not to meet us later; and yet others joined in discussions with us in later years and months until 2015. These interviews spanned some critical moments, not least the panicked attack on lawyers surrounding the supposed threat of a "Jasmine Revolution" in early 2011 and the unprecedented massive crackdown on activist lawyers across China beginning in July 2015. These data, interior to the lives and work of notable activists, are supplemented by systematic analysis of international organizations and international media which maintain linkages of various sorts with many of the notable activists.

On the bases of the complementary sources of empirical materials, we argue that Chinese activist lawyers persist in their unique style of lawyering for three main reasons. First, their grievances from life experiences propel them onto a path of activism. Second, their legal, political, and sometimes religious beliefs inspire them to sacrifice for a reformed legal and political system in China. Finally, they obtain vital and sustaining support from social networks inside and outside China in which they are structurally embedded.

THE COSTS OF ACTIVISM

Since the zealous advocacy of activist lawyers can readily be construed as acts of political subversion (Teng 2012a), the defenders of the Party-state deploy an array of weapons in their armories to silence, quash, domesticate, marginalize, isolate, or exile these stubborn defenders of the weak. The personal costs of rights advocacy and defense have been widely reported in the media and analyzed by scholars (Pils 2007, 2015). From our own interview data and the writings of others, we summarize three types of costs paid by activist lawyers, namely, professional sanctions, state security repression, and violence of the black mafia. Any one of these could be disincentive enough for them to turn to safer practice. Yet many activist lawyers have experienced all three forms of suffering and still continue the fight unbowed.

Professional Punishments

All activist lawyers in China are acutely sensitive to threats of professional sanctions from the regulatory troika of the justice bureau, the bar association, and their law firms. Because all lawyers require a license, which must be renewed annually, to practice and especially to appear in court, notable activists in Beijing consider the Beijing Bureau of Justice (BBOJ) and Beijing Lawyers Association (BLA) to be agents of government control. As their law firms also need to renew their practice licenses annually at the BBOJ, activist lawyers often face pressures from their non-activist colleagues to avoid making trouble for the firm. Accordingly, they live in constant apprehension that their practices and livelihoods will be truncated or their legal careers summarily foreclosed.

The notable activist lawyers in Beijing that we interviewed detailed the array of pressures the regulatory troika brought to bear on them. They were contacted by the BBOJ or the BLA on particular cases where the government wanted them to withdraw, whether inside Beijing or in response to requests by provincial justice bureaus or bar associations. Lawyers were accustomed to being called into the BBOJ to justify why they were taking on a particular case and why they were pursuing or publicizing it. If they failed to respond, then the government agencies could suspend a lawyer's license (B1138), refuse to renew a lawyer's license (B1311; B1323), remove a lawyer's license (B1005; B1320), or send a lawyer back to his home province to renew his license. Lawyers also reported, sometimes wryly, that they had been placed on the BBOJ "blacklist" for higher levels of surveillance (B1323).

Furthermore, indirect pressure was exerted by the BBOJ and/or the BLA on individual lawyers through their law firms by the following methods: (1) threatening managing partners of firms; (2) compelling firms to expel lawyers from the firm; (3) forcing lawyers to find new firms that may be more compliant; (4) shutting down especially troublesome firms; and, (5) undertaking a "tax audit" of mischief-making firms (B1130).

In addition to the BBOJ and the BLA, in recent years the state security apparatus has also publicly targeted several law firms where a density of rights activists has made them centers of controversial practice. The earlier pressures on the Global (全球), Anhui, and Yitong law firms (see below) has been amplified dramatically in July 2015 with the nationally publicized assault on the Fengrui law firm. Its managing partner, Zhou Shifeng, was detained in humiliating fashion and subsequently paraded on CCTV to make a televised "confession," which very likely was compelled under pressure, or so informed observers outside China believe. Other lawyers and law firm personnel were detained and interrogated and the files of the firm ransacked and seized. Members of the Fengrui firm, including Zhou Shifeng and Wang Yu, were charged in January 2016 with the serious crimes of "subverting state power" and of "inciting subversion of state power" (Article 105 of the PRC Criminal Law).

Public and State Security Repression

If the professional threats do not lead to compliance from activist lawyers, then the state security apparatus has its own gradient of coercive threats and punishments it ratchets up and down, depending on the severity of the threats that the lawyers supposedly present to public and state security. Its escalating repertoire of "terror," as one activist lawyer called it, includes: (1) calling lawyers into a public security office for a "cup of tea"; (2) tapping lawyers' homes and mobile phones; (3) placing lawyers under house arrest and intervening in their meetings with clients or families, sometimes traumatizing family members; (4) detaining, beating, and torturing lawyers for days or even months; (5) threatening to send lawyers out of Beijing during sensitive periods or even "disappear" them so that neither the lawyer, her/his family, or anyone else knows where he or she is or whether or not he or she is alive or dead (B1104; B1108; B1114; B1119; B1125; B1127; B1130; B1204; B1320).

Police are routinely placed outside the homes of veteran activists. As one relayed, "every time we come to a sensitive period, e.g., the National People's Congress meeting, there are guards in front of the house" (B1104). Lawyers families have been traumatized by direct confrontations with security officials, by false rumors that family members have been harmed, or by indirect pressures, such as loss of jobs (B1130) or the arrest or detaining of other family members, such as happened to Wang Yu's husband and teenage son, or Li Heping's brother, Li Chunfu (GD_20161701). Several lawyers stated that they might be able to bear repression, but they feared its consequences for their families (B1108). The following quote is a good example:

> I feel bad that I brought a lot of trouble to my mother and wife and brother. They are all harassed. I feel I owe them a lot. For example, last Wednesday, my mother, who is 83, got a phone call. They said "your son is kidnapped. You must prepare money to release him in half an hour. If you don't find the money, we will kill him." She was very scared.
>
> (B1130, Beijing)

Psychological pressures can be ratcheted up as a prelude to coercion. One lawyer described how a state security official over several months gradually escalated threats that the lawyer would be sent back to his home province without a license (B1108; B1130). Others reported receiving threats; as veteran activist lawyer Teng Biao publicly reported in the *Wall Street Journal* in 2010, he was told he would be thrown into "a hole to bury you" (WSJ_20101228).

Among the most feared extremes of state violence is the threat and actuality of being "disappeared" so that neither the lawyer, her or his family, or anyone else knows where she or he is, or whether or not she or he is being tortured, or even whether or not she or he is alive or dead. This casts a shadow of fear over many lawyers, especially when it is accompanied by being "black hooded" (B1320). Such extreme measures by the state security apparatus have not diminished, despite the predictions of optimistic international observers. In the repressive crackdown beginning July 2015, several notable activists, such as Li Heping, have remained "disappeared" for more than one year, inaccessible to their chosen lawyers or family. Li Heping's state of limbo precipitated two courageous lawyers to begin a public campaign as they undertook a "desperate search" from one police or security building after another, each case recorded by photographs to show the hopelessness of their undertaking and to build public pressure on the security apparatus (GD_20150810).

The potency of the Party-state's weapons has been increased and skillfully disguised as "legal" by revisions to provisions on residential surveillance in Article 73 of the 2012 CPL. As Rosenzweig (2013) shows, the use of residential surveillance as an alternative to detention in a designated facility has a long history, dating back to 1949. In more recent years, however, the provision has authorized residential surveillance as a punitive and often harsh site for persons detained on the grounds of "endangering state security and terrorism." Many activist lawyers were deeply troubled by what they perceived to be dangerously vague wording in Article 73 that would enable the state security apparatus to place them in "designated residential surveillance" (指定监视居住) with very weak or no protections of notification or legal defense. Their fears were real after reports from the 2011 disappearances of artist Ai Weiwei and lawyers Liu Shihui and Li Tiantian, and numbers of other lawyers, revealed "round-the-clock surveillance, continuous interrogations and ... sleep deprivation, beatings, denial of personal hygiene, threats and humiliation, use of restraints such as handcuffs for days on end, and being forced to sit or kneel in stress positions or confined to bed for extended periods of time" (Rosenzweig 2013: 17). The wave of detentions and disappearances commencing in July 2015 instantiated precisely these fears as provisions of Article 73 and their interpretations by the MPS have variously manipulated provisions on residence and notification to skirt any legal or humanitarian rights protections while offering no form of legal redress.

Most drastic are not forms of torture that leave lasting diminishments of health, but an emerging practice of denying or restricting medical care to the detained lawyers (e.g., Pu Zhiqiang in 2014–2015) such that their health is impaired while in custody. This disguised form of physical depredation through withholding of medical care reflects yet another means of state retribution skillfully disguised so its ultimate costs appear to be something other than what they are. At the extreme this could become a prolonged sentence to death by denial of medical treatment.

Compounding the ultimate fears of what might happen, much of the anxiety generated by the security apparatus came not from the sure knowledge that a certain action by a lawyer would bring a predictable reaction from repressive authorities, but much more from the almost complete unpredictability of when and how the coercive agencies of the state would act (Pils 2015). Every notable activist has his or her own theory about where the red line might be crossed, but veterans admit that the theories are likely illusions since the reasons why some are detained while others remain untouched often remain incomprehensible – a style of policy enforcement characterized by uncertainties and mixed signals, which Stern and O'Brien (2012: 186) call the "guerrilla policy style."

Violence of the Black Mafia

While the harms that can be visited on lawyers by the state are fearsome enough, even more frightening are the several incidents of lawyers being abducted or attacked by the "black mafia" (黑社会). These "black muggings" can occur randomly, the perpetrators remain unknown, and even the reasons for the assaults may remain opaque. International media have reported on violent assaults by "gangs" and "thugs" suffered by Li Heping, Zhang Kai, Jiang Tianyong, and Liu Xiaoyuan, among others. Li Heping was grabbed in Beijing and tortured with electric rods. Zhang Kai was trapped on the third ring road in Beijing by three black cars as persons wielding iron rods sought to smash their way inside his car. Jiang Tianyong disappeared for ninety days and his captors refused to say who they were. It is usually supposed by the lawyers that the assaults relate to a current case, but they have little notion whether the assaults are another darker, arms-length form of state terror or the actions of private groups or companies taking matters into their own hands (B1311; B1320; B1323; B1405).

THE BIOGRAPHICAL AND IDEAL FOUNDATIONS OF COURAGE

When aggregated and compounded, the costs of rights activism discussed in the previous section amount to a massive and terrifying barrier to effective rights defense. As a result, many notable activist lawyers come to live fragmented professional lives – punctuated by threats, by their changing lawyer's license status, by fears and moments of terror that move in and out of their lives (B1108; B1127). Why do they maintain their courage as political activists when fear hovers in the background and terror can burst without warning into their lives? To further explain this question, we begin by relating the biography of their paths to activism and then proceed to their legal, political, and religious beliefs.

Paths to Activism

What inspires a lawyer to follow a path that is guaranteed to produce hardship, fear, and deprivation? Of the twenty-nine notable activist lawyers we interviewed over several years, no clear path or accumulation of life experiences can explain why they, and not others, chose to specialize in politically sensitive cases. Nevertheless, there are some differing paths among them whereby several share commonalities with each other, not least by what Fu and Cullen (2011) term "climbing the *weiquan* ladder."

The lawyers' educational trajectories can be sorted into three groups. The largest group (twelve out of twenty-nine) obtained their education either through "self-study" (自考) or distance learning, or by taking one or more degrees, usually not in law, at provincial universities, most often from provinces more proximate to Beijing, such as Henan and Jilin, although some activists originate from as far as Sichuan in the southwest or Heilongjiang and Inner Mongolia in the northeast. They usually migrated to Beijing after several years of law practice in their home provinces (Liu, Liang, and Michelson 2014). A smaller group (consisting of nine interviewees) undertook studies initially in a provincial university and followed this with a law degree at elite law schools such as Peking University, CUPL, or the Chinese Academy of Social Sciences. Only a handful (four) received all their education from elite universities in Beijing. In other words, most longstanding notable activists are not part of the legal elite in China in terms of their social origins and educational credentials. However, there is unsystematic evidence that this may be changing as rapidly expanding ranks of younger activist lawyers pursue rights practices because they were inspired through their own heightened rights consciousness in leading law schools.

The overwhelming proportion of activist lawyers are men, though a few women activists such as Ni Yulan and Wang Yu have also been core members of this group. Each of the activist lawyers constructs his/her biography around moments that mark the turn to human rights and legal activism as a calling. For several this had been a longtime aspiration well before they began practicing law. A lawyer recalled wanting to be a lawyer in high school because he learned from reading the histories of France and the United States that lawyers participated in social and civil rights movements and made a substantial impact on society (B1108). Another lawyer started his work life as a migrant worker and then a manager, but it was broadcasts from Radio Free Asia and the Voice of America that inspired him with stories of human rights lawyers (B1117).

For several others, the call to activist practice grew out of suffering. As a child, one lawyer experienced periodic political campaigns that targeted his father during the Cultural Revolution, which generated his personal sense of "loneliness, insecurity, and helplessness" (B1005). He received very little care from others, but when he did receive a little support it "warmed his heart." When he became a lawyer two decades later, he determined that he would use the law to help others when they experienced what he had known only too well. It was their personal experiences of the events that led to the 1989 Tiananmen student movement that motivated two others. One of these lawyers "suffered a lot" (B1106) as a result of his leadership of student protests in the movement culminating in the June 4 crackdown, as did another (B1119). Many years later, both of them took a human rights turn in their law practice against that backdrop of subsequent expulsion from university, isolation, and joblessness.

Others identify a turning point, on occasion an event that is tantamount to a conversion experience. Several recount a personal injustice that shocked them into a new understanding of themselves and their political society. A lawyer described his turn to activist litigation as an "accident" because he was compelled to defend himself and his family in a property rights dispute (B1120). Another lawyer spoke of a successful early career until he offended local officials, which led to his arrest on charges of bribery and corruption. Disillusioned with this "illegal arrest," he realized that without rule of law, everything a person had achieved and accumulated through his own hard work might be lost "in a single night" (B1111). Consequently, he focused his career on promoting human rights and rule of law in China. One lawyer recalled that after he became a Christian while he was working in a police station, he was summarily fired (B1107). From then on he turned to the defense of Christian house churches. Yet another pointed back to the moment when the police arrested and detained him because he was representing persons whose land was taken by the government: "We were accused of larceny because of the techniques we used in defending the farmers. I was really angry. This accusation had a huge impact on us" (B1112). Another person was wrongfully imprisoned, she alleged, and upon release she turned away from commercial practice to take on some of the most challenging rights and criminal defense cases in China (B1522).

Confrontation with egregious injustice in specific legal cases turned several lawyers towards activist defense of the weak. An intellectual leader of activist lawyers with impeccable academic credentials, including a doctoral degree from an elite law school in Beijing, assigned the beginning of his "civil rights defense movement" (B1204) to the notable Sun Zhigang case in 2003, when a college graduate was detained as a migrant worker and tortured to death (Hand 2006). Led by several Beijing intellectuals and lawyers, this became a national *cause célèbre* and convinced him that lawyers, in coalition with journalists and others, might force legal change to protect vulnerable persons.

Another lawyer used to practice commercial law on behalf of corporate clients, just as many of his elite law school classmates did. He became a Christian and got drawn into a widely publicized house church case with several other Beijing Christian activist lawyers (B1127). That led to an expanded practice seeking to protect legal rights of house churches. But it was the infamous 2008 Sanlu infant formula case that became a turning point for him. After that he switched from civil and commercial law to human rights and the defense of victims – "Falun Gong, torture, some freedom of speech and AIDs cases, and also the one-child policy" – all these had in common the feature that "the private rights of citizens are violated by the public power of the state" (B1127). The Sanlu case vividly demonstrated how little a citizen's constitutional rights could be protected against the power of state-owned enterprises and complicit state authorities.

A former Party cadre, later known for his defense of widely publicized cases, vividly recalled how he was stunned to discover in 2005 that a peasant in Hebei had been sentenced to death twice, detained for seven years, bailed for fifteen years, and still his case had not been settled (B1319). "At first I thought he had a mental problem. I didn't think such things could happen in China." Yet the more he investigated, the more certain he became that the peasant had indeed been treated wrongfully. More fundamentally, after successfully pressing for redress, he came to the conclusion that "the Chinese judiciary has very serious problems." Even so, a lawyer sometimes can help people solve their problems, particularly if exposure of the case through the Internet, TV, and print media stirs public opinion. "Afterwards," he said, "many weak parties came to find me." And from that moment his identity and legal vocation have been encapsulated in his statement that "I represent the weak parties" (B1319).

These paths to activist lawyering were neither entirely solitary nor purely personalistic. Charismatic leaders, progressive firms, and supportive networks engaged most of the activists at critical junctures. Gao Zhisheng, a charismatic, long-imprisoned, persecuted, and badly tortured activist lawyer, inspired many younger lawyers (B1110; Pils 2015). One recalled being introduced to him in 2004 and thereafter shifted from mainly commercial work to acting with Gao Zhisheng on public interest cases and those that "defended the weak" (B1125). Similarly, another veteran activist, one of our research subjects and thus cannot be named, "had a huge impact" on several activist lawyers. One lawyer describes how the seasoned activist kept pressing him to come to Beijing, "'Come on, come with me and we will do something' . . . I knew he meant now I am going to defend human rights and use our legal skills to establish a rule-of-law of society" (B1108). The human rights practice and then persecution of Chen Guangsheng, the blind barefoot lawyer (Chen 2015), also brought together many of the most prominent activist lawyers in Beijing to plan his defense.

The small but cohesive network of notable activists was capable of not only mutual moral support but also mobilization on each other's behalf. In fact, two law firms acted as incubators for activist lawyers until they were dismantled by the BBOJ. The Global Law Firm, where Li Heping was a senior partner and managing director, at various points employed several activist lawyers. Gao Zhisheng's former firm, Yitong, employed several others. As one Yitong activist lawyer said, "there were a group of lawyers with a similar mind and I was greatly encouraged and it was very helpful to me" (B1110). Activist lawyers also gravitated to Beijing because famous names and networks of lawyers had a magnetic attraction for persons isolated in the provinces.

In sum, the "entry points" (Fu and Cullen 2011: 42–44) of notable activist lawyers vary from grievances in early life history to troubles in ordinary legal work to the influence of other political activists. There is, however, not always a process of "climbing the *weiquan* ladder" as the origins of activism do not necessarily show a progressive trajectory. In particular, some lawyers may have reduced their political activism or even exited from the network of notable activists after experiencing professional sanctions or personal threats from the regulatory troika. To further explore the motivations of those lawyers who have persisted, therefore, requires a close examination of their legal, political, and religious values.

Legal and Political Ideals

Activist lawyers exercise courage in their risk-taking practices because every case for them is more than a legal case. They observe fundamental institutional flaws in China's current criminal justice system and the broader legal and political system. Accordingly, they are motivated by ideals that ultimately envisage a new kind of law, society, and politics in China (Michelson and Liu 2010). Like lawyers in many other countries, their concept of a reformed legal and political system has at least three aspects: (1) constraining and fracturing state power; (2) representing and empowering civil society; and, (3) protecting and exercising basic legal freedoms (Halliday and Karpik 1997; Halliday, Karpik, and Feeley 2007, 2012).

When asked who were the most powerful players in China's criminal justice system, activist lawyers broadly converged on similar responses that often implicitly, and sometimes explicitly, amounted to a fundamental critique of power in Chinese law. With few exceptions, these lawyers concurred that "police power is still the primary power" in China's criminal justice system (B1005; B1113). The exercise of police power was frequently through the interventions in court cases by the Communist Party's Political-Legal Committee (PLC) (B1319). Usually comprised of the police chief, the chief procurator, and the court president for the locality, the PLC was often headed and dominated by the police chief, who had "a higher rank in the Party than a chief judge or prosecutor" (B1311). As a result, in sensitive cases, or any case "that involves politics," the PLC was "the deciding agency" (B1001; B1128). Rather than a rule-of-law state, therefore, "we are a police state," charged several activist lawyers (B1001; B1313).

Moreover, the PLC provides the institutional means by which the Party controls the judicial process, particularly in politically sensitive cases (Liebman 2007; Minzner 2011; Li 2012). It is "a ghost behind everything" and has several deleterious effects (B1101; B1313; B1315). As a result, "judges are kidnapped by power" and are often not the ultimate decision-makers (B1001; B1002; B1005). It is inconceivable in these circumstances that there can be any "separation of powers, or checks and balances, or an independent judiciary" (B1126). Since activist lawyers disproportionately take on cases thought too sensitive or political for other lawyers, there are three broad consequences: "You either surrender," you mount a "defense without effect," or you stand and fight "and stick to your opinions and thereby encounter all sorts of difficulties" (B1002; B1005).

What then is to be done? Activist lawyers fall into three broad camps about how to practice when confronted with this shared critical analysis of power.

The first cluster of lawyers assumes practice must continue while having no expectation of fundamental changes. These lawyers propose structural changes within the legal system while leaving the present configurations of the one-Party state intact. One proposed reform, shared by several, would keep the PLC away from litigation, let judges decide on the evidence before them, and let judges control the process (B1002). A variant on this would recognize that it is impossible to abolish the PLC in the current system, but to keep them at arms length from the courts except in "extremely important cases" (B1319). And quite apart from the PLC, it would be a significant step forward if "every agency did its own work, and the police did not control the whole criminal process" (B1001).

The second cluster of lawyers implicitly looks to change in the political structure of the society through incremental steps. For instance, if the PLC is the means by which the Party controls the judicial process, then to abolish the PLC is a means of removing the Party from intervention in court cases, which is in effect an attenuation of authoritarian power. As an experienced activist lawyer said, "everyone in the legal profession" agrees that separation of powers and checks and balances is the way forward (B1105). Although this statement is obviously an exaggeration, it nevertheless represents a value at least shared by the great majority of activist lawyers and it motivates their behavior in individual cases and in their broader calls for reform.

A third cluster of lawyers is explicitly motivated by a desire to produce the political transformation of the state itself. Several activist lawyers express this view in terms of constitutionalism. It might originate from below, as "constitutionalist lawyers" take on cases with the clear intent of changing the constitutional system (B1311). It might be from above, in the creation of a real constitutional order where there is separation of powers among the agencies of state, there are checks and balances between the central and local governments (B1311), and there is "quintessential protection for human rights" by a constitutional court (B1103). Even more pointed are blunt assertions that judicial independence is impossible under the Chinese Communist Party (B1104). "Obviously we have to change the system – where one Party decides all" (B1321).

In addition to constraining state power, activist lawyers are motivated by ideals of active citizens in a vibrant civil society in both their daily work and as a vision for the social and legal order for which they fight. They fight for a shift from passive subjects with limited awareness of rights or recognition of their potential collective force to an empowered citizenry aware of its rights and able to exercise them for itself and in claims against the government. Notable activist lawyers speak of the need for individuals in China to conceive of themselves as rights-bearing citizens who are not simply objects of government action but "active subjects" who recognize their rights and act upon them (B1005). Most commonly they insist that "if people do not have rights consciousness, we cannot have civil society" in China (B1103). Every case simultaneously becomes an instance of protecting a particular client's rights and promoting legal consciousness (Gallagher 2006). Through specific cases, activist lawyers can "help individuals understand the proper relations between individuals and the government" (B1005; B1103) and "wake up the rights consciousness of Chinese citizens" (B1108; B1123).

Speaking for the public becomes an integral component of rights advocacy. As one lawyer states, "When lawyers intervene, they criticize and speak out on behalf of the public, and hopefully that will reduce the government attacks on individual rights" (B1101). Speaking out may be instrumental: it is frequently a way to put pressure on officials and decision-makers in a particular case. Speaking out can also be informative or expressive. More than one lawyer noted that the families of Falun Gong defendants hold little hope that "the evidence, or procedure, or whatever happens in court" will change the final verdict, but they are eager that those trials provide yet another occasion "to tell the public what has happened" (B1204). Use of social media, most notably blogs and microblogs (both Weibo and Twitter), has transformed the capacity of notable activist lawyers to reach domestic and international publics quickly and mobilize them instantly.

Some lawyers are motivated by their beliefs that religious groups must be protected. A natural affinity exists between the many leading activist lawyers who themselves are Christians and the increasingly large number of Chinese Christians who form a major civil society bloc in China.

Unofficial house churches have opened up public spaces where participants "exercise freedom of speech and association according to international standards and the Chinese constitution" (B1108). Christian activist lawyers lend their standing to house churches by attending their services and sometimes "speaking for the church" (B1001). Several activist lawyers state forthrightly that the real test of courage for human rights lawyering in China is the readiness to defend Falun Gong believers, for whom many activist lawyers have admiration, precisely because of the great courage of the believers themselves who have been imprisoned, tortured and executed in large numbers (B1001; B1005; B1131).

Other activist lawyers believe it is their duty to facilitate and empower victims, who often organize in networks and incipient associations. According to one lawyer, "The victims of pollution – they get to know each other, hang out, start a casual group, it gets stronger and stronger and can have a huge impact on society, so strong they can defend themselves before the government." (B1108) Another example he gave is the victims of AIDS – "they are not only concerned about themselves and other victims, but also public health and the entire public health system . . . extended to the safety of blood, safety of medicine, the drugs problem, etc." (B1108). In sum, activist lawyers act as defenders and promoters, as spokespersons and as fellow-travelers, for the emergence of civil society in China (B1204). In doing so they also create conditions for their own enhanced potency as the vanguard of a liberal political society.

Besides concerns for the moderate state and civil society, the language of rights and freedoms permeate activist lawyers' expression of their political ideals. We asked which rights they rated as being most important. Two notable activist lawyers resisted the notion that any particular right has primacy. They insisted that "all rights are important" and both amplified this view by quoting Franklin Roosevelt's concept of the four freedoms: freedom from fear, freedom of worship, freedom from want, and freedom of speech (B1125). The combination of these will "help build the rule-of-law society." It is the responsibility of activist lawyers to take any case that "clients bring in the door" which builds upon these rights.

By far the strongest view, however, as expressed by many lawyers, gave primacy to freedom of speech and freedom of religion. "If we could have freedom of speech," declared a well-known activist lawyer, "it would be a great and splendid thing" (B1101). The ability to speak openly "is the basis for supervision and checks and balances on power" (B1321) and "to reveal the truth to the public" (B1103). As another lawyer who has suffered much from the security apparatus said, "if we don't have freedom of speech we cannot really express our ideas. Freedom of speech also stimulates people's thoughts and creativity" (B1005).

Perhaps because many of these lawyers are Christians, and because both they and some non-Christians have represented brutally repressed Falun Gong believers, religious freedom is repeatedly stressed, usually in tandem with freedom of speech. Religious freedom, they say, speaks to the inner qualities of a person, to "the freedoms of your soul, your mind, your heart" (B1108). It is a "basic standard for a free human being to think and believe" (B1123). To fight for this freedom addresses a spiritual vacuum, a collapse of belief, in contemporary Chinese society. As a non-Christian activist lawyer opined, "If we only have economic prosperity but no prosperity in peoples' spiritual lives, the whole economic prosperity will be wasted" (B1005).

Chinese activist lawyers frequently link freedom of speech with freedom of association. One believes that once you have "freedom of religion, speech and association," then "the other freedoms will be easily protected," such as the "freedom to give birth and private property rights" (B1123). Once human beings can "live autonomously and independently" (B1123), then an accompanying freedom of association allows "people to solve problems by themselves. You wouldn't need the government to solve everything" (B1005). These foundations for a vibrant civil society "would balance the relationship of the state to society" (B1005).

Since many notable activist lawyers have been involved in cases of land takings in the countryside and/or forced evictions in cities (B1003; B1101; B1131; B1204), they are acutely sensitive to property rights as well. Time and again they report on the widespread public anger and wide-ranging social conflict around property grievances, which one lawyer called "a leading force of social chaos" (B1113). As another declared, "Forced evictions are a major problem. It is the biggest reason for petitioners" (B1204) and also "affects trust in the government" (B1001). Activist lawyers frequently become involved in land and housing conflicts because such conflicts can quickly turn into mass incidents or physical confrontations with police, which lead to arrests on criminal charges.

However, for these lawyers the fundamental need for secure property rights is much less an economic than a political issue. Like the freedom of belief or the freedom of expression, property rights speak to core elements of human dignity. As one lawyer said, "When the government violates property rights it is not just about specific materials, but the violation of human value. In that sense the government does not think of each individual as a worthy person" (B1001). If human dignity were respected by the protection of property rights it would have far-reaching implications for political society. Another lawyer argues that full protection of property rights "might change the relationship between citizens and the government" because "if my private property rights are protected, then the government depends on me" (B1123). Moreover, having property rights frees citizens to be active participants in the championing of their own rights and those of others: "Only if someone's living conditions are stable, then he can spend time being active socially, fighting for the rights of others. If your own rights cannot be protected, how can you protect the rights of others?" (B1005).

Several activist lawyers state that the existence of fundamental political rights to free speech and association are necessary conditions for protection of property rights. "If there is no proper protection for political rights, there is no proper protection for property rights" (B1106). Or, as another leading figure stated, "if there is not freedom of expression in a society, there will not be real property rights" (B1204). And thereby the logic of argument circles back to the moderation of the Chinese state. Freedom of expression or freedom of association and property rights cannot be sustained without an institution to protect those rights, and that institution must be an independent judicial system (B1204).

Religious Beliefs

Despite the strength of legal and political ideals, they are not the only sources of ideological motivations for Chinese activist lawyers. A subset of activist lawyers is motivated by religious ideals. They believe they are engaged in a spiritual battle, even a struggle between the laws of God and the laws of man. At least ten of the longest-standing twenty-nine notable activists in our study, and some asserted that possibly 40 percent of China's notable activist lawyers (B1313), were or now are Protestant Christians. This figure hugely exceeds the proportion of Christians in China's population (Yang 2012). The values and motivations of these Christian activists offer yet another layer of ideals and diversity that strengthen the resiliency and courageous practices of the activist lawyer community as a whole. It requires further research to understand whether or not Roman Catholic Christians or in Buddhist, Taoist, or Muslim believers are self-consciously or readily identified among the few hundred notable activist lawyers in China, but we have not encountered any in our fieldwork, except for one lawyer who converted to Christianity from Buddhism in the mid-2000s (B0502).

Several Christian lawyers asserted that there are affinities between faith and law. One lawyer explained his conversion to Christianity in terms of such affinities: "When I first went to a church and saw how they worshipped God, to be honest, it totally scared me. But I kept going to church anyway, [and] later I found out in the Bible there are lots of ideas that are consistent to what I am pursuing – democracy, constitutionalism, rule of law." (B1104) Another lawyer argued that "all rule-of-law societies have the Christian faith behind them" and he regarded the leaders of Christian churches as admirable figures such as "George Washington and Sun Yat-sen" (B1104).

A number of Christian lawyers contrast Christian understandings of human nature with Confucian, Communist, and popular beliefs. Said one: "For Confucianism, man can be perfect; Communism requires a person to be morally perfect" (B1001). Christians, by contrast, believe that "everyone is a sinner before God" (B1114). This radical equality of all persons means that "because we are all sinners, Chairman Mao is the same sinner as I am" (B1104), that "all sinners are equal whether you are an ordinary citizen or the president" (B1001; B1111; B1114; B1125). It follows that "we also commit sins in reality" and that in turn should shape law and politics. Since "all sinners are created by God and in the image of God and all sinners have dignities and rights, they should be protected" (B1125).

When we asked Christian lawyers what Christian doctrines motivated their human rights work, five clusters of responses recurred. Not all activist lawyers mentioned all the five beliefs, but each was presented by several persons, which suggests they are fairly widely shared.

(1) *Freedom* "Jesus came," said a well-known activist lawyer, "to set us free" (B1116). Our freedoms and rights are not grants from the government but "are given by God" (B1001). Any limitation or restriction on rights or freedoms," therefore, "is against the law of God" (B1125). These freedoms should lead to "freedom from the terror of power," including "bad things from China's traditional culture and Communist control" (B1001).

(2) *Justice* Because justice and righteousness derive from the very character of God, who is "righteous and just," one said, they are foundational to Christian rights aspirations (B1108). For Christians, justice should be focused disproportionately on the weakest in society – the "widows and orphans" repeatedly privileged in the Bible (B1111). The principle of defending the weak should extend to all "people who are violated by the public power, whether rich or poor," "Han or Tibetan," including even "government officials themselves" (B1001).

(3) *Love* For Christians, said several lawyers, the most important of the Biblical ideals is love – "that God loves us and we need to love others and to help and defend others" (B1101). "Justice can only be built on love,"

said another, "and at the same time justice guarantees that love can continue" (B1138).

(4) *Fairness* Several pointed to parts of the Bible that influenced them, most particularly "those concerning justice and fairness, especially fairness" (B1001). Fairness should then extend into procedural justice under the Criminal Procedure Law, said one (B1001).

(5) *Forgiveness* "The Bible teaches 'love your enemies,'" said a lawyer, "This has a huge impact on me" (B1138). It opens up the prospect of an inner peace in the face of outer persecution. "Forgiving those who persecute us will help us have a peaceful heart, to really live out God's life because the core of forgiveness is love and the core of God is love" (B1138). Forgiveness should extend, they said, to those who persecute them, including the police and state officials (B1104; B1108).

Underlying all these particularities are general convictions that their ultimate loyalty lies not to the Party-state but to their faith. "Divine rights are the Magna Carta for Christians" (B1101) and "if the teaching of God ... conflicts with the government's law," then the Christian lawyer "must obey God's word" (B1001). Building the rule of law in China, and doing rule-of-law work, therefore, is not merely a lawyerly or philosophical ideal. It is doing "work for Christ" (B1106).

Finally, the foundations of courage may require sacrifice. Most expansive was the reflection by a notable activist lawyer on the severity of such a calling:

> I believe Chinese society right now is full of hope and full of challenges. It is dangerous and this requires sacrifice. The sacrifice is to follow Christ. We believe that by sacrificing we will have new birth in return. I know the cases I have been taking might not help my clients directly but when you walk with the people when they are in great need they will be comforted. Many times I have accompanied a person who is in need. I find that Christ has done the same thing to us. When we are in difficulties, what Christ has done has to be with us and we are comforted, not necessarily to show signs or miracles. On the other hand, it requires great courage to face an evil power. To love or to suffer cannot be done by our own efforts. But we believe that Christ has set a great example for us.
>
> (B1001, Beijing)

This extended quotation has significance because it states that for some Christian activist lawyers the path that led Jesus Christ to crucifixion might lead a Chinese lawyer to martyrdom. That is a price some would be prepared to pay.

THE SOLIDARY FOUNDATIONS OF COURAGE

The legal, political, and religious ideals expressed by notable activists are one fundamental pillar on which their mobilization rests, but it would be erroneous to assume that all Chinese activist lawyers are idealistic and altruistic martyrs who do not take benefits and costs into consideration in their law practice. Consistently, the activist lawyers in our study insisted that their courage comes not only from beliefs and visions for reforms in China, but also from tangible social support. Ideals are expressed through social relations and sustained by solidary relationships. For notable activists these solidary relationships are of two kinds – domestic and international.

Domestic Organizational Strategies: The 2008
Beijing Lawyers Association Election

The domestic strategy can proceed along two potentially supporting tracks – a strategy that takes advantage of already existing organizations of lawyers; and a complementary strategy of informal networks of like-minded lawyers. We have seen that lawyers across China took advantage of the communication infrastructure provided by the ACLA to create an online forum of great vitality and lively discussions (Halliday and Liu 2007; see also Chapters 3 and 7). By 2008, however, this had been shut down. A much bolder strategy would be to abandon a minimalist approach of working within the actual structures provided by a bar association and to adopt a more expansive strategy of transforming those structures themselves. Such a bold step could be accomplished by changing how bar associations are governed and how its leaders are appointed.

In principle, the formal organizations of state justice and the bar might provide an institutional expression of collective action for activist ideals and a source of support for individual courage in the pursuit of those ideals. Yet, as Cohen (2009) rightly observed, bar associations in China are essentially in an administrative chain of command where the Party maintains ultimate control. Command is transmitted from the Ministry of Justice through provincial and local justice bureaus, and then to provincial and local bar associations. Bar association leaders are appointed from above, not elected by lawyers, even if there is a cosmetic "election" to confirm appointments.

Notable activists had been critical of bar associations in the years before 2008, most especially of the Beijing Lawyers Association (BLA), which had jurisdiction over the largest concentration of activist lawyers in China. An activist acknowledged that the BLA's Committee on Constitutional Law and Human Rights, in which several activist lawyers assumed leadership positions in the early to mid-2000s, had done "a lot of good work promoting citizen rights" but then "by shutting it down it reinforced the concern that the BLA couldn't provide support and protection" for lawyers doing human rights work, so the BLA itself needed to be reformed (B1005). Indeed, as many activist lawyers insisted, the BLA was sometimes working against lawyers. When "lawyers were in trouble it would not provide help," and indeed it sometimes restricted lawyers' participation in certain cases (B1005). For instance, when notable Beijing activists Li Chunfu and Zhang Kai were beaten in an ugly violent incident in Chongqing, rather than spring to their defense, the BLA was ineffectual and sought "to calm down this event" rather than protect the lawyers, or resolve through law the precipitating incident in which a person had been beaten to death in a Re-Education through Labor camp (B1129).

> Lawyers realized that the situation in China is not that pleasant – they have been beaten, put into prison. They realized they desperately needed an association to protect their rights and freedoms and the BLA was not capable of this . . . The bar is not independent. Lawyers felt its role was not to support but to suppress lawyers.
>
> (B1125, Beijing)

Moreover, the BLA lacked legitimacy among practicing lawyers because its leadership was not freely elected by lawyers. Its leaders, said some activists, used their position to advance their own careers, not protect the interests or rights of lawyers as a whole. There were allegations that officers of the BLA were corrupt (B111), undoubtedly fueled in good measure because the BLA published no accounting of its income or expenditures. And to add insult to injury, the annual membership fees of RMB2500 were too high for many political activists and routine practitioners, a dark irony if those same burdensome fees were used to fund actions against the very lawyers who paid.

A convergence of events in 2008 presented an opening in which activist lawyers saw a rare opportunity to transform the BLA itself so that it would serve and protect lawyers. The 2007 Lawyers Law came into effect on June 1, 2008, and expressed promising ideals, some of which might be infused into the revision of bar association charters, which were being drafted or revised at the same time. Some Beijing notable activists thought this might be a moment when the legal profession could become self-regulating, emancipating itself from the hierarchy of control by the justice bureau and ultimately the Party.

On August 28, 2008, many notable activists widely circulated a public letter entitled "An Appeal by 35 Lawyers." The letter asserted that the BLA did not attract the interest of lawyers so it did not act in ways consistent with the Lawyers Law's goal of protecting lawyers' rights. More often, it said, the BLA punished lawyers for lawful professional work. Furthermore, the BLA did not have formal election procedures or even a legitimate charter. Wealthy lawyers were using leadership positions for their pecuniary interests. Fees were too high. The BLA was too subservient to the BBOJ and lacked transparency in either its income or expenditures. Therefore, the BLA should emulate experiments at grassroots democracy at the village level and authorize direct elections of its leaders (Cohen 2009; B1005; B1138; B1132).

Days later, on September 5, the BLA issued a "Stern Statement" (Cohen 2009: 4) insisting that the BLA is democratic, does listen to its members, and represents all lawyers. Any persons disputing these facts through "inflamma-tory speeches" or rumors which "poison the minds" of Beijing lawyers violate the law. It further stated that a call for direct election of leaders was tanta-mount to a rejection of "our country's current management system for the legal profession, judicial system and even political system." In response, the activists stated it was "plainly lawful to call upon all lawyers to exercise their right to take part in BLA elections." In turn, the BLA published its draft charter on September 13 and a week later the activist lawyers responded with their comments on a direct election website they had created. Critics of the activists in Beijing's district justice bureaus darkly spoke of the letter writers' "evil intentions," which undoubtedly were encouraged by an "hostile external forces" and "political goals" (Cohen 2009: 2–3).

The revised BLA charter did move in the direction of the activist lawyers, insofar as it adopted a two-step election process. In step one, lawyers would elect representatives, and in step two, those representatives would elect the top leaders, a process somewhat reminiscent of an earlier experiment in Shenzhen. Although not satisfactory to the activists, they nonetheless took the opening that was provided them, and embarked on an energetic campaign to elect notable activists electoral zone by electoral zone. One activist candi-date for leadership of the BLA printed thousands of brochures about his qualifications and policy positions and handed them out during an official bar training event. In another zone, lawyers in a small firm lobbied other firms so that two of their members got elected. In yet another electoral zone, several leading activists got nominated to stand for election, but the ballot did not include their names. They took advantage of a "write-in" space on the ballot so successfully that they ranked highly in the count and precluded any candi-dates at all from reaching the necessary 50 percent plurality to be elected, thereby forcing a runoff election (B1125). Quickly perceiving this threat, the BLA ensured that in the runoff, not only were the names of the activists excluded, but so too was any space for "write-ins." Indeed, the BLA declared that any ballot with a write-in would be ruled invalid.

Most striking about this assertion of democratic principle in bar governance was the extreme reaction of the BLA, BBOJ, and even a higher-level PLC. In addition to politically charged language (e.g., "splittism") and articulation of a logic that harkened back to the Cultural Revolution (B1138), activist lawyers were struck off the ballot, meetings were called by the BLA and the BBOJ of all lawyers in Beijing to counteract the activists' momentum, and two law firms at the center of the activist network paid a heavy price. Several lawyers were pushed out of the Yitong firm (B111), which itself was suspended for six months, an action "tantamount to a death sentence for a law firm," said Yitong lawyer Liu Xiaoyuan (Cohen 2009: 5). The Anhui firm, where other activists were clustered, was later dissolved (B1125). A leading activist of the bar election movement, Yang Huiwen, was placed in an administrative limbo and has not been able to practice law subsequently. Other activists, whose licenses were subsequently suspended or not renewed or otherwise not authorized to practice, traced the official retribution back to their leadership of the BLA election struggle. Altogether, at least twenty lawyers lost their ability to practice (B1110).

Moreover, according to one leader of the struggle, from this time forward the BBOJ changed its strategy on pressuring lawyers. Before, it brought pressure directly on individual lawyers. After, it added two pressure techniques. One was on law firms, either to fire lawyers troublesome to the justice bureau, or not to hire lawyers who had been pushed out of other firms, or for law firm managers to compel lawyers to comply with justice bureau preferences. Another technique was to add an extra hurdle to annual license renewals: the justice bureau issued practice certificates but thereafter it was also necessary for lawyers to obtain a seal on their licenses from the BLA every year. The cumulative effect was to multiply pressure points to quell activism, whether in practice or in reform efforts of the bar itself (B1110).

While on its face the BLA election initiative seemed ultimately to fail, at least one veteran activist saw "several positive impacts" still observable a year later:

First, it increased the rights consciousness of lawyers all over China because all the lawyer colleagues in the country were concerned about this election. We sounded the trumpet for self-governance. Previously the legal profession was closely attached to the government. Second, it promoted the institution-building of the bar, e.g., rules for the election. We drafted our unofficial version of the rules. The government made its own rules. Of course, they were very different but we did get a change from "no-rule" to "some-rules." Third, there were some smaller changes. In the lawyer license if you were a migrant lawyer it showed on your license. From our point of view, we thought that adding the 'W' letter to show you were from out-of-town was discrimination against migrant lawyers. After the campaign, this symbol was removed. Fourth, in terms of membership fees there was talk of reducing them, and they have been reduced from Y2500 to Y2000 and new lawyers are exempt from membership fees.

(B1005, Beijing)

Nevertheless, the extreme official reactions to what appears to be a very modest proposal by the activists in turn raises the question – why was the campaign for the direct election of bar association representatives and leaders so threatening to the regulatory apparatus and the Party? Repeatedly, activists recognized that they had threatened the monopoly of power, the control of the government over lawyers. As one lawyer asserted, "Control over Chinese lawyers is like colonialism … The BLA is like the Chinese that worked for the Japanese government, a Manchuria-style government" (B1125). In part, this may be seen as the Party's general fear of civil society because "this involved a very sensitive issue on the freedom of association" (B1123). As one lawyer put it:

On the one hand, they know they cannot really stop the growth of civil society. On the other hand, they are afraid of the growth of civil society. Although we have been through thirty years of so-called economic reform, the government's idea of total control of society hasn't been changed.

(B1005, Beijing)

But freedom of association by lawyers may be qualitatively different from such freedoms exercised by other groups. One activist leader noted that lawyers are very much involved "in supervising and monitoring the corruption within the government" (B1123). Since this is such an acutely sensitive issue, potentially undermining the legitimacy of the Party-state itself, it was imperative that the power of lawyers be subordinated to the control of the government and the means of doing that was to ensure that "the justice bureau and BLA were completely under their control" (B1123). A foreign diplomat who was well acquainted with the activists had an acute perception of the magnitude of the threat:

Why the problems with the bar associations? Maybe the government is a stickler at looking at other experiences at other countries – they look to Taiwan, largely led by lawyers; a military dictatorship in Korea, in Pakistan, partially crashed by lawyers; the Orange Revolution and Rose Revolution were lawyer driven. Lawyers in China are activists, intelligent, and not afraid to talk about democracy, what the rules are. The problem with lawyers is that they will say "there is a rule, you have written it, and you should hold yourselves to it." Lawyers will say, "law is for everyone." Look also inside China – lawyers were attacked from the 1950s. You have to be consistent.

(B0905, Beijing)

If indeed this perception is correct, it would lend credence to the reflections a year or two later of some activist lawyers that this was no local matter of consequence only to the BBOJ. "The reaction was determined by the political reaction and mode of governance in China" (B1005). At the time of the BLA election struggle, said one of its key participants:

I thought that just a few individuals in the bar association leadership reacted that way. But now I think it was inevitable. If you consider what happened in the past six months, you can see that the logic they are using in dealing with all the lawyers, and also at the time of direct election – it has always been the logic of their reaction. That is, *we are in control*.

(B1138, Beijing)

It is plausible to conclude, therefore, that a small democratic revolution attempted in a strategic occupation in the national capital very likely involved higher-level decisions by the central government (Cohen 2009). A fear that any insurgency that would yield a democratically governed and self-regulating profession must thereby be extinguished decisively by the Party-state at its moment of genesis. For the activist lawyers who participated in the 2008 BLA election movement, the hope of using bar associations to advance their pursuit of political liberalism diminished substantially afterwards and, accordingly, in recent years they switched to informal network strategies.

Domestic Networking Strategies

Structurally, notable activists are in a paradoxical situation. On the one hand, they stand at the margins of the domestic power structures of the legal profession and the state apparatus, most of them remote from the core of power in the justice bureaus, bar associations, or major law firms. For most, their offices are outside of Beijing's better districts and are often crowded and humbly furnished. They usually prefer to meet in public places. On the other hand, ironically, their marginal status empowers them to mobilize as outsiders, unconventionally and uncompromisingly. Furthermore, precisely because they are marginalized and repressed within China, many are compelled to obtain international support. Indeed, many are better known to foreign public and professional audiences than they are domestically.

How then do they construct and manage these two loci of social action: obtaining support domestically when they are marginalized from power structures; and finding support internationally when they are harshly repressed by the Party-State? An answer lies in the social networks in which Chinese notable activist lawyers are embedded, including both a domestic community of human rights activists and a number of complementary sources of international support.

Most of Beijing's activist lawyers know one another and they form a loosely bound activist community. Several lawyers migrated to Beijing in the first place precisely because they heard or knew that other lawyers sharing the same cause were concentrated in the city (Liu, Liang, and Michelson 2014). Once in Beijing, several joined the same law firms, such as the Yitong, Anhui, and Global law firms, and later the Fengrui firm, doomed to forced closure in 2015, which became incubators and magnets for human rights lawyers. Lawyers in many firms became knit into networks that brought them together frequently. It became a practice for numbers to meet regularly, or in response to specific cases, at restaurants in Beijing. Around a circular table in a private room, a group of lawyers could share cases, consider tactics, and decide which of them would work together on a case.

Since the BBOJ has variously suspended, failed to renew, or removed many activist lawyers' licenses to practice, some lawyers stood in the frontline, ready to appear in court and mobilize support through the media, while others, usually the victims of BBOJ sanctions, stood behind, as they described their posture, where they could encourage their frontline colleagues and advise and draft materials for them to use. Often these arrangements involved revenue-sharing, so that those behind the front line, even if denied the right to practice as lawyers in court, could nevertheless obtain some income. Various combinations of activist lawyers work jointly on cases. Many of China's most notable and newsworthy rights trials in recent years resemble a moving cast of actors, forming and reforming from one case to another, as one combination of lawyers present a forceful front on this case, while another combination form on another case (B1204).

This sense of solidarity woven out of varieties of social interaction is reinforced by the fact that a majority of these lawyers are named by the regulatory troika and state security apparatus as "blacklisted" lawyers or persons to be subject to particular surveillance and control. After their "disappearances" during the "Jasmine Revolution" scare in 2011, several of the lawyers reported that they were specifically asked about each other by name, a line of interrogation that demonstrated that the security forces believed them to be part of a collectivity mobilizing against the Party (B1320; B1323). Later, the activists became bolder and more public when 101 lawyers signed an open letter in July 2015 decrying the disappearance of Wang Yu and urging the protection of her rights. That is to say, these lawyers were forged into a community in part because they mobilized against excesses of the authoritarian state and, in part, by naming them, and in mid-2015, systematically detaining them, the state effectively helped constitute the activists even further as a self-aware social entity.

In fact, in the mid-2015 crackdown, the authorities did not have to look far to find growing numbers of activists in close contact with each other. Leading activists Tang Jitian, Jiang Tianyong, and Wang Cheng had started a WeChat group in September 2013, and by mid-2015 more than 200 activists from across China were in close touch with each other on particular cases, exchanging views, and even posting policy positions, although sometimes only in Hong Kong (B1530). The leaders assumed that the WeChat Human Rights Lawyers Support Group was under surveillance since it provided a convenient way for security forces to keep track of individual lawyers, some of whom were then subject to direct pressure of various sorts.

Christian activist lawyers, with some of their close and sympathetic non-Christian friends, add another type of social network to forge solidarity and reduce fear (Wielander 2009; B1101). An effort was made several years ago to form a China Christian Lawyers Fellowship, but it was deemed too dangerous after the Chinese government's harsh response to the Jasmine Revolution (B1115; B1204). More than one Christian lawyer has sought to create or lead a house church, sometimes in his law firm. "I started a Bible study, kind of a house church," said a lawyer, "in my conference room in my law firm. About ten to twenty people were in that house church. Later it was dissolved" (B1103). Another charismatic Christian lawyer-intellectual, Fan Yafeng, established something of a Christian lawyers' salon for conversation about the most vexing issues of law, politics, and religious faith, until he himself was placed under house arrest (B1111; B1115). Most recently, a WeChat group for Christian lawyers was formed and had more than 100 lawyers in it as of mid-2015 (B1513).

Not least, many of the Christian lawyers attend house churches where they are "frequently inspired" and obtain emotional and spiritual support (B1111; B1116). Their courage was undergirded by the strength of fellow believers. As one lawyer recounted, "Sunday service, fellowship, sharing with brothers and sisters, and reading the Bible really gave me peace and joy" (B1108). And yet another lawyer stated that his courage "comes from interaction with the believers. Without that interaction, no matter how much courage you have, it will disappear" (B1106). However, the relationship between activist lawyers and house churches can be difficult. Some house churches do not want such lawyers as members in case their presence brings unwanted surveillance and interference by the religious affairs bureau and security agencies. One Christian lawyer stayed away from a house church led by a family member because he did not want to expose the church to interruptions by security police following him (B1104). And the presence of some notable activist lawyers in the Shouwang church, a 1,000-person-strong house church locked in a long conflict with the religious affairs bureau over its church facilities and worship sites, may have simultaneously protected the church and escalated the conflict (B1116).

International Linkages

Many Chinese activist lawyers also receive both symbolic and material support from the international community to carry on the fight against the authoritarian state. Not all lawyers seek support from international sources, nor are they equally positioned to receive it. But for those who both seek and find external resources, its value cannot be over-estimated.

Take a prominent activist lawyer in Beijing. On January 7, 2013, we observed his meeting with three other lawyers in his crowded, unprepossessing office on the nineteenth floor of a nondescript building in the south side of Beijing. At about 2pm his phone began to ring, and it rung virtually without stopping for several hours. That day the Chinese government announced that it was going to abolish its much-criticized Re-Education through Labor institution (Fu 2005). By the time the lawyer's phone calls returned to their normal volume, he had spoken to USA *Today*, the *Financial Times*, the *New York Times*, the *Wall Street Journal*, the BBC, Voice of America radio, French TV1, German TV 4, the *South China Morning Post*, as well as others he could no longer recall (B1318).

Since it proved methodologically unsatisfactory to track systematically the media connections of the activists from the activists themselves (as many could not remember all the media they had spoken to), we took an alternative approach. We identified twelve notable activists in Beijing who varied by the focus of their practice (e.g., freedom of speech, defense of Falun Gong), their religious ideals (e.g., Christian versus not-Christian), and their "generation" (e.g., "veteran" activists since the early 2000s versus younger, more recently active lawyers), and searched Google headlines in English, French, German, and Spanish for stories of any kind that mentioned them. By analyzing the top 100 stories for each lawyer, it is clear that some have extensive international networks in the four language groups in our search.

We identify five main types of international support institutions for Chinese activist lawyers.

International media include (1) public and for-profit global world services (e.g., Al Jazeera, the BBC, CNN, *Radio France Internationale*, Reuters); (2) major national news media in Europe, North America, and Asia (e.g., the *Guardian*, the *Telegraph* in the UK; *L'Express, Le Monde*, and *Liberation* in France; *Die Welt, Stern, Der Spiegel*, and *DiePresse* in Germany; *El Pais* and *ElMundo* in Spain; the *New York Times, Wall Street Journal, LA Times*, NBC, *Washington Post, USA Today* in the United States; *Melbourne Age, Sydney Morning Herald* in Australia; *South China Morning Post* in Hong Kong; *Taipei Times* in Taiwan; and regional news services such as Asia News, Voice of America, Radio Free Asia); (3) national and international religious media (including, in English and in French, Christian News Wire, Persecut ion.org, Release International, Christianity Today; *Actualité Chrétienne, Journal Chrétiene.net*); and (4) various China-focused media, including compilation services (e.g., *China Digital Times, China Daily Mail*, Falun Gong's *Epoch Times*, and New Tang Dynasty TV network).

International human rights organizations divide into several strands. One class of organizations cover the world and include a China-watch. Some of these are international non- profits (e.g, Amnesty International, Human Rights Watch). Some are nationally based non-profits with a global span (e.g., Human Rights First), and others are government sponsored (e.g., Irish Aid's Frontline Defenders). Another class of organizations have a specifically China focus, such as Human Rights in China (New York-based) and China Human Rights Defenders (Hong Kong/US based). Dui Hua (San Francisco-based) also has had a monitoring of China human rights cases.

Lawyer-specific international organizations sometimes commit themselves to supporting human activist lawyers. Some of these non-profits narrow their focus to China, most notable among which are the China Human Rights Lawyers Concern Group (Hong Kong), Chinese Human Rights Defenders (Hong Kong/United States), and China Aid Association (United States). A Fordham University group, the Committee to Support Chinese Lawyers, also speaks out periodically on China developments. Other international professional associations exhibit periodic concerns with developments in China, such as the Dutch non-profit association (Lawyers for Lawyers/ Advocaten voor Advocaten), the European Bar Human Rights Institute, and the French Observatoire Internationale Des Avocats/International Observatory for Lawyers.

Several international religious organizations maintain a watch on China because of their global monitoring of persecution of Christians and infringements on religious freedom. Since persecuted Christians in China frequently seek legal representation, and Christian lawyers seek international support, these organizations maintain relationships with some activist lawyers (e.g., Release International: Voice of Persecuted Christians, a UK based non-profit; China Aid, a US-based association).

Foreign governments, finally, sometimes provide tangible and intangible support to Chinese activist lawyers. Such support can be indirect, where governments fund non-profits and media groups with a China impact, or direct, where governments intercede with Chinese officials on behalf of individuals or give symbolic recognition to China's persecuted lawyers.

These categories are not mutually exclusive. A great deal of cross-fertilization and cross-publication occurs between human rights groups and the media, which pick up their stories (e.g., Human Rights Watch and Frontline Defender bylines regularly appear in the international and European media respectively). A Christian organization like China Aid simultaneously focuses on religious freedom and lawyers. Nor do these organizations seek similar levels of visibility. Some organizations rely on visibility for their influence (e.g., Amnesty International, China Aid, Human Rights in China); others deliberately maintain a very low profile so as to not imperil their activities inside China (e.g., China Human Rights Defenders).

Our analysis of the content of international media reports and interviews with international organizations and activist lawyers demonstrates that international institutions offer varieties of support. Some are generalist, while others are more specialized. Together they create a global network of support that can fortify lawyers under tremendous pressure inside China. We observe five major forms of international support: monitoring, intervening, funding, affirming, and analyzing.

(1) *Monitoring* International institutions encourage activist lawyers and effectively warn the government that they are visibly monitoring actions of China's security apparatus, especially at times of crackdown. Every category of international institution produced stories and issued statements when activist lawyers were "disappeared" and subjected to physical and psychological torture. Some organizations, such as China Aid, on occasion make public announcements about particular cases where the names, ID numbers, and behavior of particular public and state security officers, judges, and officials are recorded. Sometimes photos accompany these stories. Activist lawyers with international connections also actively use the international media in their cases.

A result is that local officials cannot be confident that actions they consider to be local and shielded from public eye will not break into the spotlight of international attention.

(2) *Intervening* Intervening occurs where there are direct efforts by an international organization to make a difference in a specific instance. One kind of intervention occurs with specific cases, when a private person outside China may negotiate directly with government officials inside China. A more common type of intervention occurs on behalf of particular lawyers. Some of these are highly publicized, for example, in diplomatic meetings when a high-ranking US government official asks about the whereabouts of Gao Zhisheng or enables the departure of Cheng Guangcheng from China. Others are deliberately not publicized in order not to jeopardize their impact. A Scandinavian government, for instance, would regularly bring a list of names to bilateral consultations and ask for a response from China's government. A private organization, Dui Hua, has specialized in high-level face-to-face meetings where it often successfully sought information, lightened sentences, and the release of particular individuals (I1003; I1102).

(3) *Funding* Many human rights cases involve individuals who cannot afford to pay lawyers and reach lawyers who might not be able to take a case because of its costs. While some activist lawyers also do commercial and other work in order to subsidize their human rights work, a major trial in a distant part of China for a defendant unable to pay essentially denies any kind of legal representation and rights-defense for that person. At least two international organizations, which must remain unidentified, provide modest fees and travel expenses for key cases. Sometimes they work alone with a given lawyer; at other times they work together. Support sometimes also goes to the families of lawyers detained or imprisoned. In one organization, cases are chosen to give priority to cases where torture is imminent or alleged, or where women face particular danger. These organizations may have their budgets for support of activist lawyers partially underwritten by aid programs of governments.

(4) *Affirming* International connections can also lift the visibility of causes and lawyers. This is a double-edged sword: some believe it offers protection, others that it makes them more vulnerable. Within China, it is a mark of recognition and encouragement to be invited for dinner with foreign diplomats. US Ambassador Gary Locke invited Zhang Kai to dinner at the US Embassy. The US government's National Endowment for Democracy honored several Chinese activist

lawyers with its 2008 Democracy Award. Several lawyers have testified in print and person before the Tom Lantos Human Rights Commission in the US Congress. Others have appeared before the European Parliament in Strasbourg. Sometimes the invitations to meet with foreign political leaders have led to repercussions. In 2008, activist lawyers Li Baiguang and Teng Biao were prevented from meeting with US Congressmen Chris Smith and Frank Wolf, who had been active supporters of human rights in China. On another occasion, an activist lawyer was arrested as he arrived at the Beijing Capital Airport after having met with President Bush.

(5) *Analyzing* The US Congressional Executive Committee on China (CECC) writes extensive annual reports that include analysis of human rights protection in China. The US State Department produces an annual report on human rights worldwide, which includes a section on China. Other organizations are more focused. Human Rights Watch, Human Rights in China, and China Human Rights Defenders issue periodic reports on rights abuses (HRIC 2007; I1003; I1004). China Aid releases annually a report on religious persecution in China. Often these reports include detailed information about cases and situations, including the involvement of activist lawyers (Teng 2009). Periodically, these and other human rights focused groups release special reports (Justice 2015).

In sum, the political activism of Chinese activist lawyers is sustained not only by their strong ideals, but also by the social networks in which they are embedded. These networks include collegial networks among lawyers, human rights networks, religious networks, as well as transnational networks that include foreign journalists, international organizations, and foreign governments. These social networks provide not only tangible funding and resource supports, but also emotional and relational strength for the activist lawyers to carry on their highly risky practice against a repressive state apparatus. They convert individual experiences and struggles into collective action and serve a vitally important function in the growth of Chinese human rights lawyers over the years (Pils 2015).

CONCLUSION

Our research on lawyer activism in China confirms what other scholars have observed, namely, that a small number of notable activist lawyers stand at the frontline of Chinese lawyers committed to rule of law and constitutionalism

(Fu and Cullen 2008, 2011; Pils 2015). Since these lawyers take on cases that make them highly visible, and often bring them into sharp conflict with local and national authorities, we have asked – where do these lawyers get their courage from and how do they sustain that courage in the face of repression? Our repeated interviews with notable activist lawyers in Beijing from 2009 to 2015 points to three explanations. First, their life histories reveal that at certain moments, either before they became lawyers, or during their legal careers, they personally were confronted with situations they considered so unfair, unjust, and intolerable that they must use law to remedy individual grievances and to restructure the legal and political systems. As Fu and Cullen (2011) demonstrate, in many cases the growing sense of injustice moved them up a *"weiquan* ladder" to increased radicalism where systemic change became an imperative aspiration.

Yet lawyer activism is not merely a process of escalation, but rooted in deeper legal, political, and religious ideals. Extended conversations with Chinese notable activist lawyers reveal that they share legal and political ideals that cluster together with a degree of coherence, although this must not be overstated. Almost without exception they strive for reforms in China that will limit the arbitrary power of the state, that will enable citizens to mobilize actively through associations in a vibrant civil society, and that will institutionalize basic legal freedoms such as freedoms of speech, association, and religion, and property rights. With this cluster of legal ideals they are motivated by a powerful assurance that they are engaged in something far greater than earning a living or defending an individual. Furthermore, for the substantial proportion of Protestant Christian activist lawyers, they are also motivated by their religious belief that basic Christian doctrines require them to fight for equality, justice, fairness, and protection of the weak.

Finally, we find that courage is not only an individual attribute derived from a personal experience or character. It is fortified through social support, particularly among the networks of activist lawyers themselves, in both their collective struggle for an autonomous bar association and their mutual support in highly sensitive cases, and by the close association that Christian lawyers have with unofficial churches. For a smaller number of notable activist lawyers, a great deal of moral and tangible support comes from international institutions – the media, human rights organizations, professional groups, and even governments.

Many activist lawyers persist courageously because they believe they are engaged in an historic cause. In this respect their sense of a long, historical drama within China echoes elements of other instances of lawyer mobilization across the world (Karpik 1995; Halliday and Karpik 1997; Halliday,

Karpik and Feeley 2007, 2012; Moustafa 2007; Rajah 2012). Nevertheless, considerable caution and contingency must be exercised in predicting the effectiveness of activist lawyers as a driving force for legal and political change in China. Their numbers are small. Their structural positions in the Chinese legal and political system are marginal. Some recent cases, such as the Li Zhuang trial discussed in Chapter 6, suggest a potential alliance between activist lawyers and some progressive elite lawyers in promoting the rule of law and constitutionalism in China, but the collective solidarity of this alliance and the tolerance of the Chinese state towards it remain wide open questions at this point, especially after the July 2015 crackdown and the severity of charges against leading activists in 2016 (see Chapter 7). To study lawyer activism in China, therefore, requires the simultaneous recognition of lawyers' courage and heroism in individual cases and the daunting structural constraints that they face in their everyday practice.

6

The Trial of Li Zhuang

On November 20, 1980, the historic trial of the Gang of Four began in Beijing. The trial lasted for two months, with ten recently rehabilitated lawyers serving as defense counsel for ten major criminals of the Cultural Revolution that included Chairman Mao's wife (Ma 2007). This was the first time in the history of the Chinese legal profession that lawyers appeared in front of the nation and the world. Nearly thirty years later, from December 12, 2009 to February 9, 2010, under the rule of Bo Xilai, Chongqing also staged its own criminal trial that captured the nation's attention. This time, the defendant was a criminal defense lawyer named Li Zhuang, a partner of Beijing Kangda Law Firm. As the verdict stands, Li spent one and an half years behind bars, permanently lost his license to practice law, and was prosecuted again in 2011 for another crime without being convicted.

The sharp contrast between these two landmark cases signifies the contorted development of China's legal reform in the past three decades. Since the leadership change of the Supreme People's Court in 2008, talk of a "backward movement" (倒退) of the legal reform has become a popular discourse both in China's legal community and among foreign observers (Jiang 2010; Minzner 2011). Slogans such as "judiciary for the people" (司法为民) and "proactive judiciary" (能动司法) suggest a notable change in judicial ideology, which embodies the populism of the socialist period that dates back to the judicial practice in Communist areas in the 1940s (Zhu 2010). This populist approach clashes with orientations toward legal professionalism increasingly displayed by Chinese lawyers and legal scholars. Consequently, in recent years, we have witnessed an increase in the mobilization of Chinese lawyers against populism.

Perhaps no other case better illustrates the collective action of Chinese lawyers against the populist legal ideology than the trial of Li Zhuang, which one legal scholar called "China's trial of the century" (Xu 2010). Thousands of

Chinese lawyers and other legal professionals, as well as the general public, closely followed the dramatic unfolding of the Li Zhuang case. They used their words and actions to help, support, or criticize the defendant. Meanwhile, the Chinese government relaxed its grip on the professional and public discussions around this highly political case, which, as it turned out, even had an impact on the central leadership change in 2012. The Li Zhuang case became one of the contributing events that led to the fall of Bo Xilai, who had been widely speculated to join the incoming Politburo Standing Committee but eventually fell from power and was sentenced to life in prison. All these exceptional characteristics made the Li Zhuang case a rare and remarkable event in China's recent legal history.

This chapter uses the trial of Li Zhuang to analyze the political mobilization of Chinese lawyers, especially progressive elites, as well as the deeper ideological contradictions within the Chinese legal system. We argue that China's ongoing legal reform is characterized by the coexistence of two competing ideologies: professionalism and populism. Professionalism prioritizes formal rationality over substantive justice or irrational decision-making (Weber 1954). It emphasizes the autonomy of legal actors and resists political influence on the legal system (Freidson 2001; Luhmann 2004). Populism, in contrast, prioritizes public accountability and political legitimacy over professional autonomy (Canovan 1981). It uses political campaign and mass mobilization to pursue substantive justice at the expense of formal legal procedure (Li 1977; Lubman 1999; Tanner 1999; Trevaskes 2010). As the chapter will demonstrate, Chinese lawyers' collective action in the Li Zhuang case became both a fight against populism and a critical turning point for the political mobilization of progressive elites and the rise of "die-hard lawyering" afterwards (see Chapter 7). It was a crucial battle not only for their own survival, but also for the future development of China's legal and political reforms.

In the following pages, we first provide a summary account of the Li Zhuang trial. Then we proceed to analyze three episodes in the Li Zhuang saga and the professional mobilization around this case. Three main data sources are used in the chapter: (1) legal documents from the Li Zhuang trial; (2) media reports on the trial and online discussions among legal professionals; (3) nineteen in-depth interviews conducted in Beijing, Shanghai, and Kunming during 2010–2012 in which we systematically asked questions regarding this case. Our informants include several lawyers who played key roles in the Li Zhuang case, two journalists who reported on the case, and a number of ordinary law practitioners who followed the case from afar, but their names must remain anonymous in compliance with research ethics. We have also restricted the use of direct quotes in the chapter to further protect the identities of our informants.

THE LI ZHUANG CASE

In 2009, Bo Xilai, the then-Party Secretary of Chongqing, launched a massive "anti-black" (打黑) campaign against organized crimes. Within months, the local authorities arrested over 1,000 criminal suspects. Among the arrested was Gong Gangmo, a local businessman who was charged with organized crime activities, murder, illegal trading, purchasing of firearms, drug trafficking, and extortion. On June 20, 2009, the Chongqing police detained Gong, and soon afterward, his family approached the nationally renowned Beijing Kangda Law Firm (LHZB_20100101). The firm appointed Li Zhuang, a partner specializing in criminal defense, to handle Gong's case.

On November 20, 2009, the Chongqing Jiangbei District People's Procuracy formally charged Gong and thirty other suspects for organized crime activities. Once the Gong family made the 200,000 RMB partial payment (the total legal fees allegedly amounted to some 1.5 million RMB), Li Zhuang and his assistant, Ma Xiaojun, flew to Chongqing (DSKB_20091231; CQRB_20100226; FYFZ_20100306). On November 24, Li and Ma went to the Jiangbei District Detention Center to meet with Gong. Li clashed with the police when the latter insisted that the police officers in charge of the case must be present when the lawyers meet with the suspect (LHZB_20100101; XHW_20100210).

What happened at this meeting between Li and Gong became a crucial issue in Li's own trial one month later. The media, Li's counsel, and the judicial agencies in Chongqing all had different versions of the meeting. According to a *Chongqing Daily* report, Li whispered into Gong's ear and coached him to say that he was tortured for eight days and eight nights (CQRB_20100226). In a CCTV interview, Gong said that Li winked at him to coach him (CCTV_20091215). There were notable discrepancies between what Gong told the CCTV and what he provided in his testimony to the procuracy. According to Li and his counsel, Gong confided in Li the details of his forced interrogation, its date and time, and the names of the police officer present and those of the two doctors who treated him afterward (LHZB_20100101; FYFZ_20100306).

In addition to meeting with Gong again on November 26, Li also made preliminary efforts to collect evidence in Chongqing. According to the procuracy's prosecution letter, Li met with several employees from Gong's Baoli nightclub at a restaurant and coached them to give false testimonies and deny that Gong was the CEO of the company (TY_20100109). In his own defense, Li insisted that he had never met with the three employees that Gong's brother supposedly introduced to him. He was also unaware of the reason as to why Gong's brother arranged these individuals to testify (TY_20100109).

On November 31, the Chongqing authorities contacted Beijing regarding Li's clash with the police. The Beijing Lawyers Association and his law firm immediately had a talk with Li, who was directed to communicate with the Chongqing authorities before the hearing began (TY_20100109). On December 1, a division chief from the Chongqing No. 1 People's Intermediate Court telephoned Li, asking him to return to Chongqing before the trial for a debriefing. The next day, Li invited four distinguished legal experts in Beijing to review the files for Gong's case and acquired their expert opinion (TY_20100109).

On December 3, Li flew back to Chongqing. That same morning, he met with judges at the Chongqing No. 1 People's Intermediate Court, briefed them on the procedural problems that he had found in Gong's case, and requested that the hearing be postponed (TY_20100109). That same night, Li met with Gong's former counsel, Wu Jiayou, at the Continental Grand Hotel and allegedly asked Wu to contact the two doctors who treated Gong after his interrogation. Wu refused. According to the procuracy's prosecution letter, Li asked Wu to bribe the police officers who were present at Gong's interrogation to make false statements (DSKB_20091231; TY_20100109). Li denied the allegation and argued that he was merely performing his duty as Gong's counsel in finding witnesses (TY_20100109). On December 4, Li met with Gong for the third time. To get Gong to tell him details of the interrogation, Li requested the police officers to leave the room and, as a result, had another serious argument with the police (TY_20100109; FYFZ_20100306).

In the end, Li was able to postpone Gong's hearing, which was originally scheduled for December 7. On December 10, however, things suddenly changed for the worse. Gong made a statement accusing Li of coaching him to revoke his previous confession, be disruptive at his trial hearing, and claim that he was tortured during police interrogation (LHZB_20100101). That same day, Li received a call from the Chongqing No. 1 People's Intermediate Court inviting him to return to Chongqing for a "nice talk" (TY_20100109; FYFZ_20100306). Li told the court that his firm had already decided to terminate its representation in Gong's case. Afterward, Li visited the Beijing Cancer Center where Gong's wife was undergoing treatment in order to have her sign the agreement of termination. Shortly after he arrived at the hospital, Li was arrested by seven plainclothes police officers and escorted back to Chongqing (FYFZ_20100306). On December 12, Li was charged with violating Article 306 of the Criminal Law, the crime of lawyer's perjury (CQRB_20100226). Within the next few days, Li's arrest made headlines across the country.

On December 19, the court formally charged Li with Article 306, and Li's wife asked Gao Zicheng, a colleague of Li's from Beijing Kangda Law Firm, to defend him. In the next two days, Gao met with Li twice at the Chongqing No. 2 Detention Center and requested bail and to have Li's case transferred to a different jurisdiction (ZGFYW_20091230). The court refused both requests and set the trial date for the Li Zhuang case on December 30 – before Gong's trial. On December 22, Gao text-messaged Chen Youxi, a prominent criminal defense lawyer in Zhejiang Province who wrote several insightful online commentaries on the Li Zhuang case, and asked Chen to join him in representing Li (FYFZ_20100306). After consulting with the local justice bureau, Chen decided to accept Gao's invitation (FYFZ_20100306).

On December 25, Gao and Chen requested the court appearances of eight witnesses that included Gong and his cousin. They also asked to review the videotapes of Li's three meetings with Gong and to have Gong medically examined. However, all the witnesses refused to appear in court, and the Jiangbei District Detention Center did not hand over the tapes, which did not have sound due to equipment problems (ZGFYW_20091230; DSKB_20091231; FYFZ_20100306). On December 28, Gong underwent an official medical examination ordered by the Jiangbei District People's Court. The following night, Li's lawyers received a copy of Gong's medical report, which noted that a blunt object caused the injury marks on Gong's left wrist (CQRB_20100226; FYFZ_20100306).

On December 30, Li's first hearing began at 9:10 a.m. For this high-profile case, the Chongqing Municipal People's Procuracy appointed two procurators from intermediate-level procuracies to represent the Jiangbei District People's Procuracy. While the presiding judge read Li his rights, Li interrupted and requested that the Jiangbei District People's Court, the Procuracy, and all their associates to abstain from the case. At each occasion, the judge denied or ignored Li's request. Afterward, Li acted dramatically in court, first refusing to answer any questions and then arguing rigorously against the procurators with the assistance of his two defense lawyers (CQRB_20100226).

Over one hundred pieces of evidence were presented in court, including Gong's testimonies. Still, according to Li's counsel, none of them proved or could prove that Li fabricated evidence, for Li had neither made notes nor submitted a witness list to the court. During the cross-examination, Li admitted that he taught Gong some techniques in preparing for his trial but nothing that was illegal. Further, Li admitted that he hoped Gong would revoke his confession, for he suspected Gong gave his confession under forced interrogation. "I was only doing what an outstanding and dutiful lawyer should do," Li declared (CQRB_20100226). After sixteen hours, the "marathon" hearing finally ended at 1:30 a.m. the following day with no verdict.

On January 8, 2010, the Chongqing Jiangbei People's Court found Li guilty of forging and tampering with evidence, and he was sentenced to two and an half years in prison. After the chief judge announced the sentence, Li strongly objected and shouted, "The court's sentencing is illegal!" (XHW_20100108). In the following ten days, Li's counsel Gao Zicheng met him twice in Chongqing, and Li continued to insist that he was innocent (FZWB_20100118; FZWB_20100209). On January 18, Li's counsel formally submitted an appeal on behalf of Li to the Chongqing No. 1 Intermediate People's Court (CYXXSW_20100131).

On February 2, Li's second hearing began. Unlike other criminal appeal hearings in China, which are often closed-door sessions with no witnesses present, Li's hearing was not only open to the public, but it also had six criminal suspects, including Gong and two police officers, who appeared in court as witnesses. In addition, the Chongqing authorities invited representatives of the People's Congress, the People's Political Consultative Conference, and the Beijing Lawyers Association, along with reporters from about twenty media outlets, and faculty and students from local universities to observe the hearing (JHSB_20100202; CQRB_20100226).

Minutes into the hearing, Li suddenly declared: "I admit to my charges. The evidence from the first hearing was sufficient, the law was rightly exercised, and procedures observed. I withdraw my causes for appeal, the previous reasons for appeal are invalid, but I insist on appealing" (XHW_20100202; CQRB_20100226). Chen Youxi, one of Li's defense lawyers, requested Li to clearly state his position and asked him whether he knew the consequences of the withdrawal. Li said he understood the consequences. The procurators then asked Li whether he had coached Gong to make a false statement on being under forced interrogation, asked Gong's former counsel to bribe the police officers present at Gong's interrogation, and taught Gong's wife to say her husband was being blackmailed by his business partner. Li admitted to all these charges. When asked why he did so, he replied he wanted to deceive the police, the procuracy, and the court to get his client off (SHSB_20100203; XHW_20100203).

Although Li admitted the charges, his counsel insisted on proceeding with their not-guilty defense. Throughout the hearing, both sides carefully cross-examined Gong and the other witnesses. Li himself also reviewed their testimonies and raised several important questions. Li's counsel examined Gong's

wrist injuries, but Gong repeatedly denied of undergoing any forced interrogations (XHW_20100203; CQRB_20100226). During the cross-examination, Gong
and other witnesses all insisted on speaking in the Chongqing dialect, which the
defense lawyers could not understand and which required the judges to appoint
a translator (CQCB_20100203). Yet Gong spoke fluent standard Mandarin in
his CCTV interview in November 2009 (CCTV_20091215). The hearing lasted
two days and ended on February 3. Li made a six-point final statement and
admitted to his charges again (BJQNB_20100206).

On February 9, the Chongqing No. 1 Intermediate People's Court upheld
the charges from the first trial but reduced the original sentence from two and
an half years to eighteen months. Upon hearing the verdict, Li became outraged and shouted,

> My earlier admissions were forced. I was forced to do it. The police and
> procuracy said they'd reduce my sentence to probation if I admitted to
> [wrongdoing]. They said if I pleaded guilty, then the second hearing would
> be an open trial. And still I'm sentenced. If you read my written confession
> carefully, you would see I was just deceiving the police and procuracy.
>
> (XHW_20100210)

As the judicial police was taking him out of court, Li shouted again, "How
many martyrs have written confession letters, but this did not change the fact
that they were martyrs . . . I hope the 160,000 Chinese lawyers out there would
continue to appeal for me" (FZWB_20100209).

While most observers thought that the dramatic Li Zhuang case concluded in
2010, a surprising new development occurred a year later. On March 29, 2011,
the news office of the Chongqing Municipal Government publicly announced
that Li was now being investigated again for some "missing criminal activities"
(漏罪) and the new case was already transferred to the Chongqing Jiangbei
District People's Procuracy for prosecution (CX_20110422). The news quickly
spread on the Internet and many lawyers and journalists promptly labeled
the new prosecution "Li Zhuang Case Season 2" (CJ_20110407; FT_20110419).

Over the next few days, the media gradually unveiled the details of the
new Li Zhuang case. The Chongqing police investigated three cases: one was
the original Gong Gangmo case in which Li was accused of contract fraud,
and the other two were cases that Li did in Shanghai and Liaoning Province
back in 2008. In these two cases, Li was accused of inducing a witness to
provide false testimony (CX_20110422). After the procuracy reviewed the three
cases, the contract fraud charge and the Liaoning case were dropped. Only the
Shanghai case was prosecuted to the court. In other words, the new Li Zhuang
case in 2011 became yet another case concerning the crime of lawyer's perjury.

The new prosecution of Li Zhuang shocked the Chinese legal community. Many lawyers pointed out that, according to the Criminal Procedure Law, the case should be under the jurisdiction of Shanghai and not Chongqing (FYFZ_20110410; FYFZ_20110411; FYFZ_20110412), but the Chongqing authorities were determined to bring Li to trial again. In a later interview, a key informant told us that Bo Xilai was angry at what Li had said during the sentencing session of his appeals trial in February 2010. Li mentioned the fact that Bo's father, Bo Yibo, a veteran Communist leader and a high-ranking official in the 1950s, also signed a confession letter to the Kuomintang government while in a Tianjin prison in 1936 (B1201). Consequently, Bo ordered the Chongqing police to make a thorough investigation of all the cases that Li had handled, which led to the new prosecution in 2011.

While the Chongqing procurators were preparing for the trial, several leading criminal defense lawyers also began to discuss how to defend Li Zhuang in this new case. Chen Youxi, one of Li's counsel in the original case, expressed his pessimism in an essay posted on his website and asked, "Is it still necessary to play the game this time?" Chen and many other lawyers suspected that the chances of getting Li off the charges would be small given the determination of the Chongqing authorities to keep him in jail (CYYXSW_20110402). Nevertheless, Chen contacted several lawyers at the request of Li's family. And eventually Wei Rujiu, a Beijing lawyer and the Director of the Constitutional Law and Human Rights Committee of the Beijing Lawyers Association, agreed to take on the case and go to Chongqing to meet with Li. Wei asked his friend Yang Xuelin, another criminal defense lawyer in Beijing, to collaborate with him for the Chongqing trip (B1102; S1101; S1104).

On April 6, Wei and Yang flew to Chongqing and met with Li Zhuang. The meeting went smoothly; the local judges and police officers were very cooperative (B1102). Then Wei flew to Shanghai to meet with Chen Youxi, Li's family, and Si Weijiang, a well-known public interest lawyer in Shanghai (B1102; S1101). Wei collected evidence in Shanghai and then in Liaoning Province. However, shortly after the Shanghai meeting, Li's wife decided to change Li's counsel from Wei to Si, claiming that Wei and Li had some "personality conflict" (S1101). Meanwhile, Si suggested that Li's wife keep Yang Xuelin as Li's counsel because it would be inappropriate to change both lawyers who met with Li in Chongqing (S1101). In the end, Si and Yang became Li's defense counsel in the new case.

Although Chen Youxi decided not to represent Li this time, he remained active behind the scene. In addition to contacting other lawyers to represent Li in court, Chen also organized a number of prominent legal scholars and criminal defense lawyers to form a "legal advisory committee" to support Si and Yang (S1104). This advisory committee included Jiang Ping and He Weifang, two of the most prominent legal scholars in China, as well as Zhang Sizhi, a 84-year-old lawyer who served as the legal counsel during the historic Gang of Four trial in 1980. Chen Youxi and Wei Rujiu also served on this twelve-person committee, which was described by a law professor in Beijing as the "12 Angry Men," borrowing the title of a classic American movie about a jury trial (Sohu_20110503).

On April 19, the new Li Zhuang trial opened at the Chongqing Jiangbei District People's Court. The hearing lasted for two days and the presiding judge adjourned the trial briefly in the afternoon of April 20, before the defendant made his final statement. Then the court announced that the trial would continue on April 22. During the hearing, Li's two defense lawyers questioned the jurisdiction of the Chongqing court and presented audio and video evidence, which showed that Li requested that the witness give "objective and true" statements (S1101; B1201). At the end of his defense statement, Si Weijiang expressed his pessimism about the outcome of the case but concluded with a strong message to all Chinese legal professionals: "Justice is not at the present, but we can still wait for it to come!" (GSW_20110420). The trial was reported in real time on the Internet by both the Chongqing media and many lawyers, most notably Chen Youxi, on their Twitter-like microblogs.

On April 22, shortly after the trial reopened, the procurators asked to withdraw the case because of the discrepancies between the prosecution's evidence and the new evidence that defense presented in court. After adjourning the court for an hour, the judges approved the prosecution's request (CX_20110422). This outcome of the new Li Zhuang case pleasantly surprised many legal professionals, including those on the legal advisory committee, some of whom even shed tears when hearing the decision (CYXXSW_20110422). However, it also generated many rumors about the reasons behind the withdrawal. Even Li's defense counsel could only speculate. Many believed that the central leadership intervened in the final stage of the trial (S1104; B1201), while others thought the Chongqing authorities corrected their own mistake to prevent further damage to their reputation (S1101).

On June 11, 2011, Li Zhuang was released from the Chongqing Nanchuan Prison after serving his eighteen-month prison term from the 2009 case. His wife and son flew to Chongqing the day before to meet him. Li was treated well in prison and spent most of his time reading, writing poems, and playing chess and table tennis (B1101; B1201). The prison also arranged for him to give lectures to other prisoners on the criminal justice system and other related topics. Upon meeting his son at the airport, Li said, "Trust your dad. I've never committed any crime before, and I would never commit any crime in the future" (B1101). However, with his practice license revoked by the Beijing Justice Bureau in February 2010, Li's lawyer career ended for good, unless his criminal sentence could be reversed in the future.

POPULISM VS. PROFESSIONALISM: THREE EPISODES IN THE LI ZHUANG EVENT

In this section, we analyze the Li Zhuang case as a social event, focusing on three key episodes, namely, (1) the controversial coverage of the case in the *China Youth Daily*; (2) the allegation of Li's patronage of prostitutes; and (3) the "hidden poem" (藏头诗) in Li's written confession. Together, these episodes forcefully demonstrate the clashes between the two legal ideologies of populism and professionalism in the case.

To some extent, sensationalist media coverage generated much of the public attention on the Li Zhuang case. The *China Youth Daily* article titled "The Surprising Exposure of 'Lawyers Falsifying Evidence' in Chongqing's Anti-Black Campaign, Nearly 20 People Arrested" (ZGQNB_20091214) is a prime example. Published on December 14, 2009, four days after Li's arrest, the article was mostly based on a standard news brief provided by the Chongqing authorities (XJB_20091217). It not only disclosed extensive exchanges between Li and Gong and presented Li in hyperbolic terms, but it also adapted the negative portrayal of lawyers that the Chongqing authorities used in their anti-black campaign. The article produced a damaging effect on the public discussion of the case and provoked outcry from the legal profession.

In the article, Li's profile runs as follows:

> Li Zhuang, age 48, has been around in the legal circle for over a decade. Kangda, the firm where he works, also has considerable 'background' in Beijing. Interested in 'price tags,' Li most certainly came to Chongqing to milk the anti-black cases. When he agreed to represent Gong Gangmo, he was not only interested in 'fishing for people' but also in 'fishing for profit.'
>
> (ZGQNB_20091214)

According to the article, Li allegedly had Gong's worried relatives amass 2.45 million RMB in a matter of days. He would receive an additional 20 to 30 million RMB if he could stop Gong from being put on death row. When he got Gong's family to agree to these terms, Li texted his colleague back in

Beijing, "black enough, stupid people, plenty of money, come quickly!" (够黑, 人傻, 钱多, 速来!) (ZGQNB_20091214). The article also quoted one anonymous Chongqing official, who said that many Beijing lawyers were coming to Chongqing to seek opportunities of "business" and "hidden rules" (潜规则). Meanwhile, the people, the Party, and the country had to foot the bill of the lawyers' unsavory means of identifying clients and winning cases. This Chongqing official also suggested that lawyers only won 5 percent of all criminal cases, but they would not even apologize to their clients for their losses despite the high fees that they charged.

Arguably, the article not only passed judgment on Li but also on the entire Chinese legal profession, including its professional and ethical image. Its narrative appeals to the populist legal ideology, rendering the conducts of lawyers mercenary and disruptive to the judicial system. By violating judicial procedures, lawyers are described as the "horses that harm the herd" (害群之马) and seen as defenders for "enemies of the people" (ZGQNB_20091214). They hurt popular interests and butt heads with the Party-state and its judicial agencies. Moreover, the 5 percent "rate of success" in criminal defense referenced in the article has no scientific basis. As a matter of fact, in China as in other continental law countries, such as Japan and France, the criminal procedure puts much weight on the investigation of the police and procuracy and the dossier that they produce. Hence, when a criminal case reaches the trial stage, the percentage of acquittals is kept to a minimum (Hodgson 2005). In most cases, all that defense lawyers can do is to plead for a lighter sentence. Therefore, it is arbitrary and misleading to define "success" and "failure" in criminal defense as the article did.

Because *China Youth Daily* is a highly regarded national newspaper, within hours the article was reprinted in many national and local media. By equating Li's name with "black lawyers" and exaggerating their abuses, the article exacerbated the plight in which Chinese lawyers have found themselves since the enforcement of Article 306 of the 1997 Criminal Law, the crime of lawyer's perjury. As discussed in Chapter 3, this so-called "Big Stick 306" discourages many lawyers from collecting their own evidence in criminal cases. Li Zhuang was not the first victim of "Big Stick 306." Hundreds of lawyers before him had been charged with fabricating evidence since the crime was established in 1997 (Halliay and Liu 2007). The difference between the Li Zhuang case and the previous cases is that Chongqing capitalized on the popular support for the anti-black campaign to lay bare before the public the problem of lawyers fabricating evidence.

The Chinese legal profession is generally critical of Article 306. For more than a decade, lawyers and bar associations had called for its revocation or revision. When the *China Youth Daily* article was published, it immediately generated much online criticism from lawyers. For instance, the day after the article was published, Chen Youxi, who later became Li's counsel, wrote a lengthy essay in response titled "The Sinking of the Rule of Law: A Critique on the Extraordinary Article of the *China Youth Daily*" and posted it on his personal website (CYXXSW_20091215). In the next few days, Chen wrote several other essays related to the Li case that generated considerable attention and discussion on the Internet. Chen's insightful analysis of the case was one of the reasons why he was invited by Gao Zicheng to represent Li.

Evidence of professionalism can be clearly observed in the thousands of lawyer critiques on this *China Youth Daily* article. Some lawyers argued that it essentially conducted a trial by media in which Li was found guilty and, thus, violated the presumption of innocence as a principle of adjudication (CYXXSW_20091215). Other lawyers suspected that the media leaked much evidence to the public before the trial began, evidence that not even the procuracy and the defense lawyers had the right to disclose (FYFZ_20091217). After reading the article, a number of lawyers contacted the two reporters demanding that they disclose the source for the exposé on the notorious text message that Li allegedly sent to his colleagues. Some even requested that the reporters formally apologize to all Chinese lawyers (FYFZ_20091215). It is not an exaggeration to say that the *China Youth Daily* article turned the plight of one Beijing lawyer in Chongqing into an event of collective action, in which the entire Chinese legal profession mobilized and fought against media and public prejudices toward lawyers. In later media reports, the rapid and strong reactions from the lawyer community presented a counter-narrative to the original negative discourse on the Li Zhuang case and made the conflict between populism and professionalism a salient theme throughout the case.

The mixture of professional and moral evaluations on Li Zhuang can not only be found in the *China Youth Daily* article, but also in another episode in which Li was accused in court of enjoying the free service of prostitutes. In the last round of court argument during Li's first trial, one of the procurators suddenly accused of Li of living in a five-star hotel suite that cost 6,000–7,000 RMB a night and where he enjoyed the service of prostitutes free of charge (TY_20091231). Li immediately replied, "What prostitute? Your friend? What is her name? You are a state procurator, you have to be responsible for your words!" (CYXXSW_20100101). Li's counsel, Chen Youxi, too, was outraged by the procurator's astonishing outburst and accused her of launching a "moral trial" to damage Li's public image and credibility.

The accusation produced the desired public outcry in court as well as strong protests from Li and his counsel. In China, it is not uncommon for procurators to put the defendant of a criminal case on moral trial as well. In appealing to this populist ideology, they effectively blur the line between law and morality. In the socialist era, populism was often used to magnify the class struggle as one between the people and their enemies (Cohen 1968; Lubman 1999). As such, defendants in criminal cases were considered enemies of the people and should be condemned legally, morally, and publicly. The procurator's moral condemnation of Li merely follows the modus operandi of populist criminal prosecution characteristic of the People's Republic of China since its early years.

Yet the most curious aspect of the prostitution episode is the premeditated and concerted effort between the Chongqing procurator and the media. The same night that the procurator made her accusation in court, a photo of Li, clad only in a bath towel while being arrested for patronizing a prostitute, appeared on the Chongqing page of China's largest online forum Tianya (TY_20091231; FYFZ_20120306). On January 3, 2010, the Chongqing Gaoxin District Public Security Bureau also began its investigation into the matter. A few days after, the *Chongqing Evening Post* published a report on the police investigation with a photo of the place where Li allegedly patronized prostitution (CQWB_20100110). However, it was not long before some Internet observers showed that the photo posted on Tianya had been digitally manipulated to incriminate Li. The police officer in the photo wore summer clothes while Li was allegedly seen hiring prostitutes in November. Indeed, many observers began to suspect that the prostitution episode was a moral trap that the Chongqing authorities set to further mar Li's public image as an unethical lawyer (FYFZ_20120306). In fact, it was curious that the procurator knew about the matter even before the police could investigate it. In this case, the local media played the role of "throat and tongue" (喉舌) in bringing the alleged incident to public attention.

Although strongly criticized by Li's counsel and many other lawyers as libelous and a serious abuse of state power (FYFZ_20100103; FYFZ_20100306), the procurator's groundless accusation of Li in court and the subsequent actions by the police and the Chongqing media had effectively manipulated the public debate and the people's opinion of Li. It is evident that the Chongqing authorities disregarded judicial procedures in this trial and used the law merely as an instrument of class struggle against the people's enemies. Together, state agencies and the media form a powerful populist machine that compels the people to accept the state's verdict of a certain person or case with little resistance. It does this by rendering Li, as well as other defendants in criminal cases, as blameworthy and unethical, deserving the wrath of the people.

Still, the most melodramatic point of the Li Zhuang case is the "hidden poem" episode during his second hearing in February 2010. Many speculated as to why Li completely changed his defense from the first hearing. Some argued that it was only a defense strategy, whereas others suspected that the Chongqing authorities threatened Li (FYFZ_20100202; FYFZ_20100203). A few days after Li made the six-point written confession at the end of the hearing, some clever Internet commentators discovered a hidden message in Li's statement. The first and last Chinese characters of each sentence of Li's confession formed the anagram "[I was] forced to admit guilty to get probation, once released [I would] firmly appeal" (被逼认罪缓刑，出去坚决申诉) (FZW_20100210). This astonishing discovery led many to speculate that Li and the Chongqing authorities made a "plea bargaining" deal.

In a blog post six months after his release from prison (SinaBlog_20111223), Li revealed that, as a defense technique, he proposed to a high-ranking public security official after the first trial that he would confess to his crime if the second trial could be opened to the public and he could get probation as the final sentence. The Chongqing authorities warmly welcomed this proposal as it would mitigate some of the procedural problems during Li's first hearing and change the unfavorable public opinions at the time. However, Li did not fully trust the Chongqing authorities and carefully prepared the "hidden poem" while in jail, which was reminiscent of some scenarios in classic Chinese novels. The Chongqing authorities also did not keep their promise to Li and gave him an eighteen-month final sentence.

Still, Li's admission to the charges was a turning point in the case. Before then, Li received support from nearly all lawyers in China as well as many legal scholars, who were disturbed by the substantive and procedural problems in the first hearing. Particularly heavy criticism followed the prostitution episode. In response, the Chongqing authorities changed their strategies in the second hearing. They permitted an open trial and let witnesses appear in court. Although these witnesses were apparently "trained" beforehand, the trial procedure itself was relatively open and just. To a large extent, the second hearing remedied many procedural problems of the first hearing. Meanwhile, Li's public image collapsed after his confession in the courtroom. Even some lawyers began to question his moral and ethical standards (FYFZ_20100204; FYFZ_20100210). If it were not for the "hidden poem," the Li Zhuang case would have become an "iron case" that clarified all the questions and observed all the legal procedures, as the Chongqing authorities claimed (CCTV_20091226; CJ_20100321).

By contrasting the first and second hearing of the 2009 case, we can see that the Chongqing authorities initially pushed populism to its limit, generating widespread negative reactions to the case. However, when they tried to correct their previous mistakes, the authorities turned toward professionalism. When the six witnesses and two police officers were cross-examined during the second hearing, and when Li's confession was recorded in the court documents, the formal rationality of legal professionalism was superimposed onto the populist substantive justice. As a result, Li did not become a martyr of Chinese lawyers or get the freedom he hoped for. Instead, he became a victim of the populist legal ideology that the Chongqing authorities embodied in this case.

A MILESTONE OF PROFESSIONAL COLLECTIVE ACTION

For the most part, populism trumped professionalism in the legal proceedings of the Li Zhuang case. Nonetheless, the case also became a milestone for the collective action of the Chinese legal profession, especially the progressive elites. It was the first time that a large number of lawyers, scholars, and other legal professionals from all over China voluntarily mobilized for a common cause, that is, to challenge the abusive use of "Big Stick 306" on criminal defense lawyers. Hence, it is important to trace the process of professional mobilization in the Li Zhuang case, in order to understand the key turning point by which the Chinese legal profession evolved from a disintegrated, sometimes polarized, occupational group to a nascent but increasingly strong and cohesive professional community.

When the Li Zhuang case first made the headlines in late 2009, the Chinese legal profession was sharply divided. Whereas many lawyers were sympathetic to Li's arrest and condemned the abusive use of Article 306, some also expressed criticism of Li's alleged unethical behavior in the Gong Gangmo case. For example, several lawyers mentioned the fact that Li was an "urban Beijing lawyer" (京城律师) whose law firm had high-level political connections (FYFZ_20100201). Some suspected that the primary motivation behind Li's defense for Gong was to make money. That was also why many Beijing lawyers became counsel for "black gang leaders" such as Gong, who could afford their exorbitant fees (FYFZ_20100206).

It is also telling to compare the opinions of lawyers with those of procurators. At the initial stage of the case, an overwhelmingly large number of procurators on the Law Blog (法律博客, fyfz.cn) website were critical of Li's behavior and supported the use of Article 306. For instance, a procurator working in a basic-level people's procuracy posted three cases of lawyer's perjury to demonstrate the validity of Article 306 in punishing lawyers who induced witnesses to fabricate evidence (FYFZ_20091222). Another procurator expressed gratitude to the *China Youth Daily* journalists for revealing the "hidden rules" (潜规则) in the Chinese legal profession, namely, lawyers often charge a large sum of money without playing a substantive role in criminal cases, whereas procurators are poorly paid but assume vital responsibilities (FYFZ_20091222).

Li's first hearing generated a notable change of tone online among legal professionals. Criticisms were prevalent on the procedural problems that emerged during the trial. A procurator, for example, openly expressed his disappointment in the performance of the Chongqing procurators in court, particularly their blunt ignorance of some key pieces of evidence such as the video of Li and Gong's meeting and the injury on Gong's wrist (FYFZ_20100103). Furthermore, the Chongqing procurator's moral accusation of Li hiring prostitutes generated nearly uniform condemnation among lawyers, judges, and procurators (FYFZ_20091231; FYFZ_20100110). A sense of professional solidarity based on the common belief in legal proceduralism began to emerge.

The growing outrage toward the Chongqing authorities and the sympathy for Li Zhuang vanished, however, when Li openly admitted to the charge in his second hearing. Although many suspected a "plea bargaining" deal between Li and the authorities, Li's confession still betrayed the faith that lawyers, scholars, and other legal professionals had in him after his defiant actions in the first hearing. This was a turning point not only for the trial itself, but also for the collective action of the legal profession. Both online and offline, many lawyers started to distinguish themselves from Li, who was no longer regarded as a brave member of the criminal defense bar, but as a coward, a reckless opportunist, or a mindless money-seeker (FYFZ_20100204; B1002; K1005). Many lawyers whom we interviewed in 2010 admitted that, after the Li case, they became more cautious in their criminal defense work (B1002; K1001; K1002; K1005).

However, the legal community also made efforts to restore the reputation of Li Zhuang and challenge the verdict. For instance, Xu Xin, a law professor at the Southwest University of Political Science and Law in Chongqing at the time, who sat in the audience during the second hearing in February 2010, pointed out in a blog post that Li's confession was merely a defense strategy and his performance in court was even more professional than his two defenders (FYFZ_20100203). He Jiahong, a law professor in Beijing, organized a virtual trial of the case on the Law Blog following the Anglo-American trial procedure (FYFZ_20100321), with dozens of participants serving various roles.

In the end, the "jury," consisting of mostly legal professionals and law students, returned a "not guilty" verdict (FYFZ_20100422).

Bar associations did not support the collective action of Chinese lawyers during the Li Zhuang case. On the contrary, bar associations and justice bureaus seek to restrain lawyers from mobilizing. Although the BLA sent a five-person investigation team to Chongqing shortly after Li's arrest, the team only held a press conference after the trip. It called for Beijing lawyers to "stay calm and rational"; at the same time, it "hoped and believed that the Chongqing judicial authorities would handle the case according to the law" (RMW_20091220). Meanwhile, after Li was convicted in the second hearing, the BBOJ promptly revoked his lawyer license on February 20, 2010. An informant in Kunming told us that the local bar association distributed relevant documents after the case to caution local lawyers (K1004). Throughout the case, the ACLA kept a low profile and only posted a few articles on its website that discussed the general difficulties of criminal defense lawyers without references to a specific case.

The powerlessness of bar associations and justice bureaus in this case clearly demonstrates their weak positions in China's political system. As we have shown in Chapter 4, in ordinary Article 306 cases, bar associations sometimes played important roles in helping lawyers in trouble; but in politically sensitive cases or cases against higher-level state agencies, their input was usually minimal because they are controlled by justice bureaus and Party mechanisms. In the new Li Zhuang case, some bar associations and justice bureaus even sent notices to local lawyers, forbidding them to "discuss, participate, or make a defense for the case" (GSW_20110422). It was not until the day Li was released from prison that the *China Newsweek* magazine published an interview with the ACLA President on the case (ZGXWZK_20110611). Deeply disappointed, one lawyer observed: "In China, it is not the criminal defendants who have the right to remain silent, but the bar associations." (FYFZ_20110630)

Yet, not all Chinese lawyers were prevented from discussing, participating, and defending in the new Li Zhuang case. In fact, it was precisely in the 2011 case that lawyers, scholars, legal journalists, and other legal professionals from all over China demonstrated an extraordinary degree of collective solidarity. Chen Youxi's behind-the-scene mobilization of progressive elite lawyers and scholars is a good case in point. Chen's bold defense for Li in the original case in 2009–2010 earned him much renown and respect in the legal community. In the 2011 case, he was able to use this asset as well as his acquaintance with a few well-known rights defenders in Beijing and Shanghai to assemble a good defense team for Li and a prestigious twelve-person legal consulting committee.

While most members of the legal consulting committee served merely a symbolic role, He Weifang, a law professor at Peking University and one of the most respected public intellectuals in China, posted on his blog an open letter to the legal community in Chongqing titled "For the Rule of Law, For the Ideal in Our Hearts" (SinaBlog_20110412). In this letter, He questioned the procedural problems during Chongqing's anti-black campaign, particularly the Li Zhuang case, and called for judges and legal professionals in Chongqing to act according to their legal obligations and independently from the political will. At the end of the letter, He directly addressed Wang Lijun, the Chongqing Public Security Bureau Chief who later fled to the US Consulate in Chengdu and triggered the fall of Bo Xilai, and asked him to reflect on the consequences of harsh justice and to respect judicial independence. Widely circulated online, the letter elevated public concerns for the new Li Zhuang case both in China and abroad.

But the mobilization of the legal profession did not stop at the elite level. On April 19, 2011, the first day of Li's new trial, hundreds of lawyers, law students, and others voluntarily gathered in front of Jiangbei District People's Court to support Li, including several grassroots activist lawyers who flew in from other provinces such as Hunan and Shaanxi at their own expense (CJ_20110422). Yang Jinzhu, a well-known Hunan lawyer who became an activist in recent years, openly declared on his blogs that he would go to Chongqing to observe the trial (SinaBlog_20110418). When Yang landed in Chongqing and walked out of the arrival hall, a group of approximately thirty locals holding banners with slogans such as "Strike down black-heart lawyer Yang Jinzhu" surrounded and shouted at him until the police came (SinaBlog_20110419). Not surprisingly, neither Yang nor any other lawyers who voluntarily went to the courthouse that day were granted permission to observe the trial.

In comparison to the diversity of opinions formed around the original Li Zhuang case, the new case in 2011 silenced most legal professionals who were critics of Li and supporters of the Chongqing authorities. Even the procurators and police officers who previously supported the crime of lawyer's perjury considered the use of Article 306 in the 2011 case excessive and unacceptable. A good case in point is a widely circulated blog post written by an anonymous member of the Chongqing police or procuracy with the pseudonym "Yan Qi" (燕七). The author admits that his and his colleagues' attitude toward the case have changed greatly over time. When Li was first arrested, many of them were overjoyed because of their long time animosity toward lawyers; after the first trial revealed the details of the case, they became silent and did not want to discuss the case anymore; and when the new case was opened in 2011, they began to discuss the case again and many considered the new prosecution unnecessary because it was "both unreasonable and intolerant" (SinaBlog_20110424).

In short, the Li Zhuang case not only unified lawyers all over China to fight for their own survival, but it also changed the attitude of the broader legal community, which includes judges, procurators, scholars, and police officers, toward criminal defense lawyers. It is a milestone for the Chinese legal profession's political mobilization because it not only generated a collective consciousness in the legal community, but also created a new pattern of collective action championed by the progressive elite members of the Chinese bar. The conclusion will discuss this point in more detail.

POLITICAL IMPLICATIONS

The trial of Li Zhuang was not only an exceptional legal case and a dramatic social event, but it is also a political incident that influenced the central leadership change of the Chinese Communist Party (CCP). Bo Xilai, the then-Party Secretary of Chongqing, was one of the contenders for the membership of the 2012 CCP Politburo Standing Committee. The anti-black campaign, from which the Li Zhuang case originated, was part of Bo's larger populist project aimed at restoring socialist values and ideologies in Chongqing. Its slogan of "singing the red and striking the black" (唱红打黑) was steeped in the fervor of the Cultural Revolution. The campaign rounded up and persecuted local gangs and private entrepreneurs involved in illegal activities, including Li's client and accuser, Gong Gangmo. Like most "strike hard" (严打) campaigns in China (Tanner 1999; Trevaskes 2010), Chongqing's massive anti-black campaign expedited the criminal process by using compulsory measures beyond the scope of the Criminal Procedure Law. It was not long before some Beijing lawyers who went to Chongqing to defend criminal suspects found evidence of police torture (FYFZ_20100809).

To prevent out-of-town lawyers from disrupting the campaign's progress, the Chongqing authorities decided to make an example of Li Zhuang. Li became the primary target for two reasons. First, unlike most Chinese criminal defense lawyers who would defer to the police in their work, Li had serious clashes with the Chongqing police when meeting his client. Second, Li's law firm, Kangda, was directed by Fu Yang, the son of Peng Zhen, a veteran Communist leader who played a vital role in reviving the legal system after the

Cultural Revolution. Some commentators saw Li's arrest as the continuation of the "generational feud" between two high-ranking Communist families (NYT_20120217). According to a key informant, for this reason, the Chinese central leadership followed the Li Zhuang case from its beginning in 2009 and eventually decided to intervene in the 2011 case (B1201).

A full assessment of the political significance of the Li Zhuang case is still premature, but its impact on the political career of Bo Xilai and his associates was remarkable. Before this case, Bo was speculated to be a likely candidate for the next head of the CCP Political-Legal Committee, the top leadership position for the political-legal system (NYT_20110419). However, the trial of Li Zhuang infuriated the Chinese legal community and demonstrated Bo's ignorance of the basic principles of the rule of law. In February 2012, Wang Lijun, Bo's right-hand man in the anti-black campaign, was removed from his position and then investigated by the central government after his unexpected visit to the US Consulate in Chengdu (NYT_20120217). On March 15, 2012, the day after the annual National People's Congress concluded, the central leadership ousted Bo from his Party post. The media identified the Li Zhuang case as one of the contributing factors to Bo's fall (NYT_20120315).

The only time that Bo officially commented on the Li Zhuang case was during the annual National People's Congress in Beijing on March 6, 2010, a month after the 2009 case concluded. He fielded questions from reporters and declared that the Li case was just "an interlude" in the anti-black campaign. Bo insisted that Li's two hearings followed all the procedures and adhered to Chinese law in bringing a lawyer to justice. He emphasized the fact that Li charged his client an exorbitant amount of money and was baffled why the case caused such a stir. To end, Bo said, "In this country, no one is above the law. Whoever violated the law will be punished accordingly. That's our attitude" (XHW_20100306). Two years later, the table turned and Bo himself was ousted from the CCP and later charged with bribe-taking, embezzlement, and abuse of power. Bo's own trial began in Jinan on August 22, 2013, with two prominent criminal defense lawyers from a Beijing law firm acting as his defense counsel. In his defense, Bo acknowledged the importance of defenders in China's criminal justice system and ironically stated, "if only the prosecution's opinions were heard, it would result in a large number of wrongful convictions" (SinaBlog_20130826). On September 22, 2013, the court found Bo guilty of all the three charges and sentenced him to life in prison.

CONCLUSION

Since the late 1970s, the ideologies of populism and professionalism have competed in China's legal discourses and law practice. While socialist popular justice remains the dominant ideology in the judiciary and law enforcement agencies, ideas of the rule of law and procedural justice have become influential in both law schools and the legal profession. The tension between these two legal ideologies is a key for understanding both the progress of China's legal reform and the collective action of the Chinese legal profession. The trial of Li Zhuang is not only a case that offers a rare look into the legal and political clashes between professionalism and populism, but it is also a key turning point in the political mobilization of Chinese lawyers. The different outcomes of the 2009 and 2011 cases suggest that, although populism remains a formidable force in striking the "enemies of the people," professionalism has maintained its ground and gained support from a growing range of legal professionals, state officials, and the public. This "birth of a liberal moment" in China echoes the fight for political liberalism by lawyers and other legally trained professionals in many parts of the world in the past and present (Halliday and Karpik 1997; Karpik 1998; Halliday, Karpik, and Feeley 2007, 2012).

For the mobilization of Chinese lawyers, the Li Zhuang case inspired a new pattern of collective action. It challenges the populist judicial system not only by mobilizing a small group of lawyers, but also by networking widely through social media, particularly Weibo and WeChat. In more recent cases (e.g., the Beihai and Xiaohe cases; see Chapter 7 for details), this new pattern of collective action has become an effective means for lawyers to gain public attention and expose the judicial agencies' procedural problems. The irony here, however, is that lawyers have to rely on media and popular support to fight for professionalism due to their weak position in the judicial system. Further, in these recent cases since the trial of Li Zhuang, it was the elite members of the Chinese legal profession that collectively mobilized and defended their unknown colleagues, whereas before it was the small network of notable activist lawyers in Beijing that took on the highly sensitive cases, as discussed in Chapter 5. The progressive elites who were active in the Li Zhuang case have deep connections with both the state apparatus and the media, and they are able to mobilize these resources to fight for the status of the legal profession and the ideals of professionalism. Toward their collective action, the Chinese government has displayed a greater degree of tolerance compared to its relentless treatment of notable activist lawyers.

Finally, the stark contrast between the Li Zhuang trial and the "Gang of Four" trial from three decades ago signifies the contorted progress of China's legal reform. Although the influence of the ten defense lawyers on the outcome of the "Gang of Four" trial was minimal, it at least showed the symbolic commitment of the Chinese government to protect the legal rights of even the worst criminals of the Cultural Revolution. After three decades, however, Chinese lawyers still suffer from a taboo on effective criminal defense, particularly in politically sensitive cases. In this sense, the Li Zhuang case serves an important educational function. It disseminates the ideologies of legal professionalism and political liberalism, epitomized in lawyer's criminal defense work, to state officials and the general Chinese public. The case is also a timely reminder that the legacy of socialist popular justice is still alive and well in China, and it deserves a more serious treatment in both scholarship and law practice than the general criticism of a "backward movement." The *cause célèbre* of Li Zhuang may have concluded, but the collective action of Chinese lawyers for their survival and the rule of law ideals goes on.

7

Lawyer Activism through Online Networking

The daunting task of survival in the criminal justice system poses significant constraints on Chinese lawyers' collective action. If political embeddedness is so important for many lawyers' self-protection, then how do lawyers mobilize to challenge state power and institutionalize basic legal freedoms? In the previous two chapters, we examined two main approaches of political mobilization for Chinese lawyers, namely, human rights activism and elite mobilization. While they present two complementary forms of collective action in different structural positions of the criminal justice system, these two approaches mostly are adopted by a small number of progressive elites or notable activists in Beijing and other major cities.

In recent years, a third approach of lawyer mobilization has emerged and reached a much larger population of Chinese lawyers, namely, online networking using new media forms such as online forums, blogs, Weibo, and WeChat (Teng 2012b). This new approach of lawyer activism has the potential to transcend occupational and geographic boundaries in the formation of professional ideologies and political agendas. Focusing on lawyers' mobilization in the cyberspace, this chapter reveals the dynamic recent history of Chinese lawyers' online networking and the interactions between their online and offline activities. We begin with a content analysis of the ACLA forum data, arguing that there is a link between stories of lawyer persecution and the rise of their politically liberal discourses in the virtual public sphere. Then we discuss the recent emergence of social media (e.g., Weibo and WeChat) and how "die-hard lawyers" use them to pursue collective action against state power in real cases. We observe that there is an iterative interplay between lawyer mobilization and state responses, a cat-and-mouse sequence of encounters with far-reaching personal and institutional consequences.

POLITICAL LIBERALISM ON THE ACLA FORUM

Until recently, Chinese lawyers had little space for undertaking collective action in their law practices owing to ideological and institutional constraints. They are closely regulated by justice bureaus through bar associations and have to work in a judicial system tightly controlled by the illiberal Party-state (Michelson 2007; Liu 2011). Except for the small number of corporate elite in major business centers (Liu 2006, 2008; Liu and Wu 2016), the vast majority of Chinese lawyers are *de facto* solo practitioners with limited collaboration with other lawyers in their everyday work. Although many of them possess liberal ideals on the rule of law, the moderate state, civil society, and citizenship as lawyers in other social contexts do (Halliday and Karpik 1997; Halliday, Karpik, and Feeley 2007), as we have shown in the previous chapters, these grassroots activists have to bury such ideologies deep in their mundane legal practice.

Consequently, cyberspace has become a rare and important site for Chinese lawyers to express and exchange their political views, an area that resembles a virtual public sphere (Lei 2011; Lei and Zhu 2015). In the earliest data collection for this research, during 2003–2005 we closely observed the nation-wide online discussions at the ACLA lawyer forum and collected sixty threads of messages most relevant to lawyers and political liberalism. A detailed description of the forum and our data collection has been provided in Chapter 1. In this section, we use the ACLA forum data to explore the initial stage of Chinese lawyers' political mobilization, which we called the "birth of a liberal moment" in an earlier work (Halliday and Liu 2007).

In Chapter 3, we presented three cases of lawyer persecution reported on the ACLA forum, but the exchanges among lawyers on this forum went beyond specific complaints about particular grievances and incidents. Frequently the language of protest emanated from underlying premises about the nature of law, professionalism, and the state. These were not often articulated expressly or systematically, but a loose coherence of ideas can be perceived across a variety of discussion threads. The ideological integration of these ideas or the degree of consensus around them must not be overstated for they exist as fragments across many conversations. It is impossible to ascertain how well they either cohere in the minds of the lawyers or represent widely held views that span lawyers and reach across the provinces of China. Yet they occurred with such frequency and through such a variety of combinations that they cannot be ignored.

Most striking in these online discussions are rudiments of an ideology of the rule of law. On one side, lawyers called for restrictions on state power and for restraints in the abuse of public power; as one lawyer articulated, "As long as the phenomenon of power substituting for law exists, the law made by the state could never be properly implemented and executed." (F#256611). There was a strong belief that state power is illicitly manifest in corruption and judicial injustice (F#268312). On the other side, the law must protect private rights. Citizens must be tried fairly, be guaranteed a right to a defense, and prescribed punishments should be publicized for specified crimes. Academic criminal procedure specialists called for defendants to have the right of silence and to be presumed innocent before conviction (F#450228). Furthermore, the due process of law and its procedural meanings were frequently mentioned in discussions of extended detention, confession by torture, judgment before trial, and the police and procuracy's obstruction of lawyers' work (F#455014). These concepts reflect a legal ideology that emphasizes proceduralism, equality, and balance of power in the justice system.

But the concept of the rule of law often sits uneasily in the online discussions alongside the belief that good law comes from a pristine state. While many lawyers believed that courts should not be subject to the will of a person, the court did "stand for the will of the state . . . for the dignity and law of the state" (F#536452). Here and elsewhere the barrier between the rule of law and rule by law is blurred (Ginsburg and Moustafa 2008). Even more prevalent among lawyers on the ACLA forum is the presumption that the rule of law is meaningless without a role for lawyers. It is not only that lawyers ensure the right of a fair trial; most fundamentally, the profession of lawyers is an inherent weapon that is used to fight against the abuse of state power. Indeed, as several forum participants argued, the status and level of influence of lawyers in a society is indicative of the extent of democracy and the rule of law (F#368312; F#536452).

To build the rule of law requires that lawyers must be able to defend themselves. However, they readily acknowledge their weakness in this area. "The unity of lawyers is a feeble, vague, weak and flabby power" (F#536976), said a lawyer from Anhui Province. Another lawyer agreed that "in front of the powerful public power lawyers are actually too feeble" and lamented that China had never witnessed lawyers objecting collectively to injustice (F#537209). Yet, protecting clients demands self-protection. "In our country, if we cannot protect the rights and interest of the lawyers themselves, how can you expect that we can protect the legal interest of the clients?" (F#576076)

To protect themselves, many forum participants proposed that lawyers built a collective identity and capacity for collective action. They needed to forge their own destiny in order to counter the powerful state machine. As one lawyer put it, "Lawyers should unite together in consciousness and respect for others in the profession. When we meet with difficulties we should support, aid and cry out for each other" (F#536976). A theme of mutual support cuts across the forum threads. In this way a professional community, united through a common consciousness, can mobilize through their collective organizations to protect their own. And in protecting their members they will shape civil society and the consciousness of the masses. By not relying on the state-controlled bar associations, which are "more interested in collecting dues than obtaining justice for lawyers" (F#528094), lawyers in China must "unite together and dominate our own destiny by ourselves" (F#537209).

It follows that there is a direct contingency between a rule-of-law society and lawyers' collective action. Yet several lawyers acknowledged that even together they could not stand alone against the power of the state or the arbitrariness of unrestrained local officials. Although many strong voices expressed these themes in one thread after another, not all lawyers agreed that the government could not be trusted. When responding to stories of lawyer persecution, some would tell the lawyers in trouble to "trust the government and the Party" and to rely upon the MOJ, the local justice bureau, or the ACLA (F#440419). Still, these were minority voices on the forum, surprisingly unrepresentative given that these conversations were taking place on a site organized by the ACLA, which in turn is regulated and constituted by the MOJ.

Throughout the threads that relate to political liberalism there are structural critiques of the system of justice and state power more generally. The plight of Chinese defense lawyers results from the continuing imbalance of power in the criminal justice system. The root of this imbalance of power in the criminal process lies in the power structure of the Chinese state. The MPS, the SPP, and the SPC are three more powerful actors in both legislative and administrative activities than the MOJ – the state regulatory agency for lawyers. Since the PPC regard themselves as an integrated "iron triangle" for striking crimes, officials and staff in these three agencies often are perceived to be hostile to defense lawyers. Lawyers' low status in the criminal process is further undermined by the fact that the ACLA and local lawyers' associations are subject to the regulation of the MOJ and local justice bureaus and thus enjoy very limited professional autonomy. A lawyer from Zibo, Shandong Province, commented on the consequence of this imbalance of power:

> Lawyers have an extremely unequal position compared with the PPC. In such conditions, relying on the self realization of the PPC to promote the change in lawyers' status is like looking for fish in the forest (缘木求鱼).
> (F#556170, August 8, 2004, 11:21pm, Shandong Province)

Overwhelmingly on the ACLA forum, however, lawyers enunciated heroic values that captured something of the revolutionary zeal of earlier generations of Chinese. There were more than a few hints that the zeal for the rule of law substituted for the loss of faith in an earlier revolutionary ideology. The heroes of the criminal defense bar were animated by their belief that they were the last bastion between abusive public power and helpless individuals. Above all, they believed that lawyers were harbingers of democracy, heralds of the rule of law. From China's far west, a lawyer from Xinjiang called upon leaders from democratization movements in East Asia:

> It is because the profession is filled with danger that we are the tower of strength in the society. Think about Chen Shui-bian in Taiwan, who passionately defended the people of Meili Island in his early life. And think about Roh Moo-hyun in Korea, who pled for the students in the democratic movement under the tyranny ruled by Park Chung-hee. So that now Taiwan and Korea have accomplished democracy and prosperity at the present time. It is just that we should pay the cost for democracy!!
> (F#556755, August 9, 2004, 10:33pm, Xinjiang Uyghur Autonomous Region)

A revolutionary rhetoric can be found in many of these hundreds of messages. It is as if the fervor for an abandoned ideology is being transferred to a new set of hopes. The spirit of sacrifice, the call to unite for the common good, and the responsibility to defend the weak and oppressed all have revolutionary resonance. And some found it in the rule of law. In response to a lawyer persecution case to be discussed below, another lawyer even appropriated the opening words of the Chinese national anthem to the plight of lawyers: "Rise, all people who are not willing to be slaves. Use our flesh to build our new Great Wall." (F#546617)

Skeptics of online activism may dismiss the strong liberal discourses on the ACLA forum as merely "talking the talk" without any concrete action or consequence. Nonetheless, we argue that this "birth of a liberal moment" represents the initial stage in the political mobilization of Chinese lawyers, namely, lawyers who share similar beliefs and ideologies finding a rare virtual space to exchange their ideas. The opening up of such a space is the crucial starting point for turning scattered ideas and thoughts regarding political liberalism into grievances and, later, collective action. It is a social process analogous to the "naming, blaming, and claiming" in the transformation of disputes (Felstiner, Abel, and Sarat 1980) – the value of naming their legal and political ideals should not be underestimated.

FROM LIBERAL IDEOLOGIES TO ONLINE MOBILIZATION

In spite of the strong liberal voices on the ACLA forum, they could not constitute mobilization without specific grievance-generating events. Not surprisingly, stories of lawyer persecution were the main triggers of Chinese lawyers' collective action that were reported in the cyberspace. In Chapter 3, we discussed three case stories reported on the ACLA forum during 2003–2004. These three cases are both ordinary and extraordinary: they are ordinary because the lawyers being persecuted were all routine practitioners with no clear political orientation, but they are also extraordinary because they display instances, and demonstrate the possibility, of collective action that turn online expressions of opinion into tangible actualities. This section analyzes in detail the strong liberal discourses and calls for collective action generated by the three lawyer persecution cases.

To build the rule of law, reiterated the commentators on these cases, requires that lawyers must be able to defend themselves. Protecting clients demands self-protection. In reply to the lawyer SOS case, a lawyer from Shandong Province asked, "Is it the case that Chinese lawyers only have the responsibilities to protect the rights of the clients, but no right or capacity to protect ourselves?" And with a touch of sarcasm he continued to wonder if this state of affairs was "the goal of the socialist system of lawyers with Chinese characteristics?!" (F#576076). In another reply he put the call for collective action more bluntly:

> Yes, lawyer colleagues, we should unite to protect our own legal rights. Lawyers are the protector of rights but we cannot protect our own rights, this is the tragedy of China's rule of law! . . . To unite is the only way out for lawyers!
>
> (F#612439, November 13, 2004, 10:15am, Shandong Province)

Over and over again, lawyers called upon each other to take collective action. In response to the SOS plea, one lawyer wrote, "What to do? There is never any Christ nor any immortal emperor. The key is our lawyers' collective cohesion and the fighting spirit" (F#526705). Lawyers cannot expect others to do what they will not do themselves; "Every lawyer needs to stand up and fight to do his/her duty, otherwise they will all go down one by one" (F#460363). And in an echo of a classic cry from internal opponents to National Socialism in Nazi Germany, another lawyer wrote:

> If we still tolerate this, the next victim might be ourselves. If lawyers cannot protect their own rights, how would you make people believe that you could protect the rights of clients? Gentlemen, if we tolerate all this just because we

haven't got hurt, just to guarantee our own good lives, then we would not be qualified as lawyers.

(F#528094, June 30, 2004, 9:36am, location unknown)

One course of action offers little prospect. Lawyers "can't rely on leaders of the lawyers association because they are appointed by the government." Bar associations are "more interested in collecting dues than obtaining justice for lawyers" (F#528094) and they are like "parents who eat dishes without managing anything . . . the parents did not fulfill their responsibilities, [and] our brothers and sisters got hurt" (F#634726). Even the Lawyers Law regulates rather than protects (F#450228). The necessity of mutual support, independent of state-controlled bar associations, rings across the forum threads. In response to the SOS appeal, another lawyer stated:

> For Whom the Bell Tolls? For you, for me, for every one of us. When we see misfortune come to other people and feel lucky, we will eventually find out: when the catastrophe comes, there is already nobody to save us. I cry to every lawyer who still has some conscience, stand up, stand together, do our best to save our colleague.
>
> (F#460363, April 25, 2004, 10:35pm, location unknown)

In this way a professional community, united through a common consciousness, can mobilize through their collective organizations to protect their own. And in protecting their members they will shape civil society and the consciousness of the masses since a vulnerable lawyer is "a misfortune for China's rule of law, a misfortune for the Chinese people!" (F#460363). By not relying on bar associations or the government, lawyers in China must "unite together and dominate our own destiny by ourselves" (F#537209).

The lawyer who posted the tragic story of lawyer Wen Zhicheng of Ruijin City understood its lessons precisely:

> Our nation should obtain the cultivation of law and establish a legal professional community. But, from this case, how far away we are from the establishment of a legal professional community! How far away from the establishment of a rule-of-law society! Every lawyer should have the spirit of sacrifice to realize the cultivation of law. All lawyers should unite together to protect our rights! The rights of lawyers should be respected, the social status of lawyers should be improved, the legal community should be truly established, the law practitioners should be universally respected in society and the rule of law should be realized. It is really a multi-benefit thing. Why do I, we, and all the people not stand up to strive for this goal?!
>
> (F#620344, December 4, 2004, 11:07am, Sichuan Province)

Efforts to construct a lawyers' collective consciousness can be exemplified through the individual lawyer who risks his or her safety by speaking on behalf of the collectivity. In a notable case reported on the ACLA forum, lawyer Shen Zhigeng defended his colleague Zhang Jianzhong, the director of Beijing Gong He Law Office, against accusations of forging evidence, with the words, "I was here at present to defend Zhang Jianzhong not only on behalf of myself, but also to express the collective voice of all the lawyers" (F#368312). Ma Guangjun saw his trial and vindication as a kind of test case: "I think that because this case not only related to me, an individual named Ma Guangjun, but it related to the issue of a professional environment for a lawyer . . . when a lawyer is fulfilling his duty in a justified and legal way" (F#536452).

It is evident from the ACLA forum discussions on the three cases that a professional and political consciousness shared by lawyers across China can be generated from the persecution of individual law practitioners at the grassroots level. Compared to the general discussions on political liberalism in the previous section, discussions in response to particular cases transformed abstract liberal ideas into specific grievances and collective consciousness. The semi-anonymous nature of the ACLA forum enabled politically liberal lawyers to openly express their desire for collective action without the threat of official sanctions. In a sense, it created a public sphere analogous to the French salons in the eighteenth and nineteenth centuries, in which political debates were staged and public opinions were formed (Karpik 1988). To be sure, this collective consciousness in cyberspace remained primitive and volatile in the heyday of the ACLA forum, but the move from abstract liberal ideologies to concrete consciousness of political mobilization is of critical importance in Chinese lawyers' collective action against arbitrary state power.

"DIE-HARD" LAWYERING IN THE AGE OF SOCIAL MEDIA

When we first began researching the ACLA lawyer forum in the mid-2000s, we labeled it the "birth of a liberal moment?" with a question mark (Halliday and Liu 2007) because it was unclear whether this collective consciousness in cyberspace would develop into something more concrete and substantial. Indeed, the ACLA forum remained an active site of online mobilization only until around 2006–2007, when it frequently became read-only and was eventually shut down altogether due to the political sensitivity of some of the discussion threads. We were fortunate to be able to systematically collect data from its most vibrant period, but the increased state control over the Internet in the mid- to late 2000s (Yang 2009) posed a serious threat to the livelihood of this and many other online legal communities.

Nevertheless, the decline of the ACLA forum and many other legal professional forums was accompanied by the rise of social media in China, notably blogs, microblogs such as Weibo, and, most recently, WeChat. In the late 2000s, blogs gained popularity among Chinese legal professionals. In addition to the general blog sites hosted by mainstream websites such as Sina or Sohu, several blog sites specializing in law-related topics were also established in this period. The most notable one was the Law Blog (法律博客, www.fyfz.cn), hosted by the website of the SPP. Despite its affiliation with the SPP, an institution seemingly unfriendly to criminal defense lawyers, this blog site soon became an important public space for scholars, lawyers, judges, procurators, and other legal professionals to post on to discuss legal news, cases, academic papers, and so on. In particular, during the first Li Zhuang trial in 2009, the Law Blog became one of the most active online spaces for lawyers, scholars, procurators, and other legal professionals to debate on various aspects of the case (see Chapter 6). That period was the climax of the blog's popularity.

Nevertheless, the blog, as a relatively self-centric form of new media, has natural defects for serving as a means of political mobilization. Compared to the earlier form of online forum, it is less interactive and often has lengthier contents. Although readers can comment on a blog post and interact with the blog host, heated discussions over a long period of time as we observed in some discussion threads of the ACLA forum were rarely seen on the Law Blog website. Even during the Li Zhuang case, the liberal sentiments expressed by lawyers on the Law Blog were not as strong as those in the earlier ACLA forum discussions over similar Article 306 cases. This may be partly due to the fact that the Law Blog is hosted by the SPP, but an equally important reason is the technical deficiency of the blog as a medium for mobilization – it is more suitable for long scholarly essays than for short and interactive exchanges among law practitioners.

But the limitation of blogs was soon overcome by the arrival of a revolutionary form of social media, namely, Twitter-like microblogs. While several microblogging service providers are still competing in the Chinese market, the most popular one since 2010 has been Weibo (www.weibo.com), hosted by Sina, one of the largest gateway websites in China. A large number of Chinese lawyers registered for Weibo using their real names, including many renowned criminal defense lawyers. In "Season 2" of the Li Zhuang case in 2011 (see Chapter 6), Li's defenders and the "legal consulting committee" behind them successfully used blogs and Weibo to increase media and public attention on this case, which eventually led to the intervention from the central leadership. It was also the first time that Chinese lawyers all over the country mobilized online and voluntarily flew to the same location to exercise influence in a real case.

Since we have provided a full-fledged analysis of the Li Zhuang case in Chapter 6, in the rest of this section we focus on a subsequent case in which lawyers used blogs and Weibo to mobilize collectively against judicial and political power, namely, the Beihai case in Guangxi Zhuang Autonomous Region. In this case, a group of lawyers formed a professional network across different regions of China through microblogging interactions and then flew to the site of the case one after another to defend the accused or to support their colleagues. An even more striking fact is that this online group consisted of lawyers who belong to the professional groupings of progressive elites, notable activists, and grassroots activists, three categories of lawyers who rarely crossed paths in their law practice before the Li Zhuang case. The following account is based on Sida Liu's online ethnography in 2011–2013 by following the blogs and Weibo accounts of several leading participants of the Beihai lawyer group.

On June 15, 2011, Yang Jinzhu, a well-known Hunan lawyer who became an activist in recent years, posted on his blog and Weibo that a lawyer named Yang Zaixin in Beihai, Guangxi Zhuang Autonomous Region, was detained under Article 306. The next day, Yang updated his post and announced that, in fact, four lawyers were detained or put under residential surveillance in this case. As the Beihai case occurred just a few days after the release from prison of Li Zhuang, who was also a victim of Article 306, it immediately drew great attention on Weibo. In one of his blog posts, Yang Jinzhu openly called for the formation of a "lawyer group" (律师团) to provide legal assistance to the four accused lawyers. Later on the same day, Yang made another post and declared the formation of a seven-person lawyer group, expected to go to Beihai on Sunday, June 19. Over the next a few days, Yang posted online photos of the case file of the original intentional injury case for which the four lawyers were defense counsel. Several other lawyers, including the progressive elite lawyer Chen Youxi, one of Li Zhuang's defenders, also openly called for the ACLA's attention on this case. Facing increasing pressure from media and Internet attention, the Beihai Municipal Public Security Bureau held a press conference and confirmed the detention or residential surveillance of the four lawyers on June 21. In the meantime, the ACLA heard the case reports from Yang Jinzhu and the Guangxi Lawyers Association and expressed support for the accused lawyers.

On June 26, 2011, six lawyers flew to Beihai from Beijing, Shandong, and Yunnan, respectively. Two days later, Chen Guangwu and Zhang Kai, two of the six lawyers, met with Yang Zaixin, one of the four local lawyers under detention. Later on the same day, the three other lawyers under compulsory measures were released and returned home, whereas Yang Zaixin was formally arrested by the order of the local procuracy on June 29. In the next two weeks, more lawyers joined the lawyer group and flew to Beihai to provide legal assistance not only to Yang Zaixin, but also to the criminal suspects and witnesses of the injury case in which Yang and his colleagues served as defense counsel. On July 11, three members of the lawyer group went to Beijing to report the case to the ACLA and the MOJ. By July 13, the total number of lawyers in this group reached twenty, and included several high-profile progressive elite lawyers in Beijing.

On July 12, Fang Ligang, a Shaanxi lawyer who recently joined the lawyer group, went to the Beihai Municipal Detention Center to meet his client Pei Rihong, a newly added defendant of the injury case. When Fang was going through security check at the Center, the local police officers asked him to go through the security door six times, searched his body repeatedly, and eventually rejected his meeting request. The incident was soon posted on the Weibo as "a discriminating and insulting treatment" suffered by the lawyer group.

In the evening of July 18, four members of the lawyer group were physically attacked by an unknown crowd of locals in their hotel rooms. Chen Guangwu, a Shandong lawyer, tried to videotape the scene but he was beaten by the crowd and his video camera robbed. The locals also took away several volumes of case files. The lawyers called the police but no police officer appeared until half an hour later. Even after the police had arrived, the local crowd continued to attack the lawyers and threatened them with violence if they did not give up their defense work. Li Jinxing, another lawyer in the group, was violently hit in the head, pushed to the ground, and then taken to hospital in an ambulance. Over the next three days, the lawyer group continued to experience sporadic attacks from unknown local crowds and the tension between out-of-town lawyers and the local police escalated. The whole incident was "broadcasted live" on Weibo, with photos of lawyers' physical injuries posted there, and it greatly increased public concern for the lawyer group in Beihai. In response to this incident, the ACLA made an announcement to express its serious concerns about the illegal violation of lawyers' right of defense.

Chi Susheng, one of the few lawyer representatives in the NPC, saw the July 18 incident on Weibo during a business trip and immediately wrote "I will go to Beihai as soon as possible" on her Weibo account. Three days later, she arrived in Beihai and met with the lawyer group. On July 22, accompanied by staff members of the local people's congress, Chi went to the Beihai Municipal Public Security Bureau to investigate the earlier conflicts between the lawyer group and the local police and residents. She also visited the municipal procuracy and court in the same afternoon and urged the judicial officials there to effectively protect lawyers' procedural rights. Despite the short period of her visit to Beihai, Chi's identity as a NPC representative not only provided conspicuous symbolic support to the lawyer group, but also curbed the growing local antagonism toward out-of-town lawyers in this case. The visit also boosted the collective solidarity among lawyers in Beihai and those observing the incident through social media, especially considering the long distance between Beihai, a city in the far southwest of China, and Chi's home province Heilongjiang in the far northeast.

On July 26, the Beihai Intermediate People's Court notified the defense counsel, mostly comprised from the lawyer group, that the trial for the injury case would be opened on August 8. The lawyer group assigned ten lawyers, including one local lawyer in Beihai and nine out-of-town lawyers from Beijing, Shandong, Shaanxi, and Guangdong, as the defense counsel for the five defendants. During August 4–6, all the defense lawyers arrived in Beihai to prepare for the trial. However, on the evening of August 6, the court suddenly notified the lawyers that the trial would be postponed to September 6 due to the procedure of calling witnesses. The nine out-of-town lawyers had no choice but to return home. On September 3, the court postponed the trial again to September 20. Many lawyers suspected that these were strategies that the local judicial agencies had adopted to increase the costs and inconveniences of the lawyer group.

When the trial finally opened on the morning of September 20, the lawyer group reshuffled their defense team and ten lawyers appeared in court. One and half hours into the trial, the presiding judge suddenly paused the cross-examination and asked one of the defendants if he agreed to use the two lawyers that his relatives had retained as his defenders. The defendant hesitated and then answered "No." Chen Guangwu, one of his defense counsel, immediately requested the court to adjourn so that he could communicate with his client. The presiding judge rejected this request and asked the two lawyers to leave the courtroom. The lawyers protested and left the courtroom as a group. The trial was adjourned. The presiding judge asked the lawyer group to discuss the defense matters in the early afternoon, but the lawyers refused and the court had to postpone the trial again. During the trial, several members of the lawyer group posted to their Weibo accounts from the courtroom to expose the procedural problems of the trial.

Due to the long duration of the Beihai case and the repeated adjournments of the trial, the lawyer group's total expenses exceeded 200,000 yuan by late September. All lawyers in the group were volunteers and paid most of their own expenses. On September 24, the lawyer group posted a fundraising letter on blogs and Weibo to ask for financial assistance from the public. In three days, the account they provided had received more than 450,000 yuan, and the total amount of funding support reached 750,000 yuan by the end of the case. The successful fundraising campaign fully demonstrated the power of social media in mobilizing Chinese lawyers. In comparison to the ACLA forum, Weibo constitutes not only a (cyber)space for observation and comments, but also a crucial link for social action between individual lawyers in real cases and the broader lawyer community and the general public.

On October 14, the trial resumed and the court designated a local lawyer for the defendant to replace the two out-of-town lawyers retained by his relatives. The court initiated a procedure for the exclusion of illegal evidence and several police officers appeared in court to give testimonies. On October 21, the victim's relatives attacked two members of the lawyer group outside the courthouse. The defense lawyers protested until midnight and the news was rapidly circulating on Weibo. Finally, the court offered to provide special vehicles for the lawyers to go to the court hearing. The twenty-two-day marathon hearing was concluded on November 4, 2011, without a verdict.

On March 15, 2012, Yang Zaixin was given residential surveillance in a building near the court, with the close monitoring of four police officers and the armed police. Six months later, on September 13, Yang was given the procedural decision of obtaining guarantor pending trial (取保候审), a procedure similar to bail in other countries. In the meantime, several members of the lawyer group continued to provide legal assistance to suspects and witnesses of the injury case. On January 19–20, 2013, a symposium on the Beihai case organized by the lawyer group was held in Beihai and the lawyers who attended the symposium published "A Letter Calling for the Immediate Release of the Defendants of the Beihai Case." On February 6, 2013, the court finally rendered the verdict of the Beihai case and acquitted five of the defendants. The procuracy also withdrew all the charges against Yang Zaixin. After more than 600 days under compulsory measures, Yang finally regained his freedom as both a lawyer and a citizen.

It took the court over a year to reach the final verdict of the Beihai case, but the online mobilization of Chinese lawyers did not pause while waiting for the result. In early 2012, Zhou Ze, a public interest lawyer who worked as a journalist in the *Legal Daily* newspaper and had extensive networks in both the media and the legal profession, organized another lawyer group through Weibo to defend fifty-four defendants in an organized crime case in Xiaohe, Guizhou Province. Although the defendants in this case were not lawyers, the size of the lawyer group grew even bigger than that in the Beihai case, with several prominent criminal defense lawyers in the Li Zhuang and Beihai cases involved (B1506; B1507). Again, using blogs and Weibo, the Xiaohe lawyer group reported on the court hearings in real time from the courtroom and exposed serious procedural violations by the judges and prosecutors. During the trial process, Zhang Lei, a Hunan lawyer with the online username "black stone lawyer" (青石律师), wrote thirty-three dairy entries on this case and posted them on his Weibo account on a daily basis. It is also during the Xiaohe case that the term "die-hard lawyers" (死磕派律师) was coined by Yang Xuelin, a progressive elite lawyer in Beijing and one of Li Zhuang's defenders, in a Weibo post (B1501). After the Beihai and Xiaohe cases, die-hard lawyering through online networking became increasingly common and a virtual community of politically liberal lawyers was emerging in social media.

Yang Xuelin summarizes the strategies of die-hard lawyers in sixteen Chinese characters: "Serious application of legal rules, exposure on the Internet, report and complaint, performance art" (法条较真, 网络揭露, 举报投诉, 行为艺术). Arguably, some die-hard lawyers are more radical than others. Some would send a bag of sweet potatoes to the SPC to caricature the court's incompetence (B1502), or organize peaceful protests or even hunger strikes in front of the courthouse (B1506; B1507), whereas others would rather adhere to legal arguments in the courtroom and official channels of complaints (B1501; B1503; B1512). As a notable activist lawyer commented, die-hard lawyers are not necessarily human rights activists because most of them are "bound by their rules," "try to avoid the most sensitive cases," and "would not receive foreign interviews" (B1405). They choose to "die-hard in specific cases, but not in every case" (B1405). Nevertheless, they mobilize as a group both online and offline, in Beijing and across the country, fighting for citizens' basic legal freedoms in a variety of criminal cases.

THE JULY 2015 CRACKDOWN AND INTERNATIONAL ONLINE MOBILIZATION

By connecting online and offline activities as well as uniting different types of lawyers under the same cause, blogs and Weibo have generated a revolutionary change in the short history of political mobilization among Chinese lawyers. The rise of die-hard lawyering, a form of activist lawyering that combines performativity in the courtroom and in cyberspace (B1502), enables lawyers to become emancipated, albeit temporarily, from their dependence on political embeddedness with the PPC in handling criminal cases (B1501).

The extensive use of social media by die-hard lawyers in the Beihai, Xiaohe, and other recent cases was applauded by many netizens, but it also generated controversies, resentment, and resistance in the PPC. For instance, Zhang Jun, a former vice-president of the SPC, criticized the behavior of lawyer groups during trials as "disturbing court order" (闹庭) at an internal judge training session in May 2012. A few months later, the SPC added a draft article on court orderliness to its implementing interpretation of the 2012 CPL, which forbids lawyers and other litigation participants to make online posts from the courtroom during the hearing. In the same article, the SPC also gave the court the power to sanction lawyers who disturb court order by forbidding them to appear in court for up to six months. Not surprisingly, this draft article caused strong reactions in the lawyer community and the final version of the SPC interpretation removed the sanction clause, yet the restriction on online posting during trial remained. As a result, the "live broadcast" of court hearings, a strategy widely and effectively used by die-hard lawyers in the Beihai case and a few subsequent cases, has disappeared from social media.

Meanwhile, the increasing popularity of WeChat, a social networking app, in China in recent years adds another powerful tool for activist lawyers to organize lawyer groups and discuss their ideas related to political liberalism. In comparison to Weibo, which is public in nature, WeChat enables lawyers to organize private group discussions that could potentially bypass the surveillance of state authorities (B1402; B1534). This was especially important for the several hundred notable activists who had discussed highly sensitive cases through a WeChat network named the "Human Rights Lawyers Group" (B1515; B1520; B1523; B1529). Christian activist lawyers also have their own WeChat group (B1513). As the state security authorities gradually increased their surveillance on such WeChat groups, some notable activists migrated their group to Telegram, a similar app developed by Russian entrepreneurs that enables encrypted exchanges of information (B1518; B1526).

By the spring of 2015, the expanded body of activist lawyers across China were not only networked to each other, principally via the WeChat communities and the immediacy of everyday contacts via Telegram, but many were deeply integrated into global networks of lawyer support groups, international human rights organizations, international governmental bodies, international religious networks, leading-edge international media outlets, and the monitoring and publicity capacities of national governments, not least the US government (see Chapter 5). Nowhere is this better illustrated than in the campaign against Wang Yu and its radical expansion into a nationwide crackdown on hundreds of lawyers and other activists that began on July 9, 2015.

In June 2015, China's official media launched an unprecedented public disinformation campaign against Wang Yu, a female commercial lawyer who had emerged as a bold notable activist in the several years following her imprisonment by the railway police for what she asserted was a false charge of beating someone on a station platform in Tianjin. The nationwide attack, labeled by many of her supporters as a "smear campaign" (B1517), included coverage in newspapers such as *People's Daily*, online at People's Net, and on CCTV. The media pieces alleged that this ex-prisoner had beaten someone to death and then "sarcastically" questioned whether she could be an authentic advocate to "represent justice and human rights" (B1522).

Wang Yu's activist peers responded immediately with their own campaign to defend her reputation. As one of them explained:

> Our human rights lawyers are a disadvantaged group and we frequently experience crackdowns. So when that happened we had the idea of "getting together and getting warm" (抱团取暖). So a lot of people tried to publicize online rebuttals. Some lawyers wrote long articles providing testimonies to [her] reputation. Even citizens published recommendations on Weibo. The article mentioned that [she] was in prison before as evidence of [her] reputation. A lot of lawyers organized an advocacy group to speak of [her] rights.
>
> (B1522, Beijing)

Nevertheless, as a relative newcomer to the vanguard of rights activists, Wang Yu did not have strong connections outside China, although her name had arisen in connection with her defense in some newsworthy cases, not least the detention of the five feminists in early 2015, which received extensive media coverage and heightened political awareness overseas (NYT_20150413).

All that changed on July 9, 2015, after Wang Yu dropped off her lawyer husband and sixteen-year-old son at Beijing Capital International Airport, where her son was headed to Australia for further study, and she returned to her apartment. At around 3am Wang Yu texted that her electricity and Internet connections were turned off, and then at 4:17am, that someone was trying to pry open her front door. Then all contact with her went dead. Neighbors later reported that some twenty to thirty police officers had gathered in the early hours for a so-called drug raid and they left the area with someone in custody (CHRLCG_20150710). In the following hours it became immediately apparent that Wang Yu's disappearance – since no one knew who took her or where she was being held – was the beginning of a pre-planned attack on her law firm Fengrui, for some years one of China's boldest centers of activity which accommodated such notable activist lawyers as Zhou Shifeng and Liu Xiaoyuan, who had long represented the controversial Chinese artist Ai Weiwei. Zhou Shifeng, the managing partner, was seized in a hotel in which he was staying. Several other lawyers and administrators in the firm were also detained. Security people entered the firm itself and seized files and computers. Nine days later, on July 18, Zhou was shown on CCTV where he "confessed" – in a manner seemingly scripted from show trials – to alleged "crimes of disturbing court order and social order" in the course of his die-hard lawyering even before he was formally charged by the procuracy.

Through smartphones and the Internet, these disappearances and detentions were almost instantly conveyed to lawyer networks inside China and, within minutes, to networks in Hong Kong and across the world. On July 9, the same day Wang Yu disappeared, 101 activist lawyers nationwide, including some of Beijing's most prominent longtime notable activists, such as Li Heping, Jiang Tianyong, Li Fangping, and Tang Jitian, took the daring step of issuing a public call for her release, which they circulated on social media as widely as censorship would allow inside China. By July 10, international scholars, lawyers, and human rights groups close to the activists, as well as activists residing outside China (e.g., longtime legal academic and rights lawyer Teng Biao), began to mobilize rapidly to inform the media, governments, and international organizations of a massive crackdown that quickly covered all of China, with at least two hundred lawyers taken in for questioning, detained, or disappeared. The lawyers daring to sign the petition to release Wang Yu seemed to be targeted in particular. Radio Free Asia broadcast on July 10 that Wang Yu was missing, "believed detained" (RFA_20150710).

Within twenty-four hours of the initial detentions, international diplomats were in direct contact with notable activists before some were detained and interrogated and after some were released to debrief them on why the government had taken drastic steps against lawyers not seen for decades in China. On July 10, the Hong Kong–based China Human Rights Lawyers Concern Group, a highly vocal NGO with close ties to China's activist lawyers, put out a statement via its Internet listserv calling for help and detailing in microscopic detail the timeline of the initial attack on Wang Yu, her family, and her Fengrui colleagues (CHRLCG_20150710).

International networks came alive. An article in Hong Kong's *South China Morning Post* on the disappearances (SCMP_20150710) was distributed on July 10 to the 1,500 plus specialists across the world in Chinese politics who communicate on the listserve ChinaPol, an instant message board that includes diplomats and many of the most influential journalists that cover

China for prominent media overseas. Amnesty International released a statement on July 11 cataloguing in detail the detainees by name, location, and occupation, criticizing China's top leadership and demanding the "unconditional release of all those detained solely for their work defending human rights" (AI_20150711). On July 12, the US Department of State issued a statement condemning the detention of human rights defenders and strongly urging China "to release all those who have recently been detained for seeking to protect the rights of Chinese citizens" (USDOS_20150712). The European Union issued a statement three days later which pressed China to "release all those detained for seeking to protect . . . the rights of all citizens as recognised by the Chinese Constitution" (EUEA_20150715) and enshrined in the Universal Declaration of Human Rights.

Rapid exchanges crisscrossed the world as lawyers, international NGOs, UN advocacy groups, and the nexus of lawyers', human rights, and international media exchanged information and approaches, confirmed facts, and sought to support one another, as well as exchanged views about forms of leverage that could be applied to China's government, amid parallel releases of stories by the media. The UN Human Rights Council Special Rapporteur issued a statement headlined "Lawyers need to be protected not harassed – UN experts urge China to halt detentions" (UNHR_20150716). The International Service for Human Rights, an international NGO, connected the new incursions on the rights of lawyers to China's rejection of the expression of concern by the UN High Commissioner for Human Rights over China's new National Security Law which "leaves the door wide open to further restrictions on the rights and freedom of Chinese citizens" (ISHR_20150711). Lawyers' defense organizations accompanied human rights appeals for information, release, and forbearance in the ongoing "raids, abductions, detentions, disappearances, summons and searches" (CHRD_20150713).

As Amnesty International's comprehensive and regular updates reinforced the extraordinary scope of the security move against lawyers and activists, divergences in the international legal community, and even between lawyers' groups within a national profession, revealed fissures in the forms of their response to China. By July 13, national and international bar associations in Asia, Australia, North America, and Europe caucused with their members and with one another about forming appropriate responses. The varieties of responses were instructive.

The top leadership of the American Bar Association (ABA) had been alerted about the crackdown by its human rights leaders and academic networks and discussions began on July 11 among the ABA, the International Bar Association, the Council of Law Societies and Bar of Europe, and the

Francophone *Union des Internationale des Avocats*. Many European lawyers' organizations issued independent statements which were brought together as 24 organizational signatories of a July 21 open letter addressed to President Xi Jinping and the MPS by the Dutch lawyers' group, Lawyers for Lawyers. The mix of signatory organizations gathered by Lawyers for Lawyers (L4L) signifies the growing nature of the international legal complex and its ability to mobilize rapidly. The signatories included national bar associations (*DeutscherAnwaltVerein*, the Norwegian Bar Association, The Law Society of England Wales, *Syndicat des Avocats de France*), provincial or city generalist bar associations (The Law Society of Upper Canada, *Ordres des Avocats des Geneve, Amsterdamse Orde van Advocaten*), specialty criminal defense associations (the European Criminal Bar Association), human rights sections of national and international bar associations (the Bar Council of Ireland Human Rights Committee, Solicitors' International Human Rights Group, Bar Human Rights Committee of England and Wales), and other international organizations for human rights or political segments of the lawyer population (The Observatory for the Protection of Human Rights Defenders, the European Democratic Lawyers/*Advocats Europeens Democrates*, and International Association of People's Lawyers). It is noteworthy that this coalition was forged within twelve days of Wang Yu's detention. Its activism and immediacy rested heavily on instant and regular online reporting and monitoring by human rights organizations and international lawyers' groups and the permeability of China's information firewall in both directions.

The Lawyers for Lawyers collective letter, widely circulated on the Internet and posted on its website, strongly condemned "the recent unprecedented and seemingly well-coordinated detention of a large number of human rights lawyers in China" (LFL_20150721). It criticized China's security apparatus for not adhering to the standards of UN global norms on the role of lawyers, human rights, fundamental freedoms, and human rights defenders. The following day, July 22, the world's peak association of lawyers' organizations, the International Bar Association, issued through its Human Rights Institute an open letter to President Xi Jinping "to express its deep concern at the unprecedented number of lawyers, human rights activists and support staff who have faced arrest, questioning and detention in China" (IBAHRI_20150722). If they were not already aware of the situation in China, this letter gave notice to its membership of 55,000 individual lawyers and more than 190 bar associations and law societies spanning all continents of the gravity of the crackdown and set the tone for lawyers' reactions to the incident.

The situation in the United States, however, provides a snapshot of the longstanding paradox of lawyers' ability to mobilize collectively across the diversity of their ideological and economic interests, reproducing a pattern earlier documented by Powell (1988) and Halliday (1987). A 145-year-old bar association with more than 24,000 members, the City Bar of New York, over the signature of its president, wrote an open letter, signed by its president, to President Xi Jinping on July 28 which expressed "grave concern" about the "intimidation, arrest, detention, and in many cases enforced disappearance" of lawyers, activists, support staff and families (CBNY_20150728). Informed by close ties between the City Bar's own members and China's activists, together with the detailed spreadsheet updated regularly by Amnesty International's Hong Kong office, President Raskin could write explicitly about 228 persons targeted and twenty-two that remained missing or in custody. She identified those persons by name. She aligned the City Bar with "the protected scope of lawyers' legitimate work" as practiced by the Fengrui law firm. She extensively contrasted China's actions with international standards and China's own CPL and, indeed, Xi Jinping's Four Comprehensives, which included a commitment to "govern the country according to the law." She ended with a call for the immediate release of detainees and for detentions to adhere to international standards, including access to legal counsel and detention in "official detention facilities."

This strong, detailed, and forthright letter contrasted noticeably with the American Bar Association (ABA), whose internal politics immediately revealed a deep cleavage between two factions. For seventeen years the ABA Rule of Law Initiative (ROLI) had maintained an office in Beijing and it had cooperated with the government in many projects to advance rule of law. The preference of ROLI supporters within the ABA was that the ABA make no statement at all in case it impaired a future ABA presence in Beijing or risked harming ABA employees, especially Chinese citizens. The ABA Human Rights Center and other rights-oriented segments of the ABA, by contrast, preferred a strong statement which registered grave concern at the detentions and urged China to respect the rights of lawyers inscribed in China's own laws and constitution as well as UN standards. Both sides brought specialist academics and lawyers to buttress their cases. In the end, the ABA President did issue a statement on August 3 (noticeably later than most other national bar associations), but it placed much greater emphasis on future cooperation with China's authorities than on the treatment of lawyers in the crackdown (ABA_20150803).

It is evident that international mobilization was substantially enabled and quickened by online listserves, messaging services, video-conferencing tools, websites, and URL links to the accumulating statements and even database of detainees. As the magnitude of the crackdown increased, the international response began to shift into a different register. One organization even called upon the International Olympic Committee to reject China's bid for the 2022 Winter Olympics (IFC_20150723). Several rights and lawyers' groups within the United States targeted the US-China Rights Dialogue, scheduled for August 13–14 in Washington, DC, as a focal point for protest. A coalition of "overseas Chinese organizations in the greater Washington DC region" staged a small public demonstration in front of the Chinese Embassy on August 13 where it read "A Letter of Protest against China's Arrest of Rights Lawyers" (IFC_20150811). In the meantime, Ambassador Samantha Power launched a US State Department publicity initiative at the UN entitled "#FreeThe20 campaign," in anticipation of the forthcoming UN Conference on Women presided over by China (USDOP_20150831). The first woman featured in the public launch was Wang Yu.

Even more remarkable was a public statement directed to the Dialogue by twenty-five lawyers and eleven human rights defenders, most of whom were inside China, and several of whom, such as Chang Boyang, Tang Jitian, and Jiang Tianyong, had themselves suffered grievously under previous crackdowns. The statement explicitly requested that "The Chinese government should release all lawyers and activists who have been arbitrarily detained and forcibly disappeared (secretly imprisoned) since July 9" and that "The US government should pay close attention to the latest legislative trend and urge Chinese authorities to abolish or substantially amend the clauses and articles of law and regulations that breach the *Constitution of the People's Republic of China* or the international standards of human rights by which China has already promised to abide" (CHRD_20150811). In addition, persons expressing views to or about the Dialogue should have their safety assured and the results of the Dialogue should be publicly reported.

By mid-August, therefore, the rich and rapid flow of information through the online media had enabled an array of local, national, and international bar associations to join forces directly or in parallel with governments, including those of China's largest trading partners (e.g., the United States and European Union), and international civil society. Further, the stream of news coverage continued in the form of op-eds, editorials, and news reporting in leading news outlets in English, French, Spanish, and other languages. And to bring this tale of worldwide mobilization back to where it began, Wang Yu herself proved a compelling figure for stories in the international media, though her fate in the Chinese criminal justice system still remains unknown at the time of writing this book.

Xi's visit to the United States in late September 2015 was met with public protests outside China's Embassy, a protest breakfast by rights protesters, NGOs, and lawyers' groups, and private meetings by Secretary Kerry with Chinese activists (RFA_20150924). Human Rights Watch China director, Sophie Richardson, attended the State Dinner, where she took the opportunity where she took the opportunity, despite the limitations of this diplomatic milieu, to represent the plight of human rights lawyers and activists before President Obama, President Xi, and those Politburo members who would speak to her. Activism then shifted to other forthcoming events that sharpened international attention, such as President Xi's visit to Britain in November 2015 and a scheduled meeting in late 2015 by the American Bar Association President with Chinese officials in Beijing.

In the following months the overwhelming majority of the more than two hundred lawyers and activists who had been questioned or detained were released without criminal charges. By the end of 2015, no more than twenty remained "disappeared," or under some form of designated residential surveillance where they had no contact with family, legal counsel, or interested parties.

Yet, in an ironic twist, the very provision in the 2012 CPL that allowed detainees to be held incommunicado for six months without being charged with a crime (Article 73), now produced a new surge of international media attention as the six-month limit for residential surveillance expired in January 2016. Those charged faced harsh and long-term prison sentences for offences of inciting subversion of state power, charges far in excess of previous crackdowns (GD_20160114). A few were released.

The powerful multiplying effect of online media can be observed from coverage of the charges brought in January 2016 against Wang Yu and other notable activists together with the coverage of a public letter addressed to President Xi Jinping and his government from distinguished international jurists that was released in January.

In Chapter 5 we identified five main types of international support institutions for China's activist lawyers. All of these institutions criticized the charges against the remaining detainees in January 2016, most especially because charges were for crimes far more serious than most international observers had anticipated.

Leading world news services (e.g., Al Jazeera, Associated Press, Reuters, BBC) released stories alongside major media outlets on several continents (e.g., *the Guardian, Le Monde, Die Welt* in Europe; the *New York Times, Washington Post, the Atlantic* in the United States; the *South China Morning Post* in Asia), and at least in France and the United States stories were echoed in regional print and online media. The international business press (e.g., *the Economist*) was paralleled by national and international religious media.

Many news stories featured the notable activists Wang Yu, Zhou Shifeng, and Li Heping. The themes echoed shock at the charges of "subverting state power" or "inciting subversion of state power" (Article 105 of the PRC Criminal Law), which could earn long prison sentences up to life imprisonment, and interpreted these as a "major escalation" and "aggressive push" in the government's attacks on lawyers (GD_20160114; NYT_20160117). The *Washington Post* editorialized that China was pulling "lawyers and activists into a dark zone of fear" (WP_20160118). The *Guardian* reported on a human interest story featured twenty-three-year-old recent law graduate Zhao Wei, a female assistant to Li Heping now charged with inciting subversion of state power (GD_20160125).

The mobilization of the international legal complex was reflected in a public letter to President Xi by twenty eminent jurists from Europe, North America, Australia, and Asia. The letter expressed great concern about those disappeared or charged with very serious crimes and appealed to both UN standards and China's constitution in order to request information, ensure access to legal counsel, and guarantee protections from torture and future control measures. In a print-only world this letter might have received limited coverage in a few print editions. In the online world of the Internet and social media the letter was released on January 18, 2016 with simultaneous news stories in the online editions of the *Guardian* and the *New York Times*, and, quickly following, the *South China Morning Post, Le Monde,* and *Die Welt.* Human Rights Watch issued an online news blast to its one-million-plus followers, other contributing organizations circulated an accompanying news release to more than 3,000 TV stations and news media in the United States, and it was redirected via international religious rights organizations (e.g., Independent Catholic News/Christian Solidarity Worldwide; ChinaAid; ACAT, the French anti-torture NGO), and sparked stories in the legal press from Nova Scotia to Melbourne.

Since the international pressure on China may have shamed its leaders in the perceptions of international public opinion, it did not prove successful in bringing any of the charged lawyers to a fair trial. In fact, the government doubled down on its repression by keeping detainees isolated from family and diplomats and adopted the cynical practice of dismissing lawyers chosen by the detainees and replacing them with lawyers acceptable to the security apparatus. The periods of their detention and prosecution were also unusually long. When this book went to press in the summer of 2016, one year after the July 2015 crackdown, none of the charged lawyers had been brought to trial yet.

A stronger wave of international criticism therefore responded to China's abuse of fundamental legal rights as the crackdown approached its one-year anniversary in early July 2016. After a long internal set of negotiations within the American Bar Association, its leadership announced on the anniversary of Wang Yu's abduction that she had been awarded the first ABA International Human Rights award, an announcement that sufficiently stung China's leaders that the *Global Times*, widely read by Party officials, editorialized against the ABA and all other ways that "the West willfully provokes over rights lawyers" (GT_20160711). The ABA was joined by bar associations in the United States, Europe, and elsewhere, and by prestigious bodies of jurists such as the International Commission of Jurists. The International Bar Association's Human Rights Institute also released a strong public statement.

While the long chill of the July 2015 crackdown, therefore, has constrained and even suppressed the use of online media in trials and networked communications among activist lawyers inside China, the proliferation of electronic media outside China appears to amplify the volume and extent of rights activist coverage. This amplification has been aided not only in the unprecedented numerical and geographic scope of the crackdown inside China and the severity of criminal charges brought against notable activists and their assistants, but also by the six-month lag before the charges were issued and a probable further lag before a likely new wave of publicity when sentences are handed down. Finally, the security apparatus appears unwittingly to have handed international media greater rhetorical influence because it has targeted lawyers (e.g., Pu Zhiqiang, Li Heping, and Zhang Kai) with strong international connections to different segments of the international public sphere, including Christians worldwide, or detained lawyers with stories of powerful human interest value, such as the female lawyer Wang Yu the and twenty-four-year-old female legal assistant Zhao Wei.

CONCLUSION

In this chapter, we have examined the short but dynamic history of online networking among Chinese lawyers and their international allies in the early twenty-first century. The ACLA forum, as well as other popular legal forums in the early to mid-2000s, provided the initial online platform for the emergence of lawyers' collective consciousness on basic legal freedoms and political liberalism, both in abstract ideas and around particular cases. However, as a medium for information flow, forums hosted by professional associations are limited in both speed and the range of coverage. Moreover, they are more vulnerable to censorship by the ACLA itself. Similar weaknesses also exist for blogs, an even less interactive medium for mobilization. In contrast, the rise of social media in the early 2010s, particularly Weibo and WeChat, provided two highly interactive and rapid information-exchange media platforms that can be used for lawyers' collective action. Although the brevity of Weibo posts or WeChat discussions somewhat limits their content, this weakness is easily compensated for by their use in combination with blogs and other traditional media forms, where much longer essays can be posted and then linked to Weibo or WeChat. Arguably, technological innovation in the past decade has greatly facilitated Chinese lawyers' political mobilization.

More important, however, is the social transformation of lawyers' liberal legal and political ideologies in cyberspace into offline collective action. In the era of the online forums, these ideologies were expressed on the Internet and led to the rise of a collective consciousness in response to specific issues such as cases of lawyer persecution. After the rise of social media, this collective consciousness began to yield concrete results in lawyers' mobilization in specific legal cases, such as the Li Zhuang case, the Beihai case, the Xiaohe case, and the Wang Yu case, among many others. The interaction between online networking and offline practice is exemplified in the formation of lawyer groups and the rise of die-hard lawyering in those cases. It is precisely the emergence of this new and highly interactive form of collective action that put the Chinese government on increasingly high alert and eventually contributed to the July 2015 crackdown.

What are the future prospects of Chinese lawyers' online mobilization? One of the most important factors here is the attitude of the state toward the emergence of the new online public sphere (Lei 2011; Lei and Zhu 2015). In the past decade, the Chinese government has shut down the politically liberal ACLA forum and repeatedly "disappeared" some "troublemaking" notable activist lawyers. The July 2015 crackdown is the latest in a series of attacks and counter-attacks against the mobilization of China's activist lawyers, who seemingly challenge the government so fundamentally that it has taken such a far-reaching set of measures despite the risk of international approbation and potential repercussions in changing international public opinion about China and its future.

The point and counter-point over the last ten–fifteen years between lawyers and the agencies of the state – the PPC, state security, propaganda, etc. – can be understood as a series of recursive encounters where norms of state control and lawyers' activism seem to settle for a brief moment, only to be disturbed by another round of confrontations. Each of the moves by lawyers to use online media have been countered by regulatory actions, such as the ACLA closing down its forum or the security apparatus attacking lawyers on WeChat networks. Moreover, there have been many reports from notable activists that they were periodically contacted by their local justice bureaus to take down a particular posting or, in sensitive periods, to have their blogs and Weibo accounts shut down altogether. Adaptations by the Party-state to lawyers' creative use of online media and performativity in their everyday work are further evident in several of the recent statutory amendments to the CPL and Criminal Law, as well as judges' actions designed to mute or restrict lawyers' capacities to represent their clients through zealous advocacy. Censors delete posts online and propaganda campaigns become coordinated with state security crackdowns.

For how long and to what extent will the state tolerate even the limited current use of social media as a form of legal and implicitly political mobilization? It is clear that both the state and the activist lawyers view Weibo and WeChat as sites of struggle, not only for individual cases but for the respective ideals of the Party and lawyers themselves. In this sense, although social media have become a powerful instrument for lawyers across China to pursue collective action, it will remain a fragile social space that contains high vulnerability and unpredictability insofar as there are high institutional stakes between the state and the legal-liberal lawyers.

Besides the state's tolerance of social media, the durability of the online networks of politically liberal lawyers is an equally important aspect. As evidenced by the online reaction to the Li Zhuang, Beihai, and other recent cases, a professional network transcending social and political boundaries seems to be emerging, and within this network several different types of lawyers coexist, including, among others, the progressive elites, notable activists, and grassroots activists featured in our analytical framework. These lawyers share a basic legal-liberal orientation in their ideologies but often adopt distinct strategies in their political mobilization. Some advocate for fundamental legal and implicitly political changes that could potentially transform the regime through peaceful revolution, whereas others believe that an incremental approach of reforming the legal system from the inside is more feasible and appealing (see Chapter 4). The extent to which these loosely connected lawyer groups can resolve such ideological and strategic differences in practice will also determine the fate of their online activism in the years to come.

The unfolding of the July 2015 crackdown further signals that online infra-structures for mobilization inside China are now complemented by a far-reaching online network of international media organizations, international rights groups, an emerging legal complex, religious NGOs, and governmental and inter-governmental bodies. Previously, these international observers, monitors, commentators, and activist organizations acted substantially in silos. Evidence has begun to accumulate that the scope and severity of the July 2015 crackdown has broken down barriers among international sup-porters and activists, with the result that they are concomitantly consolidating a tightening network of relationships even as they multiply their electronically enabled reach to readers and potential supporters. The emergence of an international legal complex of bar associations, jurists, and lawyers' rights organizations focused on China has also been precipitated by the events of 2015. This heightened international coverage and mobilization might have at least two effects on the practices of China's activist lawyers. As they have repeatedly stated in our interviews, international public opinion gives them courage and protection, hope and solidarity. At the same time, the extent of international scrutiny of the crackdown may compel China's leaders to reconsider their tactics and calculus of costs in light of the severity of the state's domestic suppression of activist and ordinary lawyers.

8

Between Reform and Repression

China's history is its own. It cannot be forced into straitjackets of institutional change and legal transformation rigidly imported from other histories and places. Yet China's history is also part of world history and China's present is increasingly embedded in international and global markets and global governance, in international educational hierarchies and ideologies of law and politics, in geopolitics and the politics of universal norms. This book has investigated China's current practices and ideals of criminal defense as they have unfolded in recent decades through the interactions between lawyers and other legal or political actors in the criminal justice system. It views those within historical and comparative contexts of lawyers' politics, not only in East Asia, and among China's neighbors with whom it shares an intimate history, but across the world where patterns of law and politics recur, albeit with many variations and contingencies.

The search for political lawyering often begins with radical lawyer activism or major political upheavals (Halliday and Karpik 1997; Karpik 1988; Halliday, Karpik, and Feeley 2007, 2012), but it rarely begins with the everyday work of ordinary law practitioners. In this book, we have taken a fresh approach by focusing on lawyers' day-to-day struggles in China's troubled criminal justice system and by examining the political mobilization around their difficulties and the dangers they face when practicing criminal defense. This approach enables us to go beyond the small number of notable activist lawyers in Beijing who have rightly attracted much international attention both in the media and in scholarship on Chinese lawyers (Fu and Cullen 2008, 2011; Pils 2015). By focusing in the first instance on apparently mundane criminal lawyering we can amplify and refine a more comprehensive and generalizable theoretical framework for understanding the variations in the relationships between lawyers and politics, as well as the different mobilizing strategies and coping tactics adopted by various types of criminal defense lawyers.

Divided by their standings with respect to legal-liberal values and institu-tional political embeddedness, each of the five types of lawyers identified in this book occupies a unique structural position in the Chinese criminal defense bar. Both liberal and embedded, progressive elites are located at the core of the Chinese bar and thus they are able to exercise political influence on both CPL lawmaking and some *causes célèbres* such as the Li Zhuang case (see Chapter 6). Notable activists, by contrast, are marginalized by the state into a peripheral position owing to their strong liberal orientations, high visibility in sensitive cases, and lack of political embeddedness. During the period of our research, many of them were disbarred, detained, or even tortured. However, such a peripheral and precarious position also makes it possible for them to forge strong social networks with one another, with domestic civil society, and with international media, foreign governments, and human rights organizations (see Chapters 5 and 7).

Somewhere between the core and the periphery lie a large number of grassroots activists, pragmatic brokers, and routine practitioners. Grassroots activists are under less state repression than notable activists not only because they are scattered all over China, but also because they hide their liberal ideologies in mundane criminal cases rather than highly sensitive cases. Without political embeddedness or access to the traditional media, the Internet becomes an important platform for the liberal voices of grassroots activist lawyers to be heard (see Chapter 7). Pragmatic brokers, on the other hand, often avoid media attention but quietly rely on their political embedd-edness to gain advantages in their criminal defense work (see Chapter 4). They are located closer to the core of the criminal defense bar than political activists or routine practitioners, yet they do not possess the liberal values and motiva-tions of progressive elites.

The vast number of routine practitioners are neither politically embedded nor motivated by ideals of political liberalism in their practice. Nevertheless, their sense of justice, fairness, or professionalism may still press them to demand in their everyday work exactly the kinds of protections for their clients and themselves that are integral to politically liberal regimes. Indeed, the difficulties and danger in carrying out criminal defense work (see Chapter 3) are shared, to various degrees, by all five types of law practitioners. Even progressive elites and pragmatic brokers constantly feel the implications of taking such risks because their political embeddedness has spatial limits.

It is precisely from the everyday work experience of battling with the "Three Difficulties" and "Big Stick 306" that the collective action of Chinese lawyers emerged in the early twenty-first century. While the vast majority of lawyers simply do their criminal defense work to earn a living, a not-insignificant number of grassroots activists, notable activists, and progressive elites believe that their everyday work is about something bigger and more institutional. Both legal practice and politics in everyday work proceed through two contrasting methods: (1) an "outside" strategy for those who turn to the media, publics, and civil society; and, (2) an "inside" strategy for those who are closer to the state. Notable activists often display sophisticated techniques and extraordinary bravery, yet their blunt opposition to the authoritarian state sometimes results in relentless repression against both their clients and themselves without immediate and ostensible substantive change to either the criminal justice system or the political regime behind it (see Chapter 5). Progressive elites, by contrast, seek a more pragmatic strategy to reform the authoritarian state from within, by strategically turning judges, procurators, and even police officers from their enemies to their allies in their everyday work (see Chapter 6). For these politically embedded yet highly liberal lawyers, the battle for political liberalism is a long and incremental process, in which survival and self-protection are more important than short-term sacrifice for drastic change.

In addition to those two major strategies for political mobilization, grassroots activists across the country rely heavily on the Internet to express their liberal political values and participate, albeit in limited ways, in collective action around specific criminal cases and cases of lawyer persecution. The rise of Internet forums and social media in the early twenty-first century provides these often anonymous activist lawyers a virtual public sphere (Yang 2009; Lei 2011; Lei and Zhu 2015) where they can exchange ideas, build solidarity, and make alliances with progressive elites and notable activists (see Chapter 7). Despite the distance between words on the Internet and actions in real cases, we have witnessed the "birth of a liberal moment" (Halliday and Liu 2007) under the close watch of a repressive authoritarian regime.

IMPULSES FROM BELOW: THE PURSUIT OF BASIC LEGAL FREEDOMS

In contrast to many studies on Chinese law that treat China as either a unique, isolated case or an Orientalist "other" to Western countries (e.g., the United States), we have taken a comparative and historical approach in this book, i.e., to approach China with hypotheses on lawyers and politics inductively derived from the histories of many other countries, enormously diverse across many criteria, in different periods of history (Halliday and Karpik 1997; Halliday et al. 2007, 2012). Comparative and historical sociology makes the contextualization of countries in time and place a central part of its explanatory ambitions. These modes of systematic inquiry seek to identify patterns of historical change, or commonalities or conjunctions in institutions or culture, that lead to some national trajectories taking one direction or another. Country specialists may resist the perspective of comparative and historical sociology to see one country, China, in the contexts of others with which it might be compared. Yet China is frequently classed with one or another group of countries, whether in comparative political economy, as a developing or transitional country; or comparative politics, as a communist or post-communist country; or geopolitics, as a rising regional or world power. All these characterizations are implicitly or explicitly comparative or historical.

Our intensive research on China's criminal defense practice permits three principal conclusions on lawyers and prospects for a liberal political society. First, there is a politics of practice and lawmaking in which basic legal freedoms are the foundations of day-to-day struggles between state officials (judges, procurators, police officers, etc.), on the one hand, and private legal practitioners and their clients, on the other hand. Second, everyday efforts to surmount difficulties and survive as criminal defense lawyers are themselves nested within ongoing meta-bargaining between the institutions of the Party-State and the collectivities of the legal complex in the struggle over the statutory and regulatory reforms of criminal procedure law and its interpretations. Third, these iterations of practice and legal change are all absorbed within a wider and ultimate politics over the legal and political order of contemporary and a future China.

The totality of these politics can be seen as a recursive process between, on the one side, lawyer advocates for basic legal freedoms, and on the other side, intermittent cycles of state reform and repression to forestall societal impulses toward civil society, moderation of state power, and legal restrictions on arbitrary state power. At this moment, no clear directionality or trajectory can be seen for the longer term outcomes of these iterative dynamics.

The practice of criminal law in China is therefore more than an analysis of social practices within a legal specialty or domain of law. While those processes warrant explication in their own right, scholarship on lawyers and legal change in other times and places has generated hypotheses that deserve empirical examination in China. Is there evidence of lawyers striving for protection of basic legal freedoms in China, as scholars have documented elsewhere in the recent history of East Asia, Southeast Asia, and South Asia (Feeley and Miyazawa 2007; Ginsburg 2007; Jones 2007; Aziz 2012; Ghias 2012; Harding and Whiting 2012; Munir 2012)? In statutory law, particularly the CPL reforms from 1979 to 2012, we find a trajectory of formal lawmaking – law-on-the-books – that appears progressively to incorporate statutory enactments into law that offer increasing protections to detainees and their legal counsel. Despite the struggles in every cycle of lawmaking and the strong resistance of the PPC in the implementation of the CPL, overall these shifts signal some convergence of China's legislation with prevailing international norms.

Moreover, a considerable majority of Chinese criminal defense lawyers believe that criminal law and procedure should prioritize protecting human rights over striking crimes, or at least give equal weight to both (see Table 4.3). When they characterize their ideologies and motivations for engaging in criminal defense work, at least three types of lawyers (i.e., grassroots activists, notable activists, and progressive elites) point to aspects of that bundle of ideals discovered in the politics of lawyers elsewhere – concepts of basic legal freedoms, an appreciation of a civil society where lawyers' themselves can organize collegially, and the emergence of a more professionalized judiciary that makes decisions based on law and facts rather than politics or extraneous interventions in the legal process. Notable activists articulate most forthrightly elements of political liberalism in their words and actions, yet the more cautious and incremental approaches to legal and political changes taken by progressive elites and grassroots activists should not be overlooked or easily dismissed.

However, even in practice there is tension among the segments of politically liberal lawyers about whether their primary role is to improve the situation of their clients (e.g., by using legal processes to get local administrative of political settlements) or to insist upon legal procedure and legal processes to resolve issues that could potentially result in harsher criminal detentions or sentences. The recent rise of die-hard lawyering not only blurs the boundary between ordinary and political lawyering, as cause lawyers in other places often do (Sarat and Scheingold 1998, 2011), but also raises important issues on the ultimate goals and workplace strategies of criminal defense work among Chinese lawyers all over the country, not merely the notable activists or progressive elites in Beijing. To what extent can the spectacles in the courtroom and in cyberspace lead to concrete progress in criminal procedure and the justice system that it regulates remains a challenging question for even the most radical activist lawyers in China.

Beyond their everyday struggles in the workplace, do Chinese lawyers mobilize collectively in defense and pursuit of basic legal freedoms? Do those struggles become collective modes of professional action? We have observed that different forms of collective action and their outcomes vary markedly.

First, there are large-scale mobilizations around specific cases, such as the SOS case on the ACLA forum, the Li Zhuang case, the Beihai case, and, most recently, the case of Wang Yu and her law firm, Fengrui. These mobilizations achieved mixed success, generating both collective consciousness among lawyers and the public and heightened alert and repression from the state.

Second, at least a small group of notable activist lawyers sought to reform the state-controlled bar associations through collective action. Despite its unfavorable outcome and strong backlash from the BBOJ, the 2008 BLA election movement (see Chapter 5) was a key event in the history of lawyer mobilization in China as it raised the professional and public awareness of the illiberal nature of professional regulation that Chinese lawyers still experience today, as well as the collective desire to make it more responsive to members and emancipate it from government control.

Third, although the Chinese government exercises harsh restrictions on any sort of organized civil society groups, incipient networks of law practitioners, such as the small groups on death penalty or torture (Belkin 2011), the die-hard lawyer groups on Weibo, and the group chat of human rights defenders on WeChat and Telegram, have emerged in recent years and made various alliances with other civic groups both in China and abroad.

Nevertheless, without the support of the wider legal complex, Chinese lawyers' political mobilization would be unlikely to succeed. Until today, the Chinese legal complex remains deeply fragmented within the criminal defense bar, between criminal defense lawyers and other lawyers, and between lawyers and the PPC (Liu 2011, 2015; Liang, He, and Lu 2014). Although both the procuracy and the judiciary have become highly professionalized in the past decade and an increasing number of judges and procurators share lawyers' liberal ideals, the antagonism between the PPC and criminal defense lawyers in the workplace remains deep. Many progressive elite lawyers acknowledge the importance of making alliances with "healthy forces inside the system" (体制内健康力量) in their pursuit of basic legal freedoms, but such alliances often collapse easily when faced with the threat of state repression.

Even within the Chinese bar, criminal defense lawyers have received relatively little support from other sectors of the bar, especially the corporate law firms specializing in high-end transactional work (Liu 2008; Liu and Wu 2016). With the exception of Li Zhuang, who was a partner in an elite corporate law firm in Beijing, the plight of Chinese lawyers in criminal defense work generated limited concern or support from their colleagues in commercial work. There are arguably many Chinese corporate lawyers who possess liberal values (Michelson and Liu 2010), but they seem content to bury those values under their largely non-political practice (e.g., civil litigation or non-litigation work), at least for now. Furthermore, as we have shown throughout the book, the criminal defense bar itself is differentiated into five sectors and collective action across these segments of practice is often a challenging task as these lawyers adopt distinct strategies to political mobilization. During the rise of die-hard lawyering, numerous conflicts and disagreements occurred among its core members, most notably on the boundaries of activist behavior and how to deal with the state.

A vanguard of a potential legal complex for basic legal freedoms would include a small segment of practicing lawyers with at least some support from a segment of judges, procurators, and law professors. For the case of China, such a legal complex remains a work in progress. Without doubt, a vanguard of lawyers has benefitted from implicit and explicit support from many legal academics in leading universities, particularly in campaigning for law reforms, but similar support from procurators and judges has been much less evident. Yet the history of the past decade has witnessed the critical transformation from the "birth of a liberal moment" in cyberspace (Halliday and Liu 2007) to the rise of collective action in real cases among Chinese legal professionals.

Furthermore, there is a more inchoate international legal complex in the making. Many Chinese legal academics and practitioners are networked into international networks of law schools and professional associations, among others. Some notable activist lawyers have formed strong international connections with lawyers, groups that are protective or aligned with lawyers, international civil society, and international media (see Chapters 5 and 7). Yet such international networks also constitute a point of tension with the state and local authorities and thus it is often a fraught relationship for politically liberal lawyers inside China.

One objection to our findings on lawyers and political liberalism might be that 10–20% of criminal defense lawyers or a few hundred notable activists amount to a tiny fraction of all Chinese lawyers, and all lawyers themselves are a tiny segment of Chinese society. This is an odd argument. Any comparative-historical study of great political and legal movements could pour such skepticism on a poor German émigré in Britain writing *The Communist Manifesto*, or a tiny proportion of India's legal elite in the vanguard of repudiating one of the world's great imperial powers, or a hidden marginal network of lawyers fueling a drive for political transformation in South Korea, or a church and a bar association standing against the power of the military in Brazil. All social, legal, and political movements have beginnings, usually with a few outspoken leaders, more discreet followers, and many more secret sympathizers. Some of those movements die. Others live and become transformative.

Is China different? In many respects, yes. It is a vast country with enormous resources, having taken immense strides to better the lives of hundreds of millions in a few short decades. It has a strong state with a security apparatus that is more pervasive and sophisticated than perhaps the world has ever known (Wang and Minzner 2015). It has enormously talented populations and a great sense of its cultural and national distinctiveness. Much of its legal profession is deeply embedded in the state's legal and political apparatuses (Michelson 2007; Liu 2011). In many other respects, however, no. China also harbors vast disaffected populations who protest against inequality, injustice, and repression (Gallagher 2006; O'Brien and Li 2006; Minzner 2011; Stern 2013). China's emergent civil society contains many idealists who believe an illiberal political order suppresses their desire for basic legal freedoms. China's hundreds of millions of migrant workers and poor peasants seek basic rights as citizens that have been long denied to them. Many of China's superbly educated professionals, not least lawyers, know that elsewhere in the world there are legal and political orders far more amenable to their professional and personal ideals.

In short, the burden of proof lies upon those who would insist that liberal-legal impulses seen across many varieties of illiberal regimes over several centuries make China the one exception. It should be clear that such impulses for political liberalism frequently do not lead in the short term to transformations in law or politics. Illiberal regimes can be sustained for decades, possibly in perpetuity, as for instance in the despotic and volatile regimes seen in the British post-colonies (Halliday, Karpik, and Feeley 2012). This could well be the case for China too – after all, the mobilization of the legal profession rarely succeeds without substantive support from the broader political society, both within and outside the state apparatus. The power of comparative and historical inquiry is that it accepts no country is *sui generis*, yet concedes that all countries exhibit distinctive characteristics. It would be a very bold conclusion indeed to claim that China alone stands apart from social and political processes observed so widely in other times and places. It is even bolder to maintain that conclusion given our data, incomplete as they are.

THE DANCE OF CHANGE: CHINESE CRIMINAL JUSTICE
IN TRANSITION

Our study of the work experiences and political struggles of criminal defense lawyers provides a unique lens for observing the changes in China's criminal justice system from 1979 to the present. To a large extent, the treatment of its defense lawyers is a sensitive indicator for the progress of a criminal justice system toward proceduralism and the rule of law, and beyond both to the threefold pillars of political liberalism observed in world history. Only when lawyers are able to represent criminal suspects and defendants rigorously and without fear can a criminal justice system achieve that always vexing balance between crime control and human rights protection. Conversely, if criminal defense lawyers are constantly fearful of professional revenge from prosecutors and police officers, or if they experience great difficulties in routine everyday work such as meeting clients or collecting evidence, then the criminal justice system is inevitably unbalanced and unfavorable to the protection of citizen's basic legal rights.

There is no doubt that Chinese criminal justice has traveled a vast distance since 1979, when the Criminal Law and the CPL were first promulgated. The "strike hard" campaigns, though still observed occasionally in various places, have been moderated and replaced by the principles of due process and "kill fewer" (Trevaskes 2010). Torture and wrongful convictions have been gradually remedied, though not systematically or on a large scale (Belkin 2011). Human rights, tabooed words in socialist China, have been written into both the 1996 CPL and 2012 CPL. Courts and procuracies have become increasingly professionalized and the dominance of the police in the criminal process has been gradually reduced. Lawyers, who had only seven days to prepare a defense in criminal trials under the 1979 CPL, have been given the full status of defender from the phase of police investigation under the 2012 CPL. Despite persistent criticisms of China's human rights records by foreign observers, today's Chinese criminal justice apparatus has become a highly sophisticated and functional system which is distinct from the lawlessness of the Mao era (Cohen 1968; Li 1978) in fundamental ways.

The great puzzle in this seemingly progressive development, as this book has shown, is that the modernization of Chinese criminal justice has not significantly improved the working conditions of its defense lawyers. With "Big Stick 306" hanging above their heads like the Sword of Damocles, Chinese criminal defense lawyers work and live in constant fear for their own freedom, let alone the freedom of their clients. Due to the difficulties in meeting suspects, collecting evidence, and accessing case files persisting in their everyday practice, many lawyers simply retreat to the safe comfort zone of court proceedings at the expense of the criminal suspects and defendants that they represent. Even so, persuading judges to adopt their defense opinions remains a challenging task. While a number of articles targeting these problems have been written into the 2012 CPL, changes have occurred slowly and unevenly across the country. And, indeed, other amendments to the criminal procedure law have been effectively subversive, essentially incorporating deep contradictions into the statutory law, which in turn precipitate domestic and international calls for further reforms that will resolve everyday conflicts and struggles in practice.

The disjunction between China's criminal justice reforms and its struggling criminal defense bar thereby exemplifies the recursive nature of legal change (Liu and Halliday 2009), particularly in the limitations of legislative and policy reforms to shape everyday legal work. As many law and society studies have shown (Halliday 1987; Scheingold [1974] 2004; Marshall and Hale 2014), without the collective action of the legal profession and other social forces, law on the books rarely makes a difference in practice. This is especially true in a justice system unfavorable or even antagonistic to lawyers. As a result, the battlegrounds for Chinese lawyers' political struggles are not only legislatures and courtrooms, but also bar associations, churches, the media, NGOs, and, occasionally, detention centers and prisons. It is certain that some of the most controversial provisions in the 2012 CPL revision (e.g., Article 73), as well as further repressive amendments of the Criminal Law adopted in 2015, will precipitate yet more pressure from ordinary and activist lawyers, and some legal academics, in alliance with restive civil society groups, to press for further reforms that protect basic legal freedoms of lawyers and citizens alike.

This book repeatedly points to a deep divide between the PPC and criminal defense lawyers, which is also observed by criminologists studying China (Liang, He, and Lu 2014). Nevertheless, although not a direct object of our inquiry, it is probable that politically liberal orientations also exist in parts of the PPC. Although many judges and procurators are constrained by their structural positions in the criminal justice system and often have to make illiberal decisions in their work, the political ideologies of many may well have converged with lawyers in recent years, particularly the younger generations who received formal legal education and passed the unified National Judicial Examination after 2001 (Minzner 2013). When conducting our research on online networking (see Chapter 7), we clearly observed signs of this shift in social media, such as the Law Blog, Weibo, and WeChat. Given the relatively weak structural position of lawyers in China's legal system (Michelson 2007; Liu 2011), any substantive criminal justice reform cannot be achieved without the support of some segments of liberal judges and procurators.

But the Chinese state is a Janus-faced leviathan (Yang 2004). Its progressive reforms are often accompanied by harsh repressions, particularly in politically sensitive cases and on human rights activists. The troubled existence of notable activist lawyers is not only a story of heroism and persecution (see Chapter 5), but also a telling indicator of the lack of a moderate Chinese state and its manifestations in the legal system. The harsh treatment of these lawyers (and the individual citizens whom they represent) is the Achilles heel of Chinese criminal justice. Although the capacity of notable activists in pushing for domestic legal reforms is limited, the international attention on this small and vulnerable lawyer population is an exogenous force that even an authoritarian state cannot ignore. Every small step of China's criminal procedure reforms is accompanied by their great sacrifice, both individually and collectively.

Law thereby has become a locus of struggle for the complexion of China's future political society. The indeterminacy and contradictions of the CPL lawmaking from 1979 to 2012 have opened up a battleground for politically liberal lawyers. The discursive swamps in which ambiguous, unpredictable, and contradictory law on the books become legal and political locales in which each side of the struggles seeks to exploit a politics of meaning (Bourdieu 1987). By ensuring that legal meaning does not become certain and predictable, the Chinese state can keep criminal defense lawyers and their allies unsettled and hence on edge, a tactic that may compel many lawyers to self-censor or to engage in legal self-restraint (Stern and O'Brien 2012).

Accordingly, the practice of criminal defense in China has become a dance, a deadly serious cat-and-mouse game, characterized by the back-and-forth encounters and confrontations between state power and ordinary citizens, between the PPC and lawyers. These struggles go well beyond the field of criminal procedure law. They reach to the primacy of the CCP and the foundations of CCP's legitimacy. Indeed, recent evidence seems to suggest that the politics of Chinese criminal justice are being absorbed into a larger politics over the contours of a dual state. This conceptualization of authoritarian law and politics has been applied in diverse settings from Soviet and post-Soviet Russia (Solomon 1995), to Li Kuan Yew's Singapore (Rajah 2012), and to contemporary China (Pils 2015). In all those cases, a dual state has one system of justice for ordinary cases (and probably the great majority of cases), and another system (or multiple systems) for cases that authoritarian rulers regard as threatening to their power – hence such cases are labeled as "politically sensitive" or even pushed beyond the mantle of law to the hands of the security apparatus (Wang and Minzner 2015).

Yet the Chinese state's adroit manipulation of its criminal justice system contains the prospects of self-subversion. It risks eroding the faith of lawyers and the general public on the sincerity and effectiveness of the legal reform that it claims to orchestrate. In our final round of interviews in August 2015,

a progressive elite lawyer who participated in the die-hard lawyering movement and witnessed the crackdown on many of her lawyer colleagues
in July 2015 said the following words, with notable stress and pessimism on
her face:

> Every person has a tomb. One individual has only one tomb. But for a Party,
> a state, its growth and demise are constituted by tombs, depending on how
> many people put it in the tombs of their hearts. This crackdown on lawyers
> can only make more people put it [the Party-state] in tombs.
>
> (B1512, Beijing)

These powerful and resonant words speak of a great struggle in which many
lawyers are deeply engaged. It is surely too early to speak of the demise or
endurance of China's current political regime, but the Party's dance between
reform and repression is a dangerous act, an act that might alienate not only its
lawyers but far more consequentially the vast number of citizens whose last
recourse for their grievances has become either law or something more
desperate and disruptive. In eighteenth-century France and late twentieth-
century Taiwan, and in many times and places between, lawyers have led
transitions in the character of their political societies. The evidence of this
book reveals that such tenacious impulses for change also exist in contemporary China, as forces for and against political liberalism engage in epic struggles
as the world watches and waits.

Bibliography

Alexander, Michelle. 2012. *The New Jim Crow: Mass Incarceration in the Age of Colorblindness*. New York: The New Press.

Aziz, Sadaf. Forthcoming. "Liberal Protagonists? The Lawyers' Movement in Pakistan." In *Fortunes and Misfortunes of Political Liberalism: The Legal Complex in the Post-Colony*, edited by Terence C. Halliday, Lucien Karpik, and Malcolm M. Feeley. New York: Cambridge University Press.

Bakken, Børge (ed.). 2005. *Crime, Punishment, and Policing in China*. Lanham, MD: Rowman & Littlefield Publishers, Inc.

Belkin, Ira. 2011. "China's Tortuous Path towards Ending Torture in Criminal Investigations." *Columbia Journal of Asian Law* 24:273–301.

Bell, David A. 1994. *Lawyers and Citizens: The Making of a Political Elite in Old Regime France*. Oxford: Oxford University Press.

Bourdieu, Pierre. 1987. "The Force of Law: Toward a Sociology of the Juridical Field." *The Hastings Law Journal* 38:805–853.

Braithwaite, John, and Peter Drahos. 2000. *Global Business Regulation*. Cambridge: Cambridge University Press.

Cai, Dingjian. 1999. "Development of the Chinese Legal System since 1979 and Its Current Crisis and Transformation." *Cultural Dynamics* 11:135–166.

Canovan, Margaret. 1981. *Populism*. London: Junction Books.

Chen, Guangcheng 陈光中. 1996. "刑事诉讼法修改的过程与主要内容 [An Overview of the Process and Content of the Revision of the Criminal Procedure Law]." Introduction to 中华人民共和国刑事诉讼法释义与应用 [*The Interpretation and Application of the PRC Criminal Procedure Law*]. Jilin: Jilin People's Press.

Chen, Guangcheng. 2015. *The Barefoot Lawyer: A Blind Man's Fight for Justice and Freedom in China*. New York: Henry Holt and Co.

Chen, Guangzhong 陈光中. 1995. "论刑事诉讼法修改的指导思想 [On the Theory of the Criminal Procedure Law Revision."]." 法制与社会发展 [*Law and Social Development*] 1995(4):43–49.

Chen, Guangzhong, and Yan Duan 陈光中、严端 (eds.). 1995. "中华人民共和国刑事诉讼法修改建议稿与论证 [*The Suggested Draft of the PRC Criminal Procedure Law and Its Reasoning*]. Beijing: China Fang Zheng Press.

Chen, Jianfu. 2002. "A Criminal Justice System for a New Millennium?" In *China's Legal Reforms and Their Political Limits*, edited by E. B. Vermeer and I. d'Hooghe, 77–122. London and New York: RoutledgeCurzon.

Clark, Donald C., and James V. Feinerman. 1995. "Antagonistic Contradictions: Criminal Law and Human Rights in China." *The China Quarterly* 141:135–154.

Cohen, Jerome A. 1968. *The Criminal Process in the People's Republic of China, 1949–1963*. Cambridge, MA: Harvard University Press.

Cohen, Jerome A. 2009. "The Struggle for Autonomy of Beijing's Public Interest Lawyers." *Human Rights in China* (April 1, 2009), URL: www.hrichina.org/en/content/3692 (last date of access: February 3, 2016).

Cui, Min 崔敏. 1995. "刑事诉讼法修改研讨中的若干争议问题 [Several Debated Issues during the Discussions on the Revision of the Criminal Procedure Law]." 公安大学学报 *[Police University Academic Journal]* 1995(3):64–69.

Cui, Min 崔敏. 1996. 中国刑事诉讼法的新发展 – 刑事诉讼法修改研讨的全面回顾 *[The New Development of China's Criminal Procedure Law – A Comprehensive Review of the Discussions on the Revision of the Criminal Procedure Law]*. Beijing: People's Police University of China Press.

Dang, Jiangzhou 党江舟. 2005. 中国讼师文化：古代律师现象解读 *[The Culture of Litigation Masters in China: Interpretations on the Phenomenon of Ancient Lawyers]*. Beijing: Peking University Press.

Dezalay, Yves, and Bryant G. Garth. 2002. *The Internationalization of Palace Wars: Lawyers, Economists, and the Contest to Transform Latin American States*. Chicago: University of Chicago Press.

Dutton, Michael. 1992. *Policing and Punishment in China: From Patriarchy to "The People."* Cambridge: Cambridge University Press.

Falcao, Joaquim. 1988. "Lawyers in Brazil." In *Lawyers in Society: Civil Law Countries*, edited by R. L. Abel and P. S. C. Lewis, 400–442. Berkeley, CA: University of California Press.

Fang, Peng 方鹏. 2005. "从律师维权案论刑事律师办案风险的避免 [An Essay on the Avoidance of Criminal Defense Lawyers' Professional Risks from Lawyers' Right Protection Cases]." Peking University Law School, unpublished manuscript (on file with the authors).

Feeley, Malcolm M. 1979. *The Process Is the Punishment: Handling Cases in a Lower Criminal Court*. New York: Russell Sage Foundation.

Feeley, Malcolm M., and Setsuo Miyazawa. 2007. "The State, Civil Society, and the Legal Complex in Modern Japan: Continuity and Change." In *The Legal Complex and Struggles for Political Liberalism*, edited by T. C. Halliday, L. Karpik, and M. M. Feeley, 151–192. Oxford: Hart Publishing.

Felstiner, William L.F., Richard L. Abel, and Austin Sarat. 1980. "The Emergence and Transformation of Disputes: Naming, Blaming, Claiming . . ." *Law and Society Review* 15:631–654.

Folsom, Ralph H., John H. Minan, and Lee Ann Otto. 1992. *Law and Politics in the People's Republic of China*. St. Paul, MN: West Publishing Co.

Freidson, Eliot. 2001. *Professionalism: The Third Logic*. Chicago: University of Chicago Press.

Fu, Hualing. 1998. "Criminal Defence in China: The Possible Impact of the 1996 Criminal Procedure Law Reform." *The China Quarterly* 153:31–48.

Fu, Hualing. 2005. "Re-education through Labour in Historical Perspective." *The China Quarterly* 184:811–830.

Fu, Hualing, and Richard Cullen. 2008. "Weiquan (Rights Protection) Lawyering in an Authoritarian State: Building a Culture of Public-Interest Lawyering." *The China Journal* 59:111–127.

Fu, Hualing, and Richard Cullen. 2011. "Climbing the Weiquan Ladder: A Radicalizing Process for Rights-Protection Lawyers." *The China Quarterly* 205:40–59.

Galanter, Marc. 1974. "Why the 'Haves' Come Out Ahead: Speculations on the Limits of Legal Change." *Law & Society Review* 9:95–160.

Galanter, Marc. 2006. *Lowering the Bar: Lawyer Jokes and Legal Culture*. Madison, WI: University of Wisconsin Press.

Gallagher, Mary E. 2006. "Mobilizing the Law in China: 'Informed Disenchantment' and the Development of Legal Consciousness." *Law & Society Review* 40:783–816.

Garland, David. 1990. *Punishment and Modern Society: A Study in Social Theory*. Chicago: University of Chicago Press.

Ghias, Shoaib A. 2012. "Miscarriage of Chief Justice: Lawyers, Media, and the Struggle for Judicial Independence in Pakistan." In *Fates of Political Liberalism in the British Post-Colony: The Politics of the Legal Complex*, edited by T. C. Halliday, L. Karpik, and M. M. Feeley, 340–377. New York: Cambridge University Press.

Ginsburg, Tom. 2007. "Law and the Liberal Transformation of the Northeast Asian Legal Complex in Korea and Taiwan." In *Fighting for Political Freedom: Comparative Studies of the Legal Complex and Political Liberalism*, edited by T. C. Halliday, L. Karpik, and M. M. Feeley, 43–64. Oxford: Hart Publishing Inc.

Ginsburg, Tom, and Tamir Moustafa (eds.). 2008. *Rule by Law: The Politics of Courts in Authoritarian Regimes*. New York: Cambridge University Press.

Gould, Jeremy. 2006. "Strong Bar, Weak State? Lawyers, Liberalism and State Formation in Zambia." *Development and Change* 37(4):921–942.

Habermas, Jürgen. [1962] 1989. *The Structural Transformation of the Public Sphere: An Inquiry into a Category of Bourgeois Society*, translated by T. Burger. Cambridge, MA: MIT Press.

Halliday, Terence C. 1985. "Knowledge Mandates: Collective Influence by Scientific, Normative and Syncretic Professions." *British Journal of Sociology* 36:421–447.

Halliday, Terence C. 1987. *Beyond Monopoly: Lawyers, State Crises, and Professional Empowerment*. Chicago: University of Chicago Press.

Halliday, Terence C. 2009. "Recursivity of Global Normmaking: A Sociolegal Agenda." *Annual Review of Law and Social Science* 5:263–289.

Halliday, Terence C., and Bruce G. Carruthers. 2007. "The Recursivity of Law: Global Norm Making and National Lawmaking in the Globalization of Corporate Insolvency Regimes." *American Journal of Sociology* 112:1135–1202.

Halliday, Terence C., and Lucien Karpik (eds.). 1997. *Lawyers and the Rise of Western Political Liberalism: Europe and North American from the Eighteenth to Twentieth Centuries*. Oxford: Clarendon Press.

Halliday, Terence C., and Lucien Karpik. 1997. "Politics Matter: A Comparative Theory of Lawyers in the Making of Political Liberalism." In *Lawyers and the Rise of Western Political Liberalism: Europe and North American from the Eighteenth to Twentieth Centuries*, edited by T. C. Halliday and L. Karpik, 15–64. Oxford: Clarendon Press.

Halliday, Terence C., and Lucien Karpik. 2012. "Political Liberalism in the British Post-Colony: A Theme with Three Variations." In *Fates of Political Liberalism in the British Post-Colony: The Politics of the Legal Complex*, edited by T. C. Halliday, L. Karpik, and M. M. Feeley. New York: Cambridge University Press.

Halliday, Terence C., and Pavel Osinsky. 2006. "Globalization of Law." *Annual Review of Sociology* 32:447–470.

Halliday, Terence C., and Sida Liu. 2007. "Birth of a Liberal Moment? Looking through a One-Way Mirror at Lawyers' Defense of Criminal Defendants in China." In *Fighting for Political Freedom: Comparative Studies of the Legal Complex and Political Liberalism*, edited by T. C. Halliday, L. Karpik, and M. M. Feeley, 65–108. Oxford: Hart Publishing.

Halliday, Terence C., Lucien Karpik, and Malcolm M. Feeley (eds.). 2007. *Fighting for Political Freedom: Comparative Studies of the Legal Complex and Political Liberalism*. Oxford: Hart Publishing.

Halliday, Terence C., Lucien Karpik, and Malcolm M. Feeley (eds.). 2012. *Fates of Political Liberalism in the British Post-Colony: The Politics of the Legal Complex*. New York: Cambridge University Press.

Hand, Keith J. 2006. "Using Law for a Righteous Purpose: The Sun Zhigang Incident and Evolving Forms of Citizen Action in the People's Republic of China." *Columbia Journal of Transnational Law* 45:114–195.

Harding, Andrew, and Amanda Whiting. 2012. "'Custodian of Civil Liberties and Justice in Malaysia': The Malaysian Bar and the Moderate State." In *Fates of Political Liberalism in the British Post-Colony: The Politics of the Legal Complex*, edited by T. C. Halliday, L. Karpik, and M. M. Feeley, 247–304. New York: Cambridge University Press.

Head, John Warren, and Yanping Wang. 2005. *Law Codes in Dynastic China: A Synopsis of Chinese Legal History in the Thirty Centuries from Zhou to Qing*. Durham, NC: Carolina Academic Press.

Hodgson, Jacqueline. 2005. *French Criminal Justice: A Comparative Account of the Investigation and Prosecution of Crime in France*. Oxford: Hart Publishing.

HRIC, Human Rights in China. 2007. *State Secrets: China's Legal Labyrinth*. New York: Human Rights in China.

Human Rights Watch. 2008. Walking on Thin Ice: Control, Intimidation, and Harassment of Lawyers in China. Human Rights Watch, April 2008. URL: www.hrw.org/reports/2008/china0408/china0408web.pdf (last date of access: February 4, 2016).

Hurst, William. 2015. "Reconsidering Grassroots Criminal Law and Justice in Maoist China." Paper presented at the Association for Asian Studies Annual Meeting, March 2015, Chicago, IL.

Jiang, Ping 江平. 2010. "中国法治处在一个大倒退的时期 [China's Rule of Law Is in a Period of Backward Movement.]" URL: http://news.mylegist.com/1604/2010–02-21/21028.html (last date of access: January 2, 2012).

Jiang, Zhan. 2011. "Environmental Journalism in China." In *Changing Media, Changing China*, edited by S. L. Shirk, 115–1278. New York: Oxford University Press.

Jones, Carol. 2007. "'Dissolving the People': Capitalism, Law and Democracy in Hong Kong." In *Fighting for Political Freedom: Comparative Studies of the Legal Complex and Political Liberalism*, edited by T. C. Halliday, L. Karpik, and M. M. Feeley, 109–150. Oxford: Hart Publishing.

Karpik, Lucien. 1988. "Lawyers and Politics in France, 1814–1950: The State, the Market, and the Public." *Law and Social Inquiry* 13:707–736.

Karpik, Lucien. 1995. *Les avocats entre l'Etat, le public et le marche: XIIIe–XXe siecle*. Paris: Gallimard.

Karpik, Lucien. 1998. *French Lawyers: A Study in Collective Action, 1274–1994*. Oxford: Oxford University Press.

Karpik, Lucien. 2007. "Postscript: Political Lawyering." In *Fighting for Political Freedom: Comparative Studies of the Legal Complex and Political Liberalism*, edited by T. C. Halliday, L. Karpik, and M. M. Feeley, 463–494. Oxford: Hart Publishing.

Karpik, Lucien, and Terence C. Halliday. 2011. "The Legal Complex." *Annual Review of Law and Social Science* 7:217–236.

LCHR, Lawyers Committee for Human Rights. 1993. *Criminal Justice with Chinese Characteristics: China's Criminal Process and Violations of Human Rights*. New York: Lawyers Committee for Human Rights.

LCHR, Lawyers Committee for Human Rights. 1998. *Wrongs and Rights: A Human Rights Analysis of China's Revised Criminal Law*. New York: Lawyers Committee for Human Rights.

Lei, Ya-Wen. 2011. "The Political Consequences of the Rise of the Internet: Political Beliefs and Practices of Chinese Netizens." *Political Communication* 28:291–322.

Lei, Ya-Wen, and Daniel Xiaodan Zhou. 2015. "Contesting Legality in Authoritarian Contexts: Food Safety, Rule of Law and China's Networked Public Sphere." *Law & Society Review* 49:557–593.

Leng, Shao-chuan. 1985. *Criminal Justice in Post-Mao China: Analysis and Documents*. Albany, NY: State University of New York Press.

Lewis, Margaret K. 2011. "Controlling Abuse to Maintain Control: The Exclusionary Rule in China." *New York University Journal of International Law and Politics* 43:629–697.

Li, Ling. 2012. "The 'Production' of Corruption in China's Courts: Judicial Politics and Decision Making in a One-Party State." *Law & Social Inquiry* 37:848–877.

Li, Victor H. 1977. *Law without Lawyers: A Comparative View of Law in China and the United States*. Boulder, CO: Westview Press.

Liang, Bin, Ni Phil He, and Hong Lu. 2014. "The Deep Divide in China's Criminal Justice System: Contrasting Perceptions of Lawyers and the Iron Triangle." *Crime, Law and Social Change* 62:585–601.

Liebman, Benjamin L. 2007. "China's Courts: Restricted Reform." *The China Quarterly* 191:620–638.

Lin, Fen. 2012. "Information Differentiation, Commercialization and Legal Reform: The Rise of a Three-Dimensional State-Media Regime in China." *Journalism Studies* 13:418–432.

Liu, Sida. 2006. "Beyond Global Convergence: Conflicts of Legitimacy in a Chinese Lower Court." *Law & Social Inquiry* 31:75–106.

Liu, Sida. 2008. "Globalization as Boundary-Blurring: International and Local Law Firms in China's Corporate Law Market." *Law & Society Review* 42:771–804.

Liu, Sida. 2011. "Lawyers, State Officials, and Significant Others: Symbiotic Exchange in the Chinese Legal Services Market." *The China Quarterly* 206:276–293.

Liu, Sida 刘思达. 2013. "法律职业的政治命运 ["The Political Fate of the Legal Profession"]." 交大法学 *[SJTU Law Review]* 2013(1):93–100.

Liu, Sida, and Hongqi Wu. 2016. "The Ecology of Organizational Growth: Chinese Law Firms in the Age of Globalization." *American Journal of Sociology* 122: forthcoming in November 2016.

Liu, Sida, and Terence C. Halliday. 2009. "Recursivity in Legal Change: Lawyers and Reforms of China's Criminal Procedure Law." *Law and Social Inquiry* 34:911–950.

Liu, Sida, and Terence C. Halliday. 2011. "Political Liberalism and Political Embeddedness: Understanding Politics in the Work of Chinese Criminal Defense Lawyers." *Law and Society Review* 45:831–865.

Liu, Sida, Lily Liang, and Ethan Michelson. 2014. "Migration and Social Structure: The Spatial Mobility of Chinese Lawyers." *Law & Policy* 36:165–194.

Lu, Hong, and Terence D. Miethe. 2002. "Legal Representation and Criminal Processing in China." *British Journal of Criminology* 42:267–280.

Lubman, Stanley. 1999. *Bird in a Cage: Legal Reform in China after Mao.* Stanford, CA: Stanford University Press.

Luo, Wei. 2000. *The Amended Criminal Procedure Law and the Criminal Court Rules of the People's Republic of China.* Buffalo, NY: William S. Hein & Co., Inc.

Ma, Kechang 马克昌. 2007. 特别辩护：为林彪、江青反革命集团案主犯辩护纪实 [*Special Defense: Notes on the Defense for the Counter-Revolutionary Groups of Lin Biao and Jiang Qing*]. Beijing: Chang'an Press.

Macauley, Melissa. 1998. *Social Power and Legal Culture: Litigation Masters in Late Imperial China.* Stanford, CA: Stanford University Press.

Marshall, Anna-Maria, and Daniel Crocker Hale. 2014. "Cause Lawyering." *Annual Review of Law and Social Science* 10:301–320.

Marwell, Gerald, and Pamela Oliver. 1993. *The Critical Mass in Collective Action.* Cambridge: Cambridge University Press.

McAdam, Doug, John D. McCarthy, and Mayer N. Zald. 1996. *Comparative Perspectives on Social Movements: Political Opportunities, Mobilizing Structures, and Cultural Framings.* Cambridge: Cambridge University Press.

McAdam, Doug, Sidney Tarrow, and Charles Tilly. 2001. *Dynamics of Contention.* Cambridge: Cambridge University Press.

McConville, Mike (ed.). 2011. *Criminal Justice in China: An Empirical Inquiry.* Cheltenham, UK: Edward Elgar.

Michelson, Ethan. 2003. "Unhooking from the State: Chinese Lawyers in Transition." Ph.D. dissertation, Department of Sociology, University of Chicago.

Michelson, Ethan. 2006. "The Practice of Law as an Obstacle to Justice: Lawyers at Work." *Law and Society Review* 40:1–36.

Michelson, Ethan. 2007. "Lawyers, Political Embeddedness, and Institutional Continuity in China's Transition from Socialism." *American Journal of Sociology* 113:352–414.

Michelson, Ethan, and Sida Liu. 2010. "What Do Chinese Lawyers Want? Political Values and Legal Practice." In *China's Emerging Middle Class: Beyond Economic*

Transformation, edited by C. Li, 310–333. Washington, DC: Brookings Institution Press.

Minzner, Carl F. 2011. "China's Turn against Law." *American Journal of Comparative Law* 59:935–984.

Minzner, Carl F. 2013. "The Rise and Fall of Chinese Legal Education." *Fordham International Law Journal* 36:334–395.

Moustafa, Tamir. 2007. *The Struggle for Constitutional Power: Law, Politics, and Economic Development in Egypt*. New York: Cambridge University Press.

Munir, Daud. 2012. "From Judicial Autonomy to Regime Transformation: The Role of the Lawyers' Movement in Pakistan." In *Fates of Political Liberalism in the British Post-Colony: The Politics of the Legal Complex*, edited by T. C. Halliday, L. Karpik, and M. M. Feeley, 378–411. New York: Cambridge University Press.

Ngok, King-lun. 2002. "Law-Making and China's Market Transition: Legislative Activism at the Eighth National People's Congress." *Problems of Post-Communism* 49:23–32.

O'Brien, Kevin J. 1990. *Reform without Liberalization: China's National People's Congress and the Politics of Institutional Change*. New York: Cambridge University Press.

O'Brien, Kevin J. and Lianjiang Li. 2006. *Rightful Resistance in Rural China*. Cambridge and New York: Cambridge University Press.

Paler, Laura. 2005. "China's Legislation Law and the Making of a More Orderly and Representative Legislative System." *The China Quarterly* 182:301–318.

Peerenboom, Randall. 2002. *China's Long March toward Rule of Law*. New York: Cambridge University Press.

Pils, Eva. 2007. "Asking the Tiger for His Skin: Activism in China." *Fordham International Law Journal* 30:1209–1287.

Pils, Eva. 2015. *China's Human Rights Lawyers: Advocacy and Resistance*. London and New York: Routledge.

Potter, Pitman B. 2001. *The Chinese Legal System: Globalization and Local Legal Culture*. London and New York: Routledge.

Powell, Michael J. 1988. *From Patrician to Professional Elite: The Transformation of the New York City Bar Association*. New York: Russell Sage.

Qianfan, Zhang. 2003. "The People's Court in Transition: The Prospects of the Chinese Judicial Reform." *Journal of Contemporary China* 12:69–101.

Rajah, Jothie. 2012. *Authoritarian Rule of Law: Legislation, Discourse and Legitimacy in Singapore*. New York: Cambridge University Press.

Rosenzweig, Joshua. 2013. "Residential Surveillance: Evolution of a Janus-Faced Measure." International Workshop on Deprivation of Liberty in China, Australian Center for China in the World, Australian National University, November 14–15, 2013.

Sapio, Flora. 2008. "Shuanggui and Extralegal Detention in China." *China Information* 22:7–37.

Sarat, Austin, and Stuart Scheingold (eds.). 1998. *Cause Lawyering: Political Commitments and Professional Responsibilities*. Oxford: Oxford University Press.

Sarat, Austin, and Stuart Scheingold (eds.). 2001. *Cause Lawyering and the State in a Global Era*. Oxford: Oxford University Press.

Sarat, Austin, and Stuart Scheingold. 2005. *The Worlds Cause Lawyers Make: Structure and Agency in Legal Practice*. Stanford, CA: Stanford University Press.

Scheingold, Stuart. [1974] 2004. *The Politics of Rights: Lawyers, Public Policy and Social Change*. Ann Arbor: University of Michigan Press.

Sheng, Yi. 2003. "A Promise Unfulfilled: The Impact of China's 1996 Criminal-Procedure Reform on China's Criminal Defense Lawyers' Role at the Pretrial Stage (Part 1)." *Perspectives* 4(4):1–18.

Sheng, Yi. 2004. "A Promise Unfulfilled: The Impact of China's 1996 Criminal-Procedure Reform on China's Criminal Defense Lawyers' Role at the Pretrial Stage (Part 2)." *Perspectives* 5(1):1–27.

Solomon Jr, Peter H. 1995. "The Limits of Legal Order in Post-Soviet Russia." *Post-Soviet Affairs* 11(2):89–114.

Southworth, Ann. 2008. *Lawyers of the Right: Professionalizing the Conservative Coalition*. Chicago: University of Chicago Press.

Stern, Rachel E. 2013. *Environmental Litigation in China: A Study in Political Ambivalence*. New York: Cambridge University Press.

Stern, Rachel E., and Kevin J. O'Brien. 2012. "Politics at the Boundary Mixed Signals and the Chinese State." *Modern China* 38:174–198.

Tanner, Harold. 1999. *Strike Hard! Anti-Crime Campaigns and Chinese Criminal Justice*. Ithaca, NY: Cornell University Press.

Teng, Biao. 2009. "I Cannot Give Up: Record of a Kidnapping." *China Rights Forum* 1:30–41.

Teng, Biao. 2012a. "The Political Meaning of the Crime of 'Subverting State Power'." In *Liu Xiaobo, Charter 08 and the Challenges of Political Reform in China*, edited by Jean-Philippe Béja, Fu Hualing, and Eva Pils, 271–288. Hong Kong: Hong Kong University Press.

Teng, Biao. 2012b. "Rights Defense (weiquan), Microblogs (weibo), and the Surrounding Gaze (weiguan)." *China Perspectives* 3:29–41.

Tocqueville, Alexis de. 2000 [1835, 1840]. *Democracy in America, Democracy in America*, edited and translated by H. C. Mansfield and D. Winthrop. Chicago: University of Chicago Press.

Trevaskes, Susan. 2007. *Courts and Criminal Justice in Contemporary China*. Lanham, MD: Lexington Books.

Trevaskes, Susan. 2010. *Policing Serious Crime in China: From "Strike Hard" to "Kill Fewer."* London and New York: Routledge.

Trubek, David M., and Marc Galanter. 1974. "Scholars in Self-Estrangement: Some Reflections on the Crisis in Law and Development Studies in the United States." *Wisconsin Law Review* 1974:1062–1105.

Wacquant, Loïc. 2009 [2004]. *Punishing the Poor: The Neoliberal Government of Social Insecurity*. Durham [NC]: Duke University Press.

Wang, Celai 王策来. 1993. 完善刑事诉讼立法研究 *[Research on the Perfection of the Criminal Procedure Legislation]*. Beijing: People's Police University of China Press.

Wang, Cheng-Tong Lir, Sida Liu, and Terence C. Halliday. 2015. "Advocates, Experts, and Suspects: Three Images of Lawyers in Chinese Media Reports." *International Journal of the Legal Profession* 21:195–212.

Wang, Gong 王工. 2001. 中国律师涉案实录 *[Records of Cases Involving Chinese Lawyers]*. Beijing: Qunzhong Press.

Wang, Yuhua, and Carl Minzner. 2015. "The Rise of the Chinese Security State." *The China Quarterly* 222:339–359.

Weber, Max. 1954. *On Law in Economy and Society*, translated by E. Shils and M. Rheinstein, edited by M. Rheinstein. Cambridge, MA: Harvard University Press.

Western, Bruce. 2006. *Punishment and Inequality in America*. New York: Russell Sage Foundation.

Wielander, Geida. 2009. "Bridging the Gap? An Investigation of Beijing Intellectual House Church Activities and Their Implications for China's Democratization." *Journal of Contemporary China* 16:849–864.

Xu, Xiaoqun. 2000. *Chinese Professionals and the Republican State: The Rise of Professional Associations in Shanghai, 1912–1937*. Cambridge: Cambridge University Press.

Xu, Xin 徐昕. 2010. "旁听李庄案二审" ["Observing the Second Trial of the Li Zhuang Case"]. The Law Blog, URL: http://justice.blog.fyfz.cn/art/579232.htm (last date of access: February 21, 2012).

Yang, Dali L. 2004. *Remaking the Chinese Leviathan: Market Transition and the Politics of Governance in China*. Stanford, CA: Stanford University Press.

Yang, Fenggang. 2012. *Religion in China: Survival and Revival under Communist Rule*. New York: Oxford University Press.

Yang, Guobin. 2009. *The Power of the Internet in China: Citizen Activism Online*. New York: Columbia University Press.

Yu, Ping. 2002. "Glittery Promise vs. Dismal Reality: The Role of a Criminal Lawyer in the People's Republic of China after the 1996 Revision of the Criminal Procedure Law." *Vanderbilt Journal of Transnational Law* 35:827–865.

Zh u, Suli 朱苏力. 2010. "关于能动司法与大调解 [On Proactive Judiciary and Grand Mediation]." 中国法学 *[China Legal Science]* 1:5–16.

Index

accessing case files, 44, 50, 53–55
   difficulties in for economic or white collar
      crimes, 61
   interview data on, 51
ACLA Criminal Law Committee, 35, 36, 86
ACLA forum, 52, 59, 145, 167
   decline of, 152
   lawyer persecution cases on, 45
   Lawyer SOS case, 45–46, 59
   political liberalism on, 145–148
   rule of law on, 146
ACLA Regulation on Lawyers' Handling of
   Criminal Cases (1999), 67
acquittal rates in criminal cases, 34
activist lawyers, 70, 160, 171, *See also* legal
      complex; motivations of activist lawyers;
      notable activists; *weiquan* lawyers
   2012 CPL and, 40
   activist community in Beijing, 113
   BLA election movement of 2008 and, 107–112
   black mafia and, 95
   Christian, 104–106, 114–115, 120
   courage of, 120
   defined, 90
   domestic networking strategies of, 112–115
   educational trajectories of, 95
   international support institutions for,
      115–119, 165
   Internet and social media use by, 173
   mobilization on behalf of each other, 98
   nationwide crackdown on (2015), 159–170
   online international networking of, 160–170
   paths to activism, 95–99
   professional sanctions against, 91–92
   repression of by public and state security,
      92–94
   rule of law and, 119

types of costs paid by, 91
   WeChat use by, 75, 158
   women, 96
   actor mismatch, 5, 22, 39
Ai Weiwei, 94, 160
All China Lawyers Association (ACLA), 14, 21
   Ma Kedong case and, 69
   silence of during Li Zhuang case, 70
American Bar Association (ABA), 38, 161
   Rule of Law Initiative (ROLI), 163
Amnesty International, 161, 163, 166
   China Human Rights Lawyers Concern
      Group, 166
Anglo-American adversarial trial system, 54
Anglo-American law, 24
Anhui Law Firm, 45, 46, 92, 110, 113
anti-black campaign, 124, 140
Article 306, 40, 44, 45, 132, *See also* Big
   Stick 306
Article 306 of the 1997 Criminal Law, 29
Article 307, 45
Article 33 (2012 CPL), 39
Article 34 (2012 CPL), 39
Article 38 of the 1996 CPL, 29
Article 73 (2012 CPL), 42
assaults, 95

backward movement of legal reform, 122
bar associations, 4, 150, 164, *See also* All China
   Lawyers Association (ACLA); American
   Bar Association (ABA); Beijing Lawyers
   Association (BLA); Chongqing Lawyers
   Association; City Bar of New York;
   International Bar Association; Inner
   Mongolia Lawyers Association (IMLA);
   Lawyers for Lawyers
   data from, 14

Books in the Series

China and Islam: The Prophet, the Party, and Law
Matthew S. Erie

Diversity in Practice: Race, Gender, and Class in Legal and Professional Careers
Edited by Spencer Headworth and Robert Nelson

Diseases of the Will
Mariana Valverde

The Politics of Truth and Reconciliation in South Africa: Legitimizing the Post-Apartheid State
Richard A. Wilson

Modernism and the Grounds of Law
Peter Fitzpatrick

Unemployment and Government: Genealogies of the Social
William Walters

Autonomy and Ethnicity: Negotiating Competing Claims in Multi-Ethnic States
Yash Ghai

Constituting Democracy: Law, Globalism and South Africa's Political Reconstruction
Heinz Klug

The Ritual of Rights in Japan: Law, Society, and Health Policy
Eric A. Feldman

The Invention of the Passport: Surveillance, Citizenship and the State
John Torpey

Governing Morals: A Social History of Moral Regulation
Alan Hunt

The Colonies of Law: Colonialism, Zionism and Law in Early Mandate Palestine
Ronen Shamir

Law and Nature
David Delaney

Social Citizenship and Workfare in the United States and Western Europe: The Paradox of Inclusion
Joel F. Handler

Law, Anthropology and the Constitution of the Social: Making Persons and Things
Edited by Alain Pottage and Martha Mundy

Judicial Review and Bureaucratic Impact: International and Interdisciplinary Perspectives
Edited by Marc Hertogh and Simon Halliday

Immigrants at the Margins: Law, Race, and Exclusion in Southern Europe
Kitty Calavita

Transnational Legal Process and State Change
Edited by Gregory C. Shaffer

Legal Mobilization under Authoritarianism: The Case of Post-Colonial Hong Kong
Edited by Waikeung Tam

Complementarity in the Line of Fire: The Catalysing Effect of the International Criminal Court in Uganda and Sudan
Sarah M. H. Nouwen

Political and Legal Transformations of an Indonesian Polity: The Nagari from Colonisation to Decentralisation
Franz von Benda-Beckmann and Keebet von Benda-Beckmann

Pakistan's Experience with Formal Law: An Alien Justice
Osama Siddique

Human Rights under State-Enforced Religious Family Laws in Israel, Egypt, and India
Yüksel Sezgin

Why Prison?
Edited by David Scott

Law's Fragile State: Colonial, Authoritarian, and Humanitarian Legacies in Sudan
Mark Fathi Massoud

Rights for Others: The Slow Home-Coming of Human Rights in the Netherlands
Barbara Oomen

European States and their Muslim Citizens: The Impact of Institutions on Perceptions and Boundaries
Edited by John R. Bowen, Christophe Bertossi, Jan Willem Duyvendak and Mona Lena Krook

Environmental Litigation in China
Rachel E. Stern

Indigeneity and Legal Pluralism in India: Claims, Histories, Meanings
Pooja Parmar

Paper Tiger: Law, Bureaucracy and the Developmental State in Himalayan India
Nayanika Mathur

Contractual Knowledge: One Hundred Years of Legal Experimentation in Global Markets
Edited by Grégoire Mallard and Jérôme Sgard

Religion, Law and Society
Russell Sandberg

The Experiences of Face Veil Wearers in Europe and the Law
Edited by Eva Brems

The Contentious History of the International Bill of Human Rights
Christopher N. J. Roberts